U.S. ARMY IN ACTION SERIES

COMBAT
SUPPORT
IN
KOREA

by

JOHN G. WESTOVER

Library of Congress Catalog Card No. 54-13365

Facsimilie Reprint, 1987

CMH Pub 22-1

Center of Military History
United States Army
Washington, D.C.

Foreword

The contributions of combat service support soldiers to the success of American armies have often been overlooked by both historians and the public. Thus, it is altogether fitting that this first volume in the Army in Action Series should be John G. Westover's compilation of short, but instructive, pieces on service and support activities during the Korean War. The Center of Military History has received many requests for a reprint of this work, which was first published by the Combat Forces Press in 1955; it is a useful companion volume to Russell A. Gugeler's *Combat Actions in Korea*, which was reprinted in 1984 as part of the Army Historical Series.

Both Westover's subject and technique are worthy of study and comment. While the details of combat actions in America's wars have been studied extensively, comparatively little has been done to enlighten the soldier of today regarding how logistical operations were conducted at the small unit level. This book will serve to repair that omission. Westover compiled this book primarily from a series of interviews conducted with men actually involved in the events "at ground level." The oral history technique, which Army historians did much to develop in World War II and later, is now an accepted historical method. The value of oral history as a means of getting to the details is amply demonstrated here.

The Center of Military History is pleased to be able to initiate the Army in Action Series with the first CMH edition of John G. Westover's *Combat Support in Korea*. This is the first volume in what we hope will be a series interesting to, and useful for, today's soldiers and leaders at every level.

WASHINGTON, D.C.

William A. Stofft
Brigadier General, U.S. Army
Chief of Military History

Introduction

This book is a collection of interviews with members of all the arms and services of the United States Army, except Infantry, Artillery, and Armor. The interviews were collected from several hundred officers and enlisted men who were serving, or had served, in the Korean conflict.

As I talked with these officers and men I could not help feeling their aggressive spirit. Each realized that his service was essential to combat and that he was moving the operation ahead. But it was more than just doing a necessary job. It was "do it better," "do it more quickly," and, above all, "get the service as close to the combat soldier as possible." These officers and men told of hot meals, daily laundering of the infantryman's socks, helicopter evacuation, ordnance mechanics working among the infantry, and airdrop of flame throwers at the point of use. I have made their surging spirit the theme of this study.

COMBAT SUPPORT IN KOREA grew from the conviction of Maj.Gen. Orlando Ward, Chief of Military History (1949–1952), that the United States Army needs a record of its service operations on the small-unit level. Interviews are sometimes better than high-level histories. They can widen the novice leader's experience before he goes into the field. They supply illustrations for instructors, and they refresh officers who have not recently been in the field. They present vividly the problems of the other services with which we are not acquainted.

The interview also lets us see how often the service troops experience the hazards of combat. No man in combat gets enough recognition, but some men have been denied honors justly earned because the word "Quartermaster" or "Chemical" was included in their unit designation. It won't dim the glory of the rifleman to give credit to other members of the team.

A year of interviewing has gone into this book. Some of the interviews were conducted in Korea by Eighth Army historians, but much more of the interviewing was done in the United States with returnees. In addition, some of the stories have been condensed from speeches, letters, and magazine articles. Much time and patience have been put into these interviews by the men who have served, and who believe that their knowledge will help the Army.

Interviews are not history. They are personal accounts. An interview can be no more accurate than the observation of the teller, no more truthful than he is candid. Different units had different operating procedures. I cannot say that the operations related here are typical of all operations in Korea, or that they are better or poorer. These are simply stories related by earnest men.

Most interviews were oral. Notes were filled in by historians and returned to the interviewee for comment. Every effort has been made to recount the incidents as they were originally related, with editorial work limited to keeping the story moving. Most of the stories returned from Korea resulted from group interviews and are, therefore, in the third person. The amount of space devoted to each service is influenced more by the stories obtained than by any evaluation of the relative importance of sister services.

While a majority of the interviews testify to the correctness of Army doctrine, some are critical of doctrine and individuals. I have usually removed the names of the individuals criticized because the criticisms are not substantiated and may be unjust, but there has been no change of unit designation and no whitewashing. The reputation of the United States Army is too great to be diminished by honest criticism of some of its doctrines or a few of its members. In this study the historian does not point out violation of doctrines or decide between the contradictory accounts. This is a factual, not a generalizing, study.

I cannot credit all of the persons who have contributed to this volume. The names of more than a hundred are recorded in the table of contents. Special credit, though, is due these historians of Eighth Army: Captains Pierce W. Briscoe, William J. Fox, B. C. Mossman, and Edward C. Williamson, and Lieutenants Bevan R. Alexander, Martin Blumenson, and John Mewha. Their contributions are labeled as they appear. Mr. John E. Lee has had the trying job of typing interviews and drafts. Miss Mary Ann Bacon has made many editorial suggestions, while my wife has been the chief custodian of the blue pencil and dictionary. Lt.Col. Joseph Rockis has given endless encouragement throughout the months when progress seemed slow. To these, and many more, I give my thanks.

JOHN G. WESTOVER
Captain, Infantry

Contents

COMBAT SUPPORT in KOREA

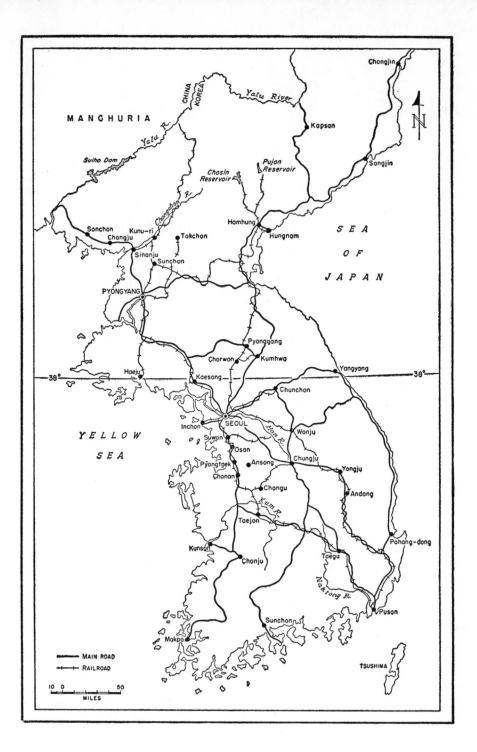

PART I

Corps of Engineers

1. Three River Crossings

Capt. Richard P. Lepke, 3d Engineer Combat Battalion

The 3d Engineer Combat Battalion (24th Infantry Division) was in a rest area at Kyongsan on 17 September 1950, after a series of long moves and fights around the Naktong perimeter. I commanded Charlie Company. At 2300 the battalion staff and company commanders were summoned by the battalion commander (Lt.Col. Peter C. Hyzer). He told us that we were to make a series of assault crossings of the Naktong River, carrying the entire 24th Infantry Division. The operation was to jump off at 0245, 19 September 1950, south of Waegwan and northwest of Taegu.

Able and Charlie Companies were to get the tough jobs of carrying the two assault regiments of the 24th Division. Able would carry the 19th Infantry, while Charlie was responsible for the crossing of the 21st Infantry. The regiments would cross the Naktong simultaneously, some six miles apart.

At the time of this meeting, not even the battalion commander had had a chance to make a reconnaissance or examine aerial photos of the crossing area, even though the operation was to begin in twenty-seven hours. The battalion had no assault boats but we were promised these at the crossing site by corps engineers. Further, we were to receive one boat per company on the following day in order to familiarize the men with the equipment.

A few days before this order was issued we had received a hundred Koreans for each company as replacements. We had started a training program for them but we had not made much progress because of our constant preoccupation with combat. We had a language barrier and all communication was channeled through their interpreters and through one of our NCOs who spoke fluent Korean. The infantry regiments also had Korean filler personnel.

None of the engineers had received any assault training in Korea, and

5

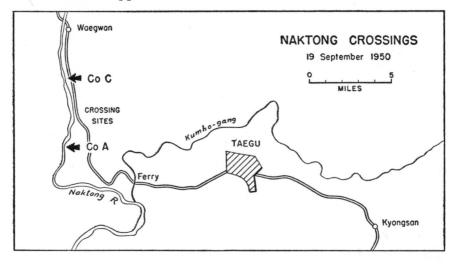

many of the people who had had practice in Japan were now casualties. Probably not over ten per cent of the U.S. personnel had launched an assault boat since their days of basic training. The infantry was also without assault river-crossing experience. There wasn't time for much coordination between the engineers and the infantry. To top it all, our Korean replacements had never before seen an assault boat.

The next day (18 September), while the engineers were familiarizing themselves with the one boat per company, the company commanders and key officers of the battalion staff joined the infantry in a reconnaissance of the Naktong. Our reconnaissance party was much too large, involving six jeeps and twenty persons. Near the river bank we came under enemy observation and received some rounds of mortar fire. No one was injured.

The engineer battalion was bivouacked twenty-five miles from the proposed crossing sites. The route to the crossing sites crossed the Kumho River, but all of the bridges had been blown. An underwater (sandbag) bridge had been operated by the North Korean Army and was being used by the U.S. troops, but this would not handle light vehicles because of the depth of the water. All jeeps had to be carried on a small ferry.

As we returned from our reconnaissance we found traffic backed up for a couple of miles, bumper to bumper, east of the ferry. The road was only one and a half lanes wide and the heavier vehicles were unable to move to the underwater bridge until the jeeps, which were mixed in the column, moved onto the ferry. These were 24th Division vehicles moving up for the crossing mixed with vehicles of corps engineers (repairing the underwater bridge), and a scattering of trucks from other units.

When I returned from my reconnaissance at 1700, I found Charlie

Company loaded and ready to go. Attached to us for this crossing were a platoon from Baker and one from Dog. Since we had only our organic personnel and equipment, and carried no assault boats to reveal our intentions, we were allowed to move during daylight. We moved independently of battalion.

There was no traffic control but we moved normally until we approached the ferry. Then we had to move slowly and lost a full hour. Still we reached our initial assembly area south of Naksan-dong by 1930.

I left Charlie Company in defilade and moved forward to the crossing site with the two platoon leaders who were each to be responsible for moving an assault infantry company. We planned to cross the two companies abreast, about a hundred yards apart. I showed the lieutenants their sites, found an abandoned foxhole near the river bank which I claimed as my forward CP, then returned alone to the company.

I had to infiltrate the company out of the initial assembly area, for it was not quite dark and enemy mortar fire was being concentrated on one flat stretch of the road. We closed unharmed in our forward assembly area at 2100. It was an apple orchard just three hundred yards behind the crossing sites. A prominent house nearby came to be a favorite target for artillery fire next day.

The Naktong River at this point was some four hundred feet wide, and had a moderate current. The river bank at one site was a sheer drop of some seven feet. This was cut down by the 2d Platoon after dark. At the second crossing point the bank was cut by a path which led to the beach. From the bank to the water's edge ran a flat, sandy beach about a hundred yards wide, punctuated only by some abandoned tactical wire. The beach was not strong enough to hold vehicles.

I assigned the 1st Platoon to the first crossing site, the 2d Platoon to the second site. The 3d Platoon was to unload the boats when they arrived and to organize the infantry into boat crews. To the attached Baker Company platoon I gave the job of laying a pierced-plank roadway (of airstrip type) over the beach as soon as the first wave was landed. This would facilitate jeep-ambulance and ammunition traffic. The attached Dog Company platoon was to stand by to await orders.

The infantry started arriving in the final assembly area at 2300 and closed in the area by 0100. We had plenty of time to break them down into boat crews and give them elementary instructions since the assault boats still had not arrived.

The commander of the infantry regiment was much upset over the delay, but there was nothing we could do. I saw him talking to Colonel Hyzer several times and I know that messengers were sent out to try to locate the missing boats. At one time the regimental commander mentioned calling off the attack, as it did not appear that the crossing could be made during darkness.

Finally, at 0400, the twenty-eight assault boats arrived. They were loaded both on pole-type trailers and in the beds of 2-½-ton trucks. It is hard to unload an assault boat from the bed of a truck, and this slowed down the operation. Worse, however, the drivers simply disappeared as soon as the trucks halted. We had to locate our own drivers to spot the trucks and trailers.

After all twenty-eight boats and their engineer crews were lined up along the road near the river`bank, the infantry came forward. Daybreak came as the first wave was on the water. There was no enemy fire at first, but as our boats reached the center of the stream an extremely heavy volume of small-arms fire hit them. Mortar and SP fire began to strike the near bank and the assembly area.

Apparently our simple instructions had not been understood by the Korean infantrymen, for they refused to leave the boats, and a few returned to the near shore. Sergeant Weird broke his carbine over the hand of one man to get him to release his hold on the guide rail.

As soon as the infantry landed on the far shore, the boats immediately started back. Eight of the twenty-eight assault boats did not make it back. In some cases the current carried them too far downstream and the inexperienced paddlers could not return them. In others, the boats were so riddled that they sank and their engineer crews returned in other boats. Of the Korean engineers who went with the first wave, none was known to return. Maybe they misunderstood their mission and stayed with the infantry. Maybe they drowned—we had no life jackets. Later, when we tried to round up all of our Koreans for replacements, we could locate only 22 of our original 100. Many had just conveniently disappeared for a short time, however.

As the returning boats reached the near shore, the enemy turned his fire on the second wave as it moved by to the beach. These infantrymen took cover on the beach by lying on their bellies near the water's edge until Sergeant Weird called for them to get loaded and help their buddies on the other side. Hearing this, one sergeant jumped up and yelled, "If the engineers can stand up and take it, so can we!" To a man the infantry hurried to the water's edge and loaded up.

As soon as we counted our boat losses we sent an urgent request to battalion for replacements. In an hour we received sixteen. We also got a boat-repair detachment which was attached to battalion for this operation—but these men claimed they had no equipment with which to make repairs. Only their sergeant would leave the cover of the orchard and go onto the beach to survey our damaged equipment.

The fire on the near beach made it impossible for the platoon of Baker Company to lay its roadway. Some self-propelled guns kept firing on our assembly area and beach until 0930.

The infantry on the far shore reorganized quickly but had strong resistance from the enemy. Our artillery helped and so did the Air Force. When the planes began to use napalm some of the North Koreans panicked and ran. These were immediately shot like quail.

The fighting on the far shore lasted about thirty minutes. The infantry carried air-identification panels on their backs and we could see little envelopments and assaults taking place. Our men were aggressive and moved right up to the enemy without hesitation. Soon we watched the panels moving up the draws, over the crest, and out of sight.

We kept crossing the infantry into the afternoon. By this time we had crossed two battalions of the 21st Infantry and were working on the third. The crossings had cost my company 42 men, only 8 of whom were U.S. troops. What happened to these men I don't know, since we had no time to locate the missing after the operation was over.

At noon, while we were still paddling the 21st Infantry across the Naktong, I was alerted for another crossing. Charlie Company was selected to cross the Naktong again that very evening, this time carrying the 5th Infantry above Waegwan. We were selected because we were the only company in the battalion assembled at one nearby site. Dog Company was to take over our present operation and support the 21st Infantry on the far shore.

I took my executive officer and a sergeant with me on a reconnaissance. We joined Colonel Hyzer and some of his staff officers, and proceeded to Waegwan where we met the commander of the infantry regiment (Colonel Throckmorton). Colonel Throckmorton told us that his regiment was clearing the bank of the Naktong as far north as Hill 303, where he was to make a juncture with friendly troops. Hill 303 was the key to the operation because of its commanding height, but it had not yet been taken. In any case, it would be necessary to cross at least one battalion that night, even if the east bank were not cleared of the enemy.

The attack was parallel to the river bank and Hill 303 was some ten miles north of Waegwan. I was given leeway to select the crossing site anywhere in this ten-mile zone. I moved my small party to the rear of the lead company of the 5th Infantry. We had to hit the ditch several times when the enemy put up small bits of resistance.

At 1430 the infantry still had not reached Hill 303, so I decided that to get a daylight reconnaissance I would have to select a crossing site somewhere between my present location and Waegwan. Two miles north of town I found a site where the banks, turnaround, assembly areas, approaches, and the far shore looked pretty good. By radio I ordered the company to meet me on the road, and I started back to Waegwan.

In Waegwan I learned that the 21st Infantry, which we had crossed that morning, was moving along the far shore of the Naktong. This meant we could make an administrative crossing. I inspected a blown-out bridge in Waegwan and decided this would be a good site. Charlie Company reached town almost as soon as I did, and the boats were delivered to us by corps engineers within another thirty minutes. By 1700 or 1730 we began to land the infantry on the far shore. We improvised a ferry and began moving men, jeeps, and equipment on it. We had one battalion across within forty-five minutes.

Our company kitchen was set up in an orchard in Waegwan and we fed the men in shifts. But before I got a chance to eat, I was ordered to cross the other two battalions of the 5th Infantry eight miles north of Waegwan near Hill 303, which we now held. I moved out to make a reconnaissance before it became completely dark.

We selected a site, but as the infantry seemed in no hurry to cross, we held off until the following morning (the 20th). We continued to operate the ferry at Waegwan all night of 19-20 September and left one platoon in Waegwan for that purpose. The other two platoons moved up to the new site.

In the crossing the next morning our site was defiladed, we had infantry on both flanks to give covering fire, mortars were emplaced, tanks and self-propelled guns were registered, and the air support was excellent. The Air Force bombed and strafed a village near the crossing site and maintained armed reconnaissance overhead. The crossing was unopposed.

We crossed two battalions before noon and I loaded my men to move on. I reported to battalion in Waegwan—hopeful that we could get a rest. Instead we were ordered to support the 19th Infantry in an attack on Sangju. We gave general engineer support in this operation. The encounter was brief because the enemy was surprised by the flanking attacks our river crossings made possible.

Within three days Charlie Company had received orders for, had planned, and had executed three river crossings, supporting two different regiments. During the same period it had given general engineer support to a third regiment in attack.

In the crossing of the Roer River in Germany, my engineer battalion had three months of preparation.[1] We actually formed the exact crews and carried the same groups of infantry in dry-run crossings of a similar river under similar conditions. How different was Korea!

---

[1] I then commanded the 2d Platoon of Company B, 121st Engineer Combat Battalion (29th Infantry Division).

2. Improvised Bridge

Capt. Richard F. McAdoo, 65th Engineer Combat Battalion

In Korea, improvising was the normal thing in bridge construction. With minefields, explosives, or fortifications we could follow doctrine closely. But bridging was different.

We usually didn't have the required materials for any job, and we never had an engineer dump close at hand. In the first six months of Korea, lack of reinforcing engineer units meant that we had to rely on our own resources. When the division needed a bridge it was up to us to build it, make it class 50 if possible, and see that it was built to last.

How important bridge construction was to a combat engineer company can be realized by looking at the record of Company A, 65th Engineer Combat Battalion—thirty-five bridges built in nine months. We built eight timber bridges, three from 120 to 180 feet long, in one week! The Nam River crossing at Chinju was typical of the improvising we had to do to accomplish our mission.

From 16 to 26 September 1950, the 25th Infantry Division made its drive out of the Pusan perimeter and captured Chinju. The 35th Infantry, with Company A, 65th Engineer Combat Battalion, attached, spearheaded the attack. Three days before we reached Chinju, the commander of the 35th Infantry (Col. Henry G. Fisher) asked me what plans had been made to bridge the Nam River. I didn't know and I had trouble getting telephone contact with battalion to find out. Even after I got to talk with the battalion executive officer, I didn't get an immediate answer. He had to call me back, and gave me the message for the engineers (and, incidentally, the infantry): "Don't worry about the Nam River. The division will halt at Chinju." But when we reached the river, the division's plans were changed and we were ordered to cross and continue the attack.

Company A worked with the infantry in the assault crossing of the river. The enemy had only a few squads of men on the far shore and they pulled out after a very short skirmish. The infantry had a few casualties; we had none. Immediately after this we began to build a bridge.

At Chinju there was a high-level concrete bridge which had been partially destroyed. We couldn't repair it because the bridge was too high and the destroyed spans were much too long. Unfortunately, we didn't have the materials to make a new bridge, either.

The Nam River at this point was 300 feet wide and about 6 feet deep, and the current was swift. Downstream from the main highway was a fordable site for tracked vehicles. We helped to cross a battalion task force of the 35th Infantry by towing the wheeled vehicles with tanks and a D7 dozer. My 3d Platoon moved out with this task force and I had only the remaining two platoons to bridge the river.

At 1600 we faced our first problem: locating materials. We had 7 pole-trailer loads of various-sized timbers, 2 truckloads of 3-inch-by-12-inch decking—and that was all. We sent reconnaissance parties out to find anything that would help. First we found 15 steel sections commonly used as sheet piling, each 50 feet long. These were in the stream bed and apparently had been discarded when the permanent bridge had been built. In addition to these, about two miles from the bridge site we located a large stockpile of heavy timbers suitable for bridging. These timbers were a better building material than the steel piles, but the narrow road from the bridge site to the timbers was bumper to bumper with trucks waiting to cross the river. The assistant division commander stayed at the bridge site giving us priority on the roads and all the help he could, but the trucks going two miles and back to load timbers took six hours for the round trip. Five of these hours were lost because of the congestion.

To speed the project we pulled the steel piles out of the river and used them. When darkness came we took a chance and used truck headlights for illumination. In spite of the fact that the enemy had been pushed off the far bank only the afternoon before, we had no interference.

The stream bed was of sand, and we knew that we could not build a lasting bridge in that strong current without spending a great deal of time making strong footings. But in this project speed was more important than permanence. We just placed 12-inch-by-12-inch timbers, 14 feet long, drift-pinned together on top of one another, to form intermediate supports. The bridge was at water level, which made it easy to float the supports out to position, set them vertically, and attach the stringers. For the first three spans we used the steel piles as stringers on 40-foot centers. The remaining stringers were made with 6-inch-by-12-inch or 12-inch-by-12-inch timbers, and varied from 15 to 20 feet in length.

We had 140 pieces of decking material—only twenty per cent of the requirement for this bridge—and we found no other suitable material nearby. We determined that this was enough, however, to build two treads. One would be 2 feet wide, the other 3. We spaced the treads so that a jeep could use them—but it would have only 2 inches of leeway on the inside of each tread. Our 2-½-ton trucks had no difficulty crossing, but wide ammunition trailers could just cross without going off on the outsides of the treads. We placed small curbings to prevent accidents. The capacity of this bridge was estimated at twenty tons.

While the engineers worked on the bridge, five hundred civilians helped on the approaches. Here we had a problem of fill and had to use rubble and everything else available for the job. We took fifteen mines out of the path of the far approach.

Traffic was moving down the approaches and across the bridge within twenty hours of our starting time. We spaced the vehicles fifty feet apart and watched the structure very closely. It was both fearful and wonderful to watch the give in those steel-pile stringers.

Soon after traffic started, Company A moved out with the 35th Infantry. Company C's men took over the maintenance and completion of our bridge. They immediately started to sandbag the base of the intermediate supports, for without footings the current had already begun to suck the sand out from under them. Company C even put in additional intermediate bracings—while traffic was moving over the bridge.

This expedient bridge lasted as long as it was maintained, and until the old bridge was repaired. I believe this was ten days or so. I wouldn't recommend this as a model structure, but it did put the division across the Nam River fast.

3. Causeway at Osan

Lt. Sam D. Starobin, S2, 65th Engineer Combat Battalion

During the withdrawal of November 1950–January 1951, the 25th Infantry Division withdrew across the Han River at Seoul and continued south on the main road as far as Chonan. At Osan we crossed the Chinwi River and there the 65th Engineer Combat Battalion blew the bridge. We believed we were withdrawing from Korea and we did thorough work on our demolitions.

The bridge at Osan was a 280-foot, two-lane, four-span, concrete structure. The abutments were fifteen feet high. The bridge was demolished by blowing alternate piers and the south abutment. This left a saw-toothed appearance.

Four weeks after we had destroyed this bridge we were back to it and were faced with the problem of crossing the Chinwi River. Osan was built up to the bank of the river, which prevented us from building a bypass alongside the bridge. We had to go east of the town with a detour, then ford the river upstream.

Our new bypass was not satisfactory. It lengthened the route by more than a mile and the river bed gave us a great deal of trouble. The spongy clay was frozen several inches deep, but the constant movement of our heavy vehicles over it soon broke this crust and the vehicles bogged down. We had to move the bypass several times.

We did not feel justified in expending materials or labor to make this bypass permanent and we feared high water would make it useless. We didn't have 280 feet of bridging, and a shorter bridge would have to cross the spongy river bed.

The battalion S3 (Major Joseph Pessa), the CO of Company A (Capt. Richard F. McAdoo) and I held a conference at the bridge site. We concluded it would be more practical to build a new bridge than to repair the damaged one. But we also found that the deck of the old concrete bridge was adequate for a causeway.

Company A placed four hundred pounds of TNT kicker charge to blow piers 1 and 3, and the north abutment. The explosions were simultaneous.

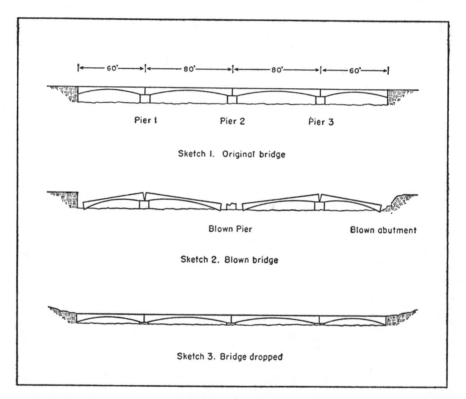

|← 60' →|← 80' →|← 80' →|← 60' →|

Pier 1   Pier 2   Pier 3

Sketch 1. Original bridge

Blown Pier   Blown abutment

Sketch 2. Blown bridge

Sketch 3. Bridge dropped

After the site cleared we could see that our calculations were accurate and that the bridge had dropped as planned. The concrete deck of the old bridge now formed a causeway over the banks and stream some four feet above the ground. There was plenty of room underneath for the river to flow at low stage.

Within six hours of our conference traffic was rolling across the new causeway. There was no limit on tonnage on this structure, but it was limited to one-lane traffic.

During the heavy spring rains several other bridges along the route were washed out. I know that this one was functioning perfectly as late as April. The river might have gone over it later, but it could never be washed away.

We used this system of stream crossing several times later. It always worked.

4. Last of the Han Bridges

Capt. D. J. Haden, Lt. Rodman M. Davis, Lt. Jack R. Wheatley, Company C; Capt. Donald E. Roush, S4, 14th Engineer Combat Battalion. (Interview by Capt. B. C. Mossman, 6th Historical Detachment.)

On 15 December 1950, the 14th Engineer Combat Battalion, supporting I Corps, was ordered to assume responsibility for the security and maintenance of the floating M2 and M4–M4A2 bridges over the Han River at Seoul. The battalion was further ordered to prepare plans for removal and for demolition of each of these bridges.

The big maintenance problem was to keep the ice broken up around the floating bridges. Ice was a particular problem because the Han River is tidal. Instead of freezing smooth, the ice froze in waves that were constantly building up on the pontons and between them. The four- to five-inch-thick ice alongside the bridges had to be chopped up—and broken by driving DUKWs over it. Ice patrols were sent along the river to report large floes.

The order to dismantle the M2 bridge on 2 January 1951 was received on 1 January. Company C was ordered to do the dismantling, assisted by a platoon of Company B, and trucks and cranes of the 55th Engineer Treadway Bridge Company.

One detail planned to take down the north and south bank trestles, one squad working at each. A second detail would disassemble the bridge into four-float rafts. A squad would work on each raft and move it to one of the thirteen disassembly sites, located downstream of the bridge on the south bank. One platoon was to operate the ponton deflation point, established near the disassembly points.

The weather on 2 January was cold and windy; the temperature was near 10 degrees. The cold made it difficult for the men dismantling the bridge, but did not hinder the work noticeably. The day was so bright that the glare from the ice was hard on the eyes.

Dismantling the M2 bridge took eleven hours. The men detailed to the job reported at the bridge site at 0530 to break the ice, and began actual disassembly at 0700. The trestles and ponton sections at each bank were first lifted, and the bridge was then broken down into four-float rafts. Once a four-float raft was removed from the bridge, a DUKW towed it to one of the disassembly sites for further dismantling. The DUKWs were needed because some of the damaged floats had become filled with water and ice, and were too heavy to tow by hand.

At the disassembly site, each four-float raft was broken down into separate floats. Ice had collected in front of the rafts as they were towed, and they could not be brought close enough to the bank to be walked out. Cranes were used to lift them.

The removal of pins between the sections was a serious problem. Some of the pins had rusted; others were frozen in place. In order to get the pins out the section had to be leveled. This was difficult to do because some of the floats were heavy with ice and water. Sledge hammers and bars were finally used successfully to remove the pins.

Each float was completely dismantled and then deflated. An officer of the 55th Treadway Bridge Company inspected each ponton and the unserviceable ones were burned. Except for the upstream anchor cable, the entire bridge was moved by 1800.

At 2300 hours, 3 January, Companies B and C received orders to begin the disassembly of the M4–M4A2 bridge on 4 January. The companies arrived at the bridge at 1600 to begin clearing ice from around the pontons, but the bridge disassembly did not begin until 1100, except for the removal of unnecessary cables, curbs, markers, and guide rails. A tactical development caused the delay. A British infantry-tank force was pocketed by the enemy north of Seoul and it was believed that a rescue force might be dispatched. This force did not materialize by 1100 and the dismantling was begun in earnest. The Eighth Army coordinator, stationed at the I Corps control point, set the time limit for dismantling at 1300. All equipment not removed at this time was to be destroyed. The I Corps engineer was able to get this extended to 1400, but at 1330 Eighth Army gave a standby order to blow the bridge, so all work halted. Half of the balk, the cables, curbs, markers, and guide rails were the only parts of the bridge salvaged.

Demolition materials were already at the bridge site. At 1100, unprimed charges were placed on the bridge while disassembly was going on. In general, the December plans for demolition were followed. Most important of the changes was the increase of TNT from 114 to 1,800 pounds, because of the shortage of tetrytol. The engineers used bangalore torpedoes to destroy the balk and, since they had no incendiary grenades, they substituted gasoline-soaked sandbags to fire the rubber pontons. At 1505 the firing order was received and the bridge was blown.

When the bridge did not sink after the first blast, a careful check was made. It was discovered that some of the charges had not fired. This was unusual. Ordinarily, sympathetic detonation will cause all charges to explode, and the failure probably was due to the explosives having become frozen. Inspection of the bridge proved it necessary to recharge and refire. After this was done the bridge was checked again. This time it was sinking. The end of the bridge was not spectacular, for the rapidly freezing water caused it to submerge slowly.

With the destruction of the M4–M4A2 bridge, all bridges across the Han River in the Seoul area were eliminated. It was a great disappointment to the engineers that they were not given time to disassemble this bridge, but all of the engineer missions in the withdrawal over the Han River were now accomplished.

5. End of the Line

Lt. Carrol W. Guth, 185th Engineer Combat Battalion. (Condensed from an interview by Lt. John Mewha, 8th Historical Detachment.)

The evacuation of Hungnam was not hurried, and each installation was demolished as soon as it was no longer needed. A railroad bridge and rolling stock were destroyed on 15 December 1950 by Company B, 185th Engineer Combat Battalion.

The 2,100-foot railroad bridge consisted of 29 spans, 8 of which were wooden-tie cribbings built up to the deck level. When Company B was ordered to destroy this bridge and all the rolling stock in the Hungnam area, it was decided that the projects should be linked. Spans of the railroad bridge would be destroyed individually and as many cars and engines as possible would be pushed into the void before blowing the next span.

About 15 engines and 275 cars were assembled for demolition. Korean railroad men helped shuttle the railroad cars from Hungnam to the bridge. When the Koreans learned that the rolling stock was to be destroyed they became reluctant—and had to be prodded to do the job. By contrast, the engineers found the job enjoyable—a release for their pent-up emotions.

At 1545 the southernmost span was blown. Ten cars and several engines were pushed into the gap until it was filled. Some of the cars were loaded with gasoline and the engines had steam up. As they were pushed into the defile the wreckage caught fire. This process was repeated at each span. When the men reached the section of wood cribbing, several carloads of POL and an engine were spotted on top of it, and the cribbings ignited. The heat was so intense that the locomotive became cherry-red and its whistle started blowing. In a few minutes the whole section had crumbled.

As some of the cars were pushed into the gaps, the ends of the rails would spread and rip. This prevented other cars from being pushed off. Blocked spans were, therefore, blown with the rolling stock on them. By mistake, a boxcar loaded with demolitions was pushed onto some flaming wreckage. The resulting blast injured two men. The destruction continued throughout the night.

6. Destruction of Wonju

Lt. William H. Champion and MSgt. Julius R. Grupe, 2d Engineer Combat Battalion. (Interview by Lt. John Mewha, 8th Historical Detachment.)

The 2d Infantry Division was defending Wonju, but on 6 January 1951 it was again necessary to withdraw. To destroy communications through Wonju and to ruin those supplies that could not be evacuated, demolitions were ordered.

Although Wonju is divided by the Wonju River, it is linked by a railroad bridge and a highway bridge. North and east of the river was the 38th Infantry. It would be necessary for the regiment to withdraw across these bridges. For this reason the 38th Infantry was charged with their destruction. The actual demolition work was to be done by the 3d Platoon of Company C, 2d Engineer Combat Battalion. This narrative is primarily concerned with the actions of the 3d Platoon.

At this time the 3d platoon consisted of forty-two men and was commanded by Lt. William H. Champion. The platoon was in direct support of the 38th Infantry and had as its normal assignment the maintenance of the Chechon and Noto-ri roads.

During the evening of 6 January the 38th Infantry ordered the 3d Platoon to prepare to demolish the highway bridge, the railway bridge, 16 freight cars loaded with 80 tons of ammunition, and two tons of Korean rifles and ammunition located in a church west of Wonju. The demolitions were to be carried out on order of the commanding officer of the 38th Infantry.

The 3d Platoon was quartered on the second floor of a concrete

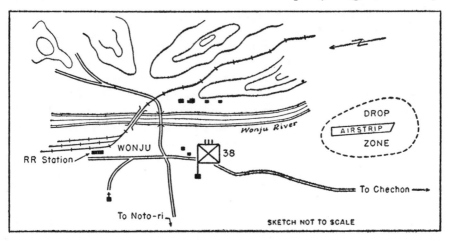

building in Wonju which was also the CP of the 38th Infantry. At 0500 next morning, the men were awakened and told that an estimated three enemy battalions had infiltrated the regimental perimeter and were entering Wonju. Each man moved to his foxhole outside the CP building. The weather was a very cold 20 degrees, with snow on the ground and a sharp wind blowing. The platoon heard sporadic firing and occasionally saw tracers and flares.

At 0700, Lieutenant Champion and his four demolitions men prepared to go to the bridge sites. A jeep was loaded with explosives, and a driver was instructed to take a ¾-ton truck loaded with demolition materials to the railroad bridge. Only 150 yards from the CP an enemy machine gun, located on high ground to the east, opened fire on the road. When the engineers saw the bullets hitting the road ahead, they concealed their jeep and took cover in a ditch. They soon saw a company of the 38th Infantry moving through town searching for the enemy. The company split, part of it moving toward the machine gun, which was silenced in five or ten minutes.

Lieutenant Champion and his demolitions crew walked with the infantry through Wonju, and the jeep load of explosives followed at a respectful distance. The infantry killed a number of enemy on its sweep through the village. They also set up a machine gun near the highway bridge and fired it at the houses east of the Wonju River. The engineers hand-carried their demolition charges to the bridge and worked under the covering fire of the machine gun.

The highway bridge was a reinforced concrete structure and the engineers had 450 pounds of Composition C3 with which to destroy it. Composition C3 is pliable and has great shattering power. It is much more easily used and will fit into places which cannot be reached by TNT. The engineers placed 200 pounds of the explosive on each of the first two piers, and 50 pounds on the deck of the bridge, to break it in the middle as the piers collapsed.

After fifteen minutes the friendly machine-gun crew departed and the demolition party was without security. To get observation, Lieutenant Champion moved northward in the river bed a few yards. Twenty minutes after he took up this new position the lieutenant noticed five or six North Koreans coming up the river bed single-file from the south. Evidently they were trying to get back to their own lines. The lieutenant shouted to his men. The lead enemy soldier, who had approached within forty feet of the bridge, reached into his blouse for a hand grenade instead of raising his rifle. Lieutenant Champion could not fire because his own men were between him and the target. One of the engineers shot this North Korean and the rest scattered behind a dike. Several more enemy soldiers joined the first group and a fire fight began. The engineers took cover behind the bridge piers and rocks in the river bed, but soon they flanked the dike and in fifteen minutes killed 9 North Koreans and took 3 prisoners.

After the fight ended, the men returned to the bridge and completed the placement of demolition charges. The engineers then moved to the railroad bridge.

The railroad bridge had nine or ten piers. The second and third were made of log cribbings, and the others were of concrete. As the railroad bridge was a stronger structure than the highway bridge, the demolition men used six hundred pounds of Composition C3 to mine it. They used 200 pounds on the first log-cribbed pier and 300 pounds on the first concrete pier. They placed 100 pounds on the top to breach the span. A five-gallon can of gasoline was hidden in the log cribbing of the third pier for emergency use. Once the work was under way Lieutenant Champion drove off to the railroad station, leaving Sgt. Lester H. Johnson in charge.

At the railroad station Lieutenant Champion found sixteen boxcars loaded with ammunition of all types, scattered on three sidings. He decided that the best demolition plan was to wire the cars with primacord so the cars would explode simultaneously. As soon as his men joined him he assigned one man to set all the explosive caps while the others placed the demolition charges in the boxcars. The men placed a case of Composition C3 in each car on top of all the other explosives, and then set a detonator cap in a block of TNT on top of the C3. A complete circuit of primacord was placed around all the cars, with a connection run from each side of the primacord net through the boxcar into the case of C3. At the end of the net, four long pieces of primacord with fifty feet of time fuze (approximately twenty-five minutes' normal burning time) were extended to the vicinity of the railroad station. This was an added precaution in case some of the fuzes failed to burn.

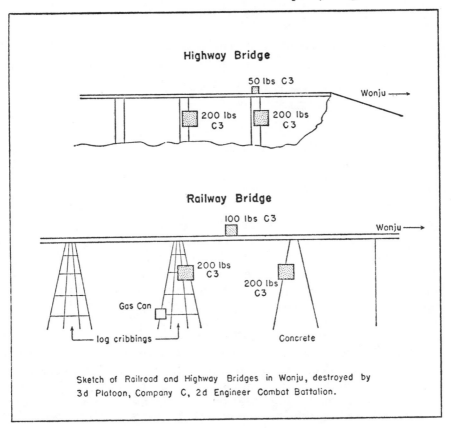

Sketch of Railroad and Highway Bridges in Wonju, destroyed by 3d Platoon, Company C, 2d Engineer Combat Battalion.

It was 1030 when this wiring was completed. The demolition men returned to the CP building, and Lieutenant Champion drove up to the church building. When he arrived he found that the munitions were already prepared for demolition. After checking to see that everything was in order, he returned to the CP building.

While the demolition crew and Lieutenant Champion were away, the S3 of the 1st Battalion, 38th Infantry, ordered MSgt. Julius R. Grupe to take a squad to the airstrip to destroy the housing, gasoline, and other supplies in this area. Before leaving, Sergeant Grupe's men gathered all the tracer ammunition they could find. Then they marched through slush and snow to the airstrip, arriving both wet and cold. Airdrops had left some two hundred drums of gasoline, small-arms ammunition, and C rations scattered throughout the area. It was disheartening to the men to have to destroy so many supplies.

One pair of men worked on each side of the field. Sergeant Grupe felt that two men would do a more effective job and that it would reduce the possibility of surprise. No effort was made to move the drums and the

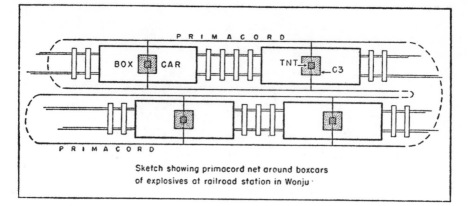

P R I M A C O R D

BOX ☒ CAR

TNT ☒ ←C3

P R I M A C O R D

Sketch showing primacord net around boxcars
of explosives at railroad station in Wonju·

men fired tracer ammunition into them where they lay. The gasoline caught fire and burned down to the bullet hole, then exploded. Some twenty cases of small-arms ammunition were piled around one gasoline drum and set afire. It took ten minutes before the heat caused the ammunition to explode, and by this time the men had withdrawn to a safe distance. Ten to twelve cases of C rations were collected and given to the 38th Infantry. Three or four buildings which might have military use were fired with torches made of gasoline-dipped rags.

When the detail returned, it mined the CP building. At about 1730, the S3 of the 1st Battalion informed the engineers that the enemy had begun to infiltrate into Wonju again. Lieutenant Champion ordered his platoon, less Sergeant Johnson, to withdraw with the infantry CP group. The demolitions were to be blown at 1800, but when the hour approached the infantry had not cleared the bridges or the town. The authority to order the demolitions had been delegated to the commander of the 2d Battalion (Lt.Col. James H. Skelton).

At 1900 Colonel Skelton and his driver went to the bridges with Lieutenant Champion and Sergeant Johnson to make certain the area was clear. Colonel Skelton halted at the highway bridge while the two engineers drove up the river bed five hundred yards to the railroad bridge. Here they heard two or three enemy soldiers talking only ten yards beyond the bridge, near the point where the fuzes were located. The Americans dismounted and as quietly as possible moved to the third pier where the five gallons of gasoline were cached. Lieutenant Champion opened the can and poured it on the two log-cribbed piers. He and Sergeant Johnson threw matches into the gasoline and fired the bridge. Then they withdrew—rapidly.

By 1920 the engineers were back at the highway bridge, but Colonel Skelton and his driver were gone. It was learned later that they had been forced to withdraw by the approach of enemy soldiers. A three-minute fuze had been stretched from the demolition charges to a ditch on the

Wonju side of the structure. As Sergeant Johnson approached the ditch a North Korean soldier jumped up and started to run. Johnson yelled and Lieutenant Champion shot this enemy soldier. The time fuze was pulled and the two men drove rapidly to the railroad station. On the way they heard the charges explode on the highway bridge.

The streets in Wonju were littered with rubble, and burning houses illuminated the area. No enemy was encountered. When the men arrived at the railroad station they ignited the time fuzes and stayed long enough to make sure the powder trains had started to burn. At the church they followed the same procedure.

All the fuzes lighted, the engineers drove south on the Noto-ri road. Within twenty minutes they had caught up with the infantry.

The powder train leading to the primacord net around the boxcars was old, and it took 1 hour 12 minutes to burn. At about 2100, when Lieutenant Champion was five or six miles south of Wonju, the sky lighted up and "it was light enough to read a newspaper."

When the Americans returned to Wonju it was found that all demolitions had exploded. The log cribbings on the railroad bridge had burned and the highway bridge had to be rebuilt. The boxcars were demolished and the CP and other buildings were completely gutted.

7. Mines Are Double-Edged Weapons

Lt. Sam D. Starobin, S2, 65th Engineer Combat Battalion

Mines are double-edged weapons. Properly employed they can be a strong instrument of defense. Improperly used they are a menace. Especially is this true for an army like ours, where vast numbers of trucks and tanks are employed. I have seen at least 150 disabled North Korean tanks —none of which had been destroyed by mines. I have also seen a great number of American tanks and trucks destroyed by our own mines. Not all of these were in minefields laid by Americans. A large percentage of the mines that destroyed our vehicles and killed our troops had been re-laid by the enemy.

This need not have been so. We could have reaped a great advantage had we employed mines intelligently. American mine warfare doctrine is sound, but after Eighth Army had shipped 120,000 mines to units, only 20,000 were recorded or on hand. The remaining 100,000 were either abandoned or buried unrecorded!

The infantry sometimes asked my company to lay undefended minefields where there were gaps in their lines. The infantry commanders were advised that this was not a sound practice. But on several occasions these hard-pressed leaders insisted and we laid the fields. I know from personal experience that this often happened in other units.

The enemy found it easy to pick up the mines in unguarded fields and lay them behind our own lines. It was a convenient source of supply of the 20-pound mines for an enemy with a poor transportation system. When we did not cover our fields with fire we invited the enemy to mine our own rear areas.

A second method of losing mines to the enemy was by abandonment. Too many mines were moved forward. A change in the tide of battle resulted in the loss of large quantities of mines. Some commanders tried to destroy the mines, but this is not easy in the field.

Failure to record minefields was a serious problem in Korea. It is not until you return to a mined area that you appreciate accurate minefield reports. We should lay mines indiscriminately only if we never intend to return and do not value the friendship of the population. Yet we had repeated instances of units laying minefields which they did not record. Under the pressure of hasty withdrawal, mine-laying sometimes degenerated to pitching armed mines from the back of a moving truck.

When the 25th Infantry Division crossed the Han River in early March 1951, we started running into unrecorded American minefields. I personally visited units that had operated in the area and inquired about minefields. The S3 of the 3d Engineer Battalion recalled minefields laid by unit near Uijongbu which, under the stress of retreat, had not been recorded. A number of our vehicles had struck mines and soldiers had been killed at the positions he indicated.

As an engineer S2, I passed along to the infantry every minefield location that I learned of. I knew that long, technical reports would not be understood and that reports to the S2s did not reach the companies. I made large-scale sketches of minefields, using graphic symbols and non-technical language. These were duplicated and distributed down to the company commanders. When an infantry company commander saw that an attack would take him through a minefield, he called on the engineers to help him. The infantry respect those minefields now.

8. Learning by Doing

Major Richard I. Crawford, Korean Military Advisory Group. (Extract from a speech of 17 February 1951.)

The necessity for some type of land mine was becoming increasingly apparent as more and more enemy armor came in. At the outset we had no source of antitank mines; however, on Tuesday, 27 June 1950, we received word that General MacArthur's headquarters would support our efforts. We immediately asked for mines, and by Friday we had received about eight hundred.

The ROK troops had not had any training in antitank mines. In fact, they had never seen an M6 mine, but in this respect they had nothing on me. I had never seen one either. However, I had an advantage in that I read and understand English fairly well, and the instructions are pasted on the inside of the individual mine's carrying case. Shortly after the first mines were received, we instituted a short course on combat operations. We spent half an hour teaching the technique of laying and arming the M6 mines, and then we went off to the front.

As long as an American was closely supervising the operation, everything went fairly smoothly, but when the ROK engineers had to act independently we ran into trouble. Our half hour of training hadn't taken too well. They would forget to put the detonators in, or having done that, would forget to arm them. Their ideas of concealing the mines left much to be desired, and, on one occasion, one of my officers caught a detail on the road, just throwing the mines—carrying case and all—off the back end of a moving truck. It actually took the Korean engineers about two weeks before they laid any genuinely effective antitank minefields.

During this two-week period, the Koreans had "a better idea." Without our knowledge they prepared charges designed to strap around the waist of a soldier and formed some "body contact squads." Members of these squads were to move into the side of a tank, pull a fuze lighter on a two-second fuze, perhaps disable the tank, and certainly join their honored ancestors. I never found out how many tanks we actually disabled by this method, but I do know that in the first four or five days we ran awfully short of "body contact" people. The ROK Chief of Engineers told me he was experiencing some difficulty in getting additional volunteers.

Again, we ran into the ever-present problem of defending an obstacle. It required herculean efforts by the KMAG advisers to keep any force behind the minefields, and seldom were we successful until we got into our final defensive positions on the Naktong perimeter. The South Koreans were loath to use mines because of their previous mishandling. However, on the perimeter they did lay both antitank and antipersonnel mines. On one of the defended antipersonnel fields, we accounted for 113 enemy casualties in a two-hour night attack. This action raised the morale of our fighting forces, and at the same time created a supply problem: we couldn't get enough mines for them.

Later, on the road between Yongchon and Uisong, engineers placed a well-sited antitank minefield on the road and to each side of the road near a bridge. Again the field was defended. This time a tank came downhill, struck a mine, and turned sideways in the road. Another tank, following closely, tried to go around the first, and struck a mine. Our troops prevented any attempt to breach the field by laying down small-arms fire on the site, and a nearby tactical air control party called for an air strike. While the F-51s were coming in, three more tanks and a self-propelled gun came down the hill. The planes dropped napalm and rocketed all six of the vehicles. They claimed six kills on that operation. Not to be outdone, and on the theory that if it hadn't been for our engineers the Air Force wouldn't have had a target, we claimed six kills, too. Thus, some of the exaggerated reports we hear about.

9. Disregarding a Minefield

Major Glade S. Wittwer, S3, 8th Engineer Combat Battalion

While we were still in the Naktong perimeter, I saw an example of reckless disregard of elementary minefield precautions. The 8th Cavalry (1st Cavalry Division) was conducting local offensive operations three miles north of Chigol. One mile north of the town was a small stream. The existing bridge had a bypass already prepared to the east. Just beyond the bridge was an ROK battalion command post, and to the left was an 8th Cavalry aid station.

The North Koreans held ridge positions to the north. From these positions enemy infantry infiltrated on the stormy night of 17-18 September 1950. They had placed 26 U.S. M6 mines in the shoulder of the road and 18 in the bypass. Then the North Koreans placed demolition charges on the bridge and blew it thirty minutes before dawn.

All of this was done so quietly that one American sentry remained within a few feet of the minelayers without noticing them. The adjacent units were so surprised at the blowing of the bridge that they called the engineers to report that the bridge had been hit by a large-caliber shell.

Shortly after the bridge was blown, three M4 tanks came up the road. The first tank took the bypass and immediately hit a mine. Because the shoulder of the road was of loose sand, the mine blew off a tread but did not injure any of the crew.

The tank commander immediately detailed two crewmen to warn all traffic. Anticipating the arrival of a tank retriever, the second tank pulled off the road. It too lost a tread.

By now the rain had washed sand from above other mines and it appeared they were widespread. The tankers' warning was not enough for most Americans. Vehicles moved up into the danger area.

The next casualty was an artillery forward observer party. A lieutenant and his two radiomen drove up, were warned of mines, but still took the bypass. They hit a mine and all three were killed.

Soon an officer and an enlisted man approached in a jeep. The officer dismounted and the jeep went ahead. The driver decided that he couldn't make it. In turning around he hit two mines, and was killed.

This was the last attempt to use the bypass until the mines were cleared by an engineer detail, but vehicles continued to move up and stop on the shoulders of the road. One brigadier general pulled off the road and discovered that he had driven within twelve inches of becoming a statistic!

10.   The Mine that Saved Sinnyong

Major David F. Campbell, Korean Military Advisory Group

From 30 August to 6 September 1950, the ROK 6th Engineer Combat Battalion engaged in unceasing mine warfare. All of its activities were in support of the ROK 6th Division in one of the most critical periods of the Naktong perimeter. If the battalion's success was greater than usual, it was because of the careful coordination of the mine warfare and the over-all tactics of the division.

The mountainous northeast sector of the Naktong perimeter was defended by Republic of Korea troops. In the center of ROK II Corps its 6th Division lay astride the Yongchon–Andong highway and the Kyonggyong South Line Railroad, with its command post at Sinnyong. In this area the highway and railroad run southeast to northwest, and are canalized by the mountains. Sinnyong served as the forward railhead for both the ROK 6th and 1st Divisions, with the main supply road of the 1st Division running through the sector of the 6th.

Opposing the 6th Division were the North Korean *1st, 8th, 14th* and *15th Divisions,* plus elements of an unidentified armored division. The enemy infantry was aggressive and applied continuous pressure. On the right flank the North Koreans occupied Hills 783 and 828, seriously threatening Sinnyong. The 6th Division had to remain on the defensive in the center and left in order to take the offensive on the right to protect the communications line. The division's front was extremely broad because its line was curved. Shrewd use of mines allowed the division to straighten its line and shift a maximum number of troops to the offensive.

Not only was there infantry pressure, but from the main highway North Korean tanks lobbed harassing shells into Sinnyong. The fire was

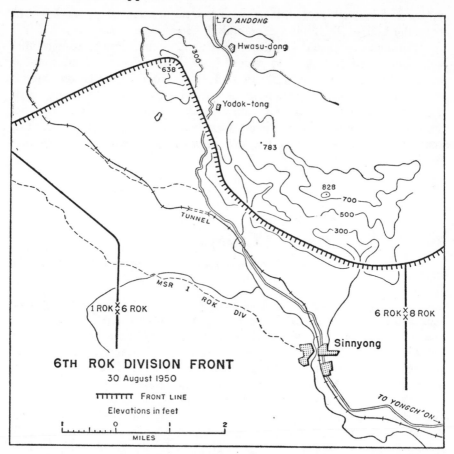

6TH ROK DIVISION FRONT
30 August 1950

⊤⊤⊤⊤⊤⊤⊤ FRONT LINE
Elevations in feet

unobserved and most of the rounds landed in the rice paddies, but small deflection shifts would have scored hits on the MSR, the marshaling yards, and military installations.

A staff conference was called on 30 August to consider ways to stop this tank menace. The division commander (Major General Kim), his KMAG adviser (Lt. Col. Martin O. Sorenson), the division engineer (Major Pak), and I were there. It was decided that the engineers would be responsible for stopping the tank fire, but any action we took must fit into the larger division defense plan.

The enemy tanks approaching Sinnyong came down the highway from Yodok-tong to a curve in the road. A crater in the road, a small minefield, and a platoon of engineers prevented them from rolling on into Sinnyong. No additional troops could be spared from the division to reinforce the position. Fortunately, the tanks could not flank our position as the road was winding and narrow and there were sheer drops of three hundred feet from its edge. Although the enemy had not tried to force the roadblock, we decided that the position must be strengthened.

That evening the corps engineer (Col. Lew Won Sik), his KMAG adviser, two KMAG advisers from the ROK 19th Infantry (in whose section the roadblock lay), Major Pak, I, and our interpreters made a reconnaissance. At the roadblock we picked up the platoon leader and two engineers. We moved 250 yards beyond our forward positions to the road crater. It was not quite dark, so we could look directly into Yodok-tong and the enemy front lines. As dusk approached we could see the North Korean infantry crawl out of their hiding places in the town and mill around.

We decided that the terrain and the steep wall flanking the road made this an ideal tank trap. We could station a bazooka team at the crater, have infiltrators mine the road near Hwasu-dong, and send tank-hunter teams along the road.

After thirty minutes at the crater we began receiving sporadic artillery fire. We returned to the division CP in Sinnyong and there continued planning our tank trap, mine program, and demolition of a railroad tunnel. Generally, the minefields were to be heaviest in the center. To undertake the minefield program I requested and received two platoons of engineers that were being used as infantry.

Later in the night the engineers emplaced forty M6 antipersonnel mines over sixty yards of the road at the point where the tanks stopped to fire (Minefield 1). Unlike our previous laying of M6 mines, these were not only armed but each was activated by placing an M3 antipersonnel mine underneath it, and then attaching a three-inch trip wire to the handle.[1] We made this field even more formidable by placing fifty-two antipersonnel mines along the narrow shoulders of the road with trip wires laced across the road and its shoulders. This would take advantage of the practice of the North Koreans of surrounding their tanks with engineers to clear mines and infantry to prevent close-in attack. Since the tanks would be canalized by the twelve-foot road, we figured that our preparations would be effective against infantry-armor attack. Fortunately, no enemy tanks arrived to interrupt our work.

While this minefield was being constructed Minefield 2 was being installed nearby and tied in with Minefield 1. About 250 M3 antipersonnel mines were laid south of Yodok-tong in an inverted chevron pattern. We worked quietly, and the enemy all around us did not recognize that we were ROK troops.

On 31 August the sketches of our previous night's activities were recorded and sent forward. A great deal of time was spent in making a

---

[1] *Arming* a mine is the process of removing all safety devices. *Activating* a mine is the process of booby-trapping it, either by setting an internal fuze or by using another mine.

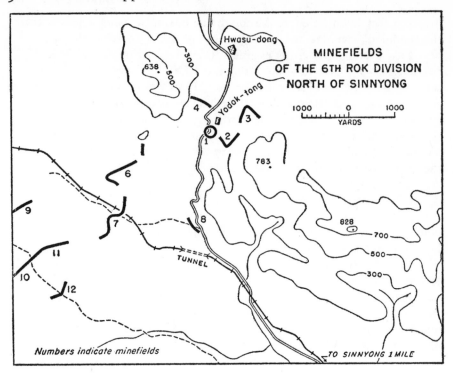

MINEFIELDS
OF THE 6TH ROK DIVISION
NORTH OF SINNYONG

Numbers indicate minefields

physical inspection of all existing minefields and making plans for strengthening them.

On the night of 31 August–1 September, Company A, ROK 9th Engineer Combat Battalion, laid ninety M3 antipersonnel mines in an extension of Minefield 2 (Minefield 3). These made a second chevron. In using the chevron pattern we were following the Soviet system, which the North Koreans employed. It was not only the efficiency of this pattern that attracted me but its deception, since the North Koreans would not expect it.

We completed our work at about 0200, and the minefield party began to withdraw. We were careful to go east of the field, to take advantage of the protection of the field itself. Just at that moment a company of North Korean infantry began an attack. They came from the direction of Yodok-tong, bunched up and running upright. Almost the entire company got into the first belt of mines before they hit the first trip wire and realized their predicament. Mines exploded and men screamed. The attackers turned in panic only to kick more of the trip wires. The whole affair lasted scarcely five minutes, yet we estimated a hundred casualties. We returned to find our minefield badly damaged. Artillery fire began falling, so we left without making the repairs. As the result of this experience I tried thereafter to get infantry protection for minelayers.

I spent a good part of the next day (1 September) teaching expedients for overcoming the shortage of activating devices, and devoted some time to instruction in booby traps. The South Koreans were especially interested in booby-trapping the little carts the enemy used to carry supplies, so I devised a method. An infiltrating party would remove a wheel, place the axle on the ground, and fasten a trip wire to the axle. When a group lifted the cart to replace the wheel the booby trap went off. This diabolical device was referred to by the ROKs as "the shaver" —from the effect it had on one's head. Teams went deep into the enemy lines and placed numerous booby traps, all of which were carefully recorded.

The same day we began to activate antitank mines. Except for Minefield 1, this had not been done before. In fields over 500 yards long, we activated 20 per cent of the mines. The smaller fields we activated 100 per cent.

That night (1-2 September) we laid two more minefields. One of these, Minefield 4, was placed to the rear of Yodok-tong to form a part of our tank trap—when we should get around to springing it. It consisted of ninety antipersonnel mines, with trip wires, laid over an area of nine hundred yards. The other field was to the left of our roadblock on the main highway. The need for more troops on the right flank of the division was so strong that even the engineer platoon at the roadblock had to be redeployed.

During the night of 2-3 September we continued with our minelaying and completed two more fields. Just before these fields were completed, the infantry on the left flank of the division was pulled behind the minefields and the gaps left for the purpose were closed. We continued to strengthen our old fields, and even repaired Minefield 2, where the attack had occurred. The enemy dead remained as a warning to others who might attempt to attack at this point.

Now that we had minefields across the division's front and had readjusted our lines, we were ready to spring the tank trap. On the night of 3-4 September we formed two engineer and one infantry 3.5-inch rocket teams. At 1900 we moved out to the crater and left Team Able (four engineers) with instructions not to fire until they heard firing from one of the other teams. Two hundred yards farther north on the road we left Team Baker from the 19th Infantry, with instructions to lay low until they heard fire from the northern end of the trap.

The third bazooka team accompanied a platoon of engineers, which I led, to the bridge at Hwasu-dong. We moved around to the left of Minefield 4, kept quiet, stayed in defilade, and were able to move into enemy territory without causing alarm. We found that the bridge at

Hwasu-dong had been damaged by the Air Force, but that the enemy had made a ford fifty yards northeast of the bridge.

North of the bridge we laid a hasty minefield from the river to the ford. Moonlight made the work easy and flashes of distant artillery increased the visibility. The rocket team selected a position two hundred yards south of the bridge and some fifty yards off the road. The engineers joined them, and all began to dig shallow foxholes. As we heard our artillery plaster the enemy, we were glad we had coordinated our movement before coming into the area.

At midnight, about forty-five minutes after we had taken up positions, we heard tanks coming down the road. These were preceded by a mine-clearing team, which easily found the mines on the top of the road. We saw the lead men drop to their knees, grab the mines without examining them, and throw them off to the shoulder. None of these mines exploded for they had not been activated. But we could see from the careless way their engineers handled the mines that they were in for a surprise!

As soon as the tanks had breached the minefield they forded the river and moved on with their foot party. I don't know how many tanks passed, but by the artillery flashes I counted five T34s. When no other tanks passed our position for twenty minutes, I sent two squads of engineers to place a deliberate minefield in the road, each mine of which was to be activated. After this was done, I knew we had the tanks.

Just as our mine squads returned to our positions, a lone enemy tank came down the road without foot troops accompanying it. I guessed it was from the same party as the first tanks, but had fallen behind. The tank approached the end of the bridge and stopped. One crewman had started to get out of the tank when our bazooka team edged up to within fifty yards and fired. The projectile struck just behind the turret. None of the crew escaped and the tank burned, blocking the road. The ROK troops became excited for a few minutes and fired their rifles to catch anyone in the vicinity. Then we withdrew quickly to our own lines. We soon heard a great deal of firing to the south, which meant that our other teams were in action.

Team Able was seventy-five feet above the road where the first tank would have to halt. It remained quiet and allowed the first tank and accompanying party to approach. Ten or fifteen enemy engineers moved along the road on their hands and knees, feeling for mines. When they reached the first activated mine and felt its pressure plate they jerked it out! The explosion killed every one of these men.

The infantry, as we had anticipated, rushed for the shoulders of the road, and immediately ran into our maze of trip wires on the antipersonnel mines. Of the 50 to 100 men, surely half were killed.

Until now neither bazooka team had fired. Five tanks had passed Team Baker but the team waited to see if there were more. By the time they knew that this was all, the last tank was masked from their fire. The rocket team moved to the road. As these men rounded the bend, the rear of the fifth tank was only fifteen to twenty yards away. The gunner heard the exploding mine and he fired directly at the tank. This tank exploded and burned, blocking the road. The bazooka men scurried up the bank and headed for home.

Within a minute of these two actions, Team Able fired down on the first tank and hit it at the junction of the turret and the motor. The force of this explosion ripped off the turret and the ammunition blew all at once. The second explosion lifted the tank off the road and hurled it down the steep bank three hundred feet into a rice paddy, where it landed upside down. As Team Able was not in a position to fire at any of the other tanks, it headed for our lines.

During the night I sent bazooka teams along that road and two more tanks were destroyed. One was destroyed by the infantry and there was a squabble between the infantry and engineers for credit for the second. The argument was heated, for the Republic of Korea offered a bonus of a hundred thousand *won* to each unit that destroyed a tank.

During the night we had destroyed five T34 tanks. In the morning Colonel Sorenson sent an air reconnaissance party forward and they called for Mosquitoes to sweep the area. These planes found nine more tanks in our trap. Air strikes destroyed all nine.

Our tank party over, there were other problems. Pressure in the north was growing and we had to move more troops to the right flank. A captured tank lieutenant told us the enemy had brought eighty-five tanks into our sector on 1 September. We knew that our bag of fourteen had hurt them, but we didn't think our present positions would hold against a heavy thrust. We began cratering the main highway and laying additional belts of mines behind a straighter front line. We also turned our attention to blocking the railroad tunnel.

Our tunnel project had waited while we collected TNT. At the east end of the tunnel we now placed 2,350 pounds of TNT pressure charge in the overburden so as to completely close the tunnel's mouth. At the west end we placed only 900 pounds. We did not place enough TNT in this end of the tunnel to completely block it since we hoped to lure the enemy into the entrance. Then we placed fifty-two booby traps with trip wires. The preparation was completed on 5 September, but the charge was not blown until the next day.

On 5 September the enemy began a drive on the front of the ROK 8th Division (on our right) and by 9 or 10 September had taken Yong-chon, some ten miles to our rear. The 19th Infantry was placed to protect our rear. Once more we had to shorten our line, and it was minefields that gave us time to move and erect a defensive barrier. Not only did we build up our own defenses; we also took the mines to the enemy, infiltrating ten miles deep and placing mines and booby traps as far back as Habon-dong.

On 6 September we blew the railroad tunnel. After this we entered the west opening and completed our job of boobytrapping it. The ROK 2d Infantry was drawing back at this time. As these men moved over the mountain which the tunnel cut through, the enemy tried to use the tunnel to cut them off. The first men ran into the booby traps and some six or seven were killed. The pursuing party withdrew and started to move northeast in hopes of taking RJ 775928 and blocking the troops withdrawing south along the main highway. They ran into Minefield 8 from the south and here lost ten or fifteen more men. The group then withdrew to the northeast in confusion and did not further interfere.

As our infantry withdrew down the Yodok-tong road toward Hill 728, the enemy attacked banzai style and a regiment strong, through Minefields 2 and 3. These minefields had been built up to contain some five hundred antipersonnel mines, and we had them covered with small-arms fire. Rifle and machine-gun fire did not stop the enemy, but the mines stopped them cold. They milled around for a few moments trying to find a passage, and the automatic weapons and mines wounded or killed five hundred. The attack soon stopped and our men withdrew without further interference.

After this engagement and the shortening of our line, we continued cratering the roads and increasing our mines. The ROKs thereafter had great faith in minefields, learning particularly that minefields supplement other means of defense.

11. Recon Dailey

> MSgt. Warren F. Dailey, Sgt. Earl J. Cayemberg, and Cpl. Elmer L. Bartley, 2d Engineer Combat Battalion. (Interview by Lt. John Mewha, 8th Historical Detachment.)

The amount of timely engineer support that can be given to the infantry squads depends greatly on the speed of the engineer reconnaissance. During the operations of the 2d Infantry Division along the Soyang River in the first week of April 1951, the 2d Engineer Combat Battalion kept a number of aggressive engineer reconnaissance teams searching for new access roads through the mountains and for obstacles requiring engineer clearing.

Two of these engineer reconnaissance teams were commanded by MSgt. Warren F. Dailey and Sgt. James G. Sulzer. Sergeant Dailey's assistants were Sgt. Earl J. Cayemberg (radio operator) and Cpl. Elmer L. Bartley (driver). The teams moved out from the engineer battalion at Samsong-dong on the morning of 2 April and headed toward Chunchon. On the way they reconnoitered two lateral roads, which had been constructed by the Marines, to see if there was any way to continue the roads across the mountains. There was not.

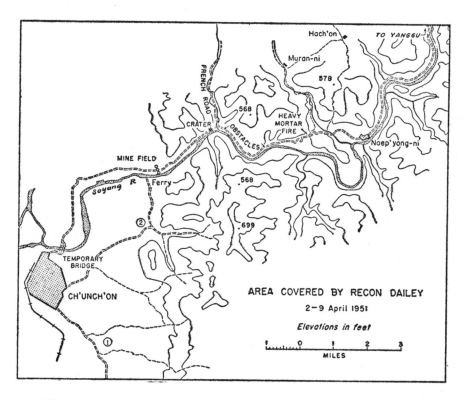

The teams reached Chunchon at 1530 and reconnoitered several roads to the east. (*1*) The roads soon dwindled into trails. That night the two teams stayed with the 8th Engineer Combat Battalion (1st Cavalry Division).

At 0715, 3 April, the teams investigated roads east of Chunchon and south of the Soyang River. (*2*) At Chamjan-ni the teams split, and Sulzer headed north to the river to look for a ford. He found the river was too swift and deep. Sergeant Dailey covered the roads to the east and southeast, only to find they ended in trails against the sharp hills.

At 1200 the teams rendezvoused (*2*) and were joined by Lt. Henry P. Leighton, who came to receive their report. He told them to recheck the first two roads. A power line crossed the mountains and the battalion commander hoped it would be paralleled by a usable trail. In any case, the teams were to remain in the Chunchon area and attach themselves to Company B as soon as it arrived. The teams were then to reconnoiter the main supply route leading east from Chunchon to Yanggu.

The teams rechecked the roads. An investigation of the power line disclosed that the towers had probably been packed into the mountains on mules. Not even a jeep could follow the rough trail. The teams checked other roads on foot, and then returned to Chunchon for the night.

On 4 April, the two teams took note of roads and bridges through Chunchon. The sixteen-span bridge over the Soyang River had been blown. The teams crossed on an improvised bridge built by the 8th Engineers and continued their reconnaissance eastward until they came to a minefield that had destroyed a tank and a truck. Following a temporary bypass around the minefield, the teams continued driving along the road between columns of men of the 23d Infantry.

By 1530 the teams reached the edge of a huge, hand-dug crater—20 feet long and 30 feet deep. The high ground northeast of the crater was still in enemy hands and the infantry were fighting in the hills, especially on Hill 568. Sulzer and Dailey walked with the infantry along the road and found a great number of obstacles. There were antipersonnel mines, wooden box mines, felled trees, and rubble blown onto the road.

Near a small bridge an enemy machine gun opened fire and hit three infantrymen. The infantry started to withdraw. The engineers ran back along the road until they were masked from the fire, and then walked carefully along. Several times they saw suspicious holes in the road and by probing with their carbine bayonets the men would feel the mine cases. Sergeant Dailey removed detonator caps from two.

At their jeeps the engineers wrote up their reconnaissance report, but as they could not make contact with battalion by radio, they called Company B. The company commander informed them that he had a message for them.

When the teams reached the Company B command post east of Chunchon, the company commander relayed the order that Sergeant Sulzer was to return to the battalion command post with maps and reports of the past three days. At 2200 Dailey received a message to continue the reconnaissance.

Next morning Dailey and his men returned to the crater. The 8th Engineers had made some temporary repairs and a jeep could cross it—with difficulty. There was evidence of road mines, and one destroyed trailer showed their effectiveness.

An infantry officer told Sergeant Dailey that "French Road" was heavily mined, so Dailey and Corporal Bartley dismounted before inspecting it. They found mines—and mangled bodies. Some mortar rounds were fired at the engineers, and they turned back, their pace increasing when small-arms fire kicked up dust at their feet. Heavy fighting continued on Hill 568, and six air strikes hit the crest.

By 0900 the team was driving east along the main road. The Antitank and Mine Platoon of the 23d Infantry was sweeping the road for mines and blasting trees and boulders out of the road. Some distance forward, the team met Lt. Russell O. Blosser with another reconnaissance party from the 2d Engineer Battalion. The lieutenant's jeep had a flat tire. While repairs were under way a mortar concentration struck near by. The engineers took cover in a ditch but later, when they had repaired the tire, moved the vehicles back out of sight. Lieutenant Blosser and Sergeant Bailey moved eastward on foot.

At a defile in the road the engineers met infantry observers and several tanks. Artillery rounds struck near the tanks, and the engineers had to duck as best they could. Forward of the defile the road was cratered. Lieutenant Blosser instructed Sergeant Dailey to return to the jeeps and radio Company B to send forward a D7 bulldozer, four truckloads of sandbags, and a platoon of engineers. The message was sent, the work done, and that afternoon traffic continued along the road.

In the afternoon Sergeant Dailey and Corporal Bartley moved beyond the defile to within three hundred yards of the enemy-held village of Naepyong-ni, and then worked northward on a small trail to Hachon. Much of this reconnaissance was through enemy territory. Minefields and trail conditions were recorded.

Recon Dailey (Dailey, Cayemberg, and Bartley) continued to operate with or ahead of the infantry for four more days before they were relieved. Their operation was typical. Their results were speedy support by the engineers and rapid advance by the infantry.

12. Inexpedient Expedients

Lt. Norman R. Rosen, 10th Engineer Combat Battalion

Field expedients are essential to combat engineer operations, especially when supplies are critical as they were in Korea. But some units disregarded sound military engineering principles in their use of expedients. When an engineer replaces a bridge with a twelve-inch culvert and uses rubble fill, this isn't expediency—it's ignorance.

In February 1951 the 3d Infantry Division was advancing toward the Han River. The railhead for the division was to be moved up from Suwon to Anyang-ni. This move would reduce the truck haul of division supplies by twenty miles. To make the shift possible, Company D, 10th Engineer Combat Battalion, was given the mission of opening the road.

At one point we lost time because someone had used an "expedient." A twelve-foot concrete bridge had been dropped, probably in the summer of 1950. Later the road was opened again. The stream was a small trickle during some seasons, a swift-flowing body of water during others. When the concrete deck of the bridge fell it left a three- or four-inch opening. The working party that opened the road made no repairs, but filled the void with rubble and trash. This was adequate at the time, since the winter of 1950 was dry, but with the rains coming in the spring of 1951 we knew we had to build a better structure.

When we started to remove the fill from the hole we ran into real difficulty. The space between the abutments was too narrow to use a bulldozer. Besides, there was limited traffic on the road and we had to keep it open. This forced us to clear the stream bed by hand.

If the fill in this case had been gravel or rock it wouldn't have been so bad, but we had to extract an ox cart, sand and rice bags, corn stalks, straw mats, and other items. All of these had become wedged and frozen in place. We had to use a full squad of men for a day and a half to clear the rubble. Each half of the bridge took less than four hours to build. In this job, like many others, the clearing of the site on which an expedient had been used took more time than the building of a new structure.

13. The Delay at K-2

Major Walter C. Henderson, 822d Engineer Aviation Battalion

The 822d Engineer Aviation Battalion was located on Okinawa in July 1950. We were special-category troops assigned to the Twentieth Air Force. Early in July we received orders from Headquarters, Far East Air Force, placing us on temporary duty with Fifth Air Force in Korea. It was intimated that we would be away only sixty days, and we were told we could leave our families, footlockers, and winter clothing on Okinawa until we returned.

When I returned to the United States in August 1951, the 822d was still in Korea. During all of these fourteen months the 822d had had all or part of its forces at the K-2 airstrip near Taegu. We had, however, received so many changes of plans that much of our time was wasted.

On 5 July 1950, the battalion commander (Lt.Col. Frank J. Polich) and I flew to Tokyo to the headquarters of Far East Air Force. Here we were oriented by the director of installations, and we submitted reports on the status of our battalion and requisitioned equipment. We explained that half of our personnel were due to return to the United States immediately, either on completion of their overseas tours, or for discharge. Later regulations issued by the Department of Defense prevented this exodus from taking place but left us with a serious morale problem.

On 8 July Colonel Polich and I accompanied the directors of installations of Far East Air Force and Fifth Air Force to the K-2 airstrip. This was the final reconnaissance for the Tokyo officers, a preliminary one for us. Colonel Polich and I remained at the field when the others left, so that we could continue our inspection and begin our planning.

Our first view of K-2 showed us an old Japanese sod-and-gravel runway, its surface scarred with pot holes. The strip was 300 feet wide and 3,800 feet long. Our job was to repair it so it could handle "moderate traffic for a minimum time." After the repairs were complete we were to lengthen the runways to 5,000 feet so that our combat planes could use the field.

Our instructions stated that the work would have to proceed without halting the air traffic. This made our job more difficult. We divided the strip to make two runways. The one closest to the control tower was designated A, and the far one B.

Work began on 18 July. Dust and the psychological effect of the wing tips were our earliest problems. We regraded the crown and hauled fill on Strip A so that eventually the center of this strip was eighteen inches above its former level. Near the west end of the old runways, we encountered "Air Force blue" clay—the soft silt that makes up the rice paddies. A truck could run over it once, but repeated trips would break through the thin crust and no bottom could be found. Of course, this would not carry a heavy plane. To strengthen the strip we excavated five to ten feet, and filled the pit with crushed rock. This made the end of the runway an island of gravel in a sea of soft clay.

We had our renovation completed and the pierced-steel planking laid on Strip A by 7 August. We opened Strip A to traffic and closed Strip B. On this second runway we intended not only to renovate but also to lengthen it to five thousand feet. When we finished Strip B we expected to lengthen Strip A.

Remembering the soil conditions we had encountered in Strip A, we decided to build the extension above the ground on a base of crushed-rock fill. Although this caused a slight grade increase, it would not raise any problems as long as the runway did not exceed six thousand feet. We didn't anticipate the airstrip going beyond that distance because of the natural obstacles at each end.

Before we had lengthened Strip B to five thousand feet, the tactical situation forced us to evacuate the battalion to Pusan. Here we began the K-9 strip and, as time moved on, we began to suspect our stay in Korea would not be limited to sixty days.

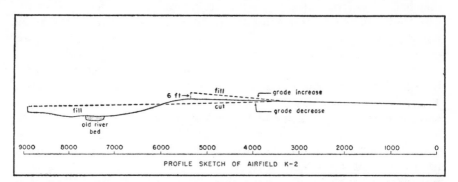

PROFILE SKETCH OF AIRFIELD K-2

When the tactical situation at Taegu improved we moved Able Company back to the K-2 strip. Shortly thereafter they had to evacuate again, and on their second return to Taegu they were ambushed by North Korean guerrillas. Able Company remained detached from the battalion and continued at K-2 while we went north to Pyongyang and then made the retreat. By February 1951, the full battalion was again assembled and working at K-2.

Under changed specifications Able Company had lengthened both runways to 5,700 feet, and then remained at the field working on the overrun. But now we received new specifications requiring us to lengthen the runways to 9,000 feet with 1,000-foot overruns at each end. K-2 was to become a jet-fighter field.

An airstrip of this length may seem unusual for fighter aircraft, but jets make this and other improvements necessary. Jets do not have the rapid take-off and climb of propeller-driven aircraft, especially in the combat zone, where they are heavily loaded. The runways have to be strong and smooth since jets have very narrow tires which are inflated up to 190 pounds. The narrowness of the tires gives a very high weight per square inch on the ground and calls for a strong surface. Smoothness is necessary because of vulnerability of high-pressure tires, and the high landing speeds (often more than two hundred miles an hour) of jets. Another important factor is the sensitivity of jets to dust.

All of these factors make the jet airstrip ideally one with an asphalt surface covered by pierced-steel planking. Yet even this surface has its difficulties. Some jet models lose a good deal of fuel on take-off, and this fuel has a corrosive action on asphalt. Tail blast and heat from later models cause the surfacing to deteriorate.

When we got out new specifications to push the runways of K-2 to nine thousand feet, we ran into two types of problems. The first were those imposed by Nature; the second, those arising from the piecemeal planning.

To the east of our runways was a hill mass which already presented a dangerous glide obstacle. To extend the field in that direction was out of the question. Going west we encountered a village and a river. We dug a new bed for the river, looping it about two miles around the end of the field and overrun. We had to demolish the village.

The piecemeal planning problem gave us the most trouble. In August we had raised our grade level at the 3,800-foot mark to overcome the unstable soil conditions. Now we were going to have to lower the grade level so we could cross the old stream bed without placing an uneconomical amount of fill. Fortunately, the drainage ditches we had dug to the north of the strip had stopped the underground water from reaching the former rice paddies that were now our airstrip. The soil was now more stable, but we had to go back to the 3,800-foot mark, take out all our original fill, and start excavating below the old ground level. Our former runway extension work was not only a complete loss, but we also lost additional time taking out the fill we had hauled in.

By the time I left Korea the runway jobs had progressed to the point where the surfacing was to be applied. The asphalt was planned to be three and a half inches deep, and the pierced-steel planking to cover it was already stored in piles on each side of the runway. At this time, however, specifications were again changed to make the asphalt six inches deep and to apply the pierced-steel planking only to the last five hundred feet of the runway. When you consider that the 1,200,-000 square feet of pierced steel planking that was not to be used at this site is both heavy and bulky, you can imagine the tremendous waste of manpower and transportation that was involved.

The building of K-2 took more than a year. Admittedly it was a big job and would have taken a lot of time and effort under ideal conditions. But the constant changes of plans led us to fill where later we were to dig, and haul pierced-steel planking to places where we were going to use only asphalt. Such changes made K-2 agonizingly slow and expensive. It also meant that jets could not come to K-2 when they were first needed. If the high-level planners had anticipated the final product, our project would have developed differently.

14. Equipment Without Operators

Capt. James E. McClure, Heavy Equipment Maintenance and Repair Officer, 76th Engineer Construction Battalion

The 76th Engineer Construction Battalion was on Okinawa when we were alerted to move to Korea. All weak equipment was exchanged and only the most aggressive officers and best-trained men were taken with the unit. In Korea we made a splendid record, but there were some occurrences that we are prone to forget.

From the moment our advance party arrived in Korea, the battalion was given an overload of work. To complete our missions we overworked our men and equipment. I shall not concern myself with the loss of morale and efficiency resulting from the long hours of work, or from assigning men the maintenance responsibility for three or more pieces of heavy equipment. I will only tell how the overload affected the equipment.

In August 1950 Ammunition Supply Point No. 1, near Pusan, had to be relocated to allow the construction of an Air Force runway. The area chosen for the new ASP was in the mountains two miles from the unloading piers. Ammunition bunkers were needed immediately since seven ammunition ships lay at anchor waiting to unload their cargos.

The engineering officer of Pusan Logistical Command assigned the construction of the ammunition bunkers to the 76th. He told our battalion commander (Lt.Col. Thomas K. Fullerton) that twelve additional D7 crawler tractors were available at the engineer depot and must be drawn to increase the battalion's work capacity. He ordered a 24-hour schedule until enough bunkers were completed to unload the anchored ships.

A battalion staff conference followed. During the discussion I pointed out that no surplus of trained equipment operators existed, and that the additional tractors would impose a hardship on the battalion without notably increasing production. Without trained operators there would be no preventive maintenance, and without that the tractors would not operate very long. In spite of these arguments, the directive to the battalion was specific and the colonel had no option but to order: "We will have to utilize the cooks and company clerks, if necessary, for operation of the additional equipment."

As equipment operators we selected carpenters and other men who had mechanical skills, and held a class on operation and preventive maintenance. We could only hope that the men would learn enough to get them by. Then the twelve D7 tractors were dispatched to the project site, and three qualified mechanics accompanied the group to support the operation.

After one day's operation the mechanics were swamped with deadlined tractors. The power-control units were all going bad, the grease seals were blowing, and the operating bands were overheating. There was no great showing of completed ammunition bunkers after forty-eight hours of continuous operation. In addition, half the tractors were out of action. The intense pressure from above to complete the project continued. Another battalion staff conference was held and it was decided to work two ten-hour shifts daily, and devote two hours of each shift to instruction and preventive maintenance. This prevented some tractors from deadlining. The work continued slowly but we kept ahead of the ammunition people because they had serious difficulties in their own operation.

On 25 August, Pusan Logistical Command again assigned us a new project with top priority. This was to build a POW inclosure, which involved draining a rice paddy and eliminating its lower areas with ten thousand cubic yards of fill. Unfortunately, the nearest fill obtainable had to be hauled five miles from a burrow pit.

Another meeting of the battalion staff was called to discuss the method of starting this project at a time when all of our battalion's personnel and dump trucks were otherwise engaged. Since we already had eight to ten top-priority projects assigned us, there was no reason to halt one to advance another. Additional dump trucks were available in the ordnance depot but again we had no drivers.

After much discussion, Colonel Fullerton accepted a tentative plan. Forty-three dump trucks would be drawn from the ordnance depot, and Korean civilian personnel would be trained as drivers. These trucks would be divided into two platoons, each to be controlled by a U.S. enlisted man with dump-truck experience. All Korean drivers would be kept in convoy with the enlisted supervisor driving the lead truck and controlling the speed. Finally, motor stables would be held daily, with the supervisor calling out each preventive maintenance point to be checked. Korean interpreters would relay the instructions to the drivers. This would insure daily preventive maintenance service on the Korean-operated equipment.

This plan was approved and put into operation. It worked very well for two months, with eighty per cent of the dump trucks serviceable and dispatched. Some time was lost at the excavator while waiting to load, but the control which the convoy plan gave us appeared to me to justify the loss of time. Colonel Fullerton, the S3, and I held several conferences concerning the time lost, but all agreed it was necessary to follow the original plan.

In October I had to be gone for two days. When I returned I found a new plan was in operation. Now, each Korean driver was individually responsible for his truck, and there was no immediate control by the enlisted supervisors. Trucks moved independently and the supervisors had little control over the forty-three trucks.

Three weeks after the initiation of this new policy, half the dump trucks were deadlined. These repairs often were necessary because the Koreans had not performed any preventive maintenance. The trucks, moving independently, were driven at excessive speeds and there was a high toll of broken springs and blown-out tires. The Korean drivers visited their homes for hours, and even sold their gasoline. Few of the drivers seemed to have any sense of responsibility.

As the efficiency of the operation declined rapidly and the number of deadlined trucks rose, the S3 came to me to complain about the trucks not operating.

I replied that the original policy of supervised operation and maintenance should be immediately re-established.

The operations officer, thinking only of immediate progress, answered: "It can't be done. We lose too much time that way."

I asked: "What are you accomplishing by your present policy?"

The S3 retorted: "You're the maintenance officer. It's up to you to keep the trucks rolling."

PART II

Transportation Corps

1. Critical Transportation

Col. John K. McCormick, G4; Major William H. Barker, Assistant Provost Marshal; Capt. Jasper N. Erskine, Highway Regulating Officer, X Corps; Major Harry J. Dodd, Executive Officer, 52d Transportation Truck Battalion. (Condensed from an article by Lt. John Mewha, 8th Historical Detachment, based on interviews with officers of X Corps.)

Highway transportation has always been critical in Korea. The limited road net has been broken down by heavy traffic, and roads through the mountains are often narrow and usable only for one-way traffic. Distances are long and turnarounds lengthy.

When the enemy attack began in May 1951, X Corps found it difficult to carry the greatly increased ammunition tonnages necessary to defend itself while maintaining supply and troop movements at the same time. The 52d Transportation Truck Battalion, which included elements of seventeen truck companies, supported X Corps. Temporary truck organizations were developed whenever it became necessary.

In mid-May the transportation officer of X Corps was directed to furnish forty trucks to assist the 3d Infantry Division's move from south of Seoul to Soksa-ri. Anticipating that the loss of forty vehicles would slow the delivery of supplies, the G4 of X Corps (Col. John K. McCormick) instructed the chiefs of X Corps' technical services to canvass their units for trucks not hauling essential cargos. The result was a collection of ¾- and 2-½-ton trucks and dump trucks, lowboys and equipment trailers. These were drawn from the 4th Signal Battalion, the 1st and 2d Mobile Army Surgical Hospitals, the 520th Quartermaster Battalion, the 69th Ordnance Battalion, and the 8224th Engineer Construction Group. The fifty to sixty trucks thus gathered were called "the Truck Bank."

Military police check points were set up by X Corps near each ammunition point. All empty trucks going north, except emergency vehicles, were loaded with ammunition. Each driver was given a note stating that his truck had been commandeered, and giving the amount of time it had been used. An average of twenty-five vehicles each day were pressed into service this way.

Under the direction of the 52d Truck Battalion, a separate truck group was established to haul ammunition exclusively. Many of the vehicles were taken from units of the 52d, others were borrowed from X Corps units.

A control point for ammunition trucks was established near the railhead at Wonju. To prevent confusion at the ammunition supply point, vehicles were dispatched in serials of five or ten. Normally twenty vehicles an hour entered the ammunition dump. At the control point a driver could get a meal from a 24-hour kitchen, and a service station provided second-echelon maintenance.

Once the ammunition trucks were loaded at Wonju, they drove to ASP No. 50 at Hongchon. Here the ammunition was usually transferred—from tail gate onto tail gate—to the vehicles of the using unit. For accounting and safety, it was against operating procedure for trucks to go directly from Wonju to the front lines, but it is believed that many of them did.

On the driver fell the burden of long hours of work. Normally each truck had two assigned drivers, and the shift was twelve hours. Many drivers, however, stayed at the wheel to the limits of endurance, and some drove eighteen or twenty hours daily.

Special operations required around-the-clock driving. To replace vehicles lost, a group of ordnance officers and men were flown to Pusan. They returned 104 trucks and 30 trailers from Pusan to Hongchon (332 miles) in 48 hours. Road conditions made driving slow and left little time for rest.

On another occasion, X Corps had only a few hours in which to gather three hundred trucks to make troop movements. The 52d Truck Battalion furnished 200 vehicles, and military police commandeered another 94. There was not enough time to notify the units that their vehicles had been taken, and no arrangements were made for gasoline or for feeding the drivers. The individual driver had to scrounge for his own supply. This system of obtaining transportation was used on other occasions.

Many other expedients had to be used when the demand for transportation was so great. Ordnance companies kept maintenance patrols on the road twenty-four hours a day, and light aircraft were used to spot disabled vehicles. Repair of the vehicles was accomplished on the spot, when possible, or the vehicles were returned to the shops for major repair.

Traffic control was carefully planned and supervised. In addition to standard highway control, light aircraft were used to direct military police to traffic jams. On one occasion, the corps commander's personal helicopter was used to patrol the roads and to assist in traffic control. X Corps approached one hundred per cent utilization of its truck capacity.

2. Truck Platoon in Korea

Lt. Alfred J. Catania, 377th Transportation Truck Company

Late in July 1950 a telegram cut short my leave and returned me to Fort Sill. There I found my unit, the 377th Transportation Truck Company, was on overseas alert.

Our assigned men were well trained, for we had completed an exercise only four months before. The training and capability of our replacements was still unknown. As we received new vehicles we ran them through our company motor shop, then through post ordnance, which prepared them for overseas shipment. Trailers were then loaded on and strapped to the beds of the trucks, and the trucks were loaded onto flatcars. This shipment preceded the company and was not seen again until after we arrived in Japan.

We landed at Yokohama on 28 August and were temporarily attached to Yokohama Motor Command. A few days later we received notice that some of our trucks had arrived at the port. It took some ten days to get all our vehicles since they came in several vessels and were unloaded at different piers.

While our vehicles were arriving in driblets we were warned to stand ready to load on one day's notice. This brought about confusion, as we had to requisition equipment from Yokohama Motor Command, and in most cases our own equipment arrived in time to be loaded. Inventories, overages, turn-ins, and paper work resulted.

While at Yokohama all our vehicles were put into running condition and combat-loaded. During the second week of September our personnel boarded a transport, and on about D plus 8 they were unloaded at Inchon. The next day our vehicles arrived and were put to work.

The beaches at Inchon were piled high with equipment. We hauled supplies over the causeway from Wolmi-do, from the beaches, and from shipside in the tidal basin. Our trucks operated around the clock. Each truck had two assigned drivers, and each worked a twelve-hour shift. The demand for transportation was so great that we did not have time to perform second-echelon maintenance. First-echelon maintenance was performed at the loading or unloading points, while the drivers waited in line. The company wrecker was posted near the tidal basin where all of our trucks had to pass. It carried parts and lubricants, and had two mechanics waiting to make emergency repairs and fix flat tires.

At Inchon we joined several newly arrived truck companies to form the 52d Transportation Truck Battalion. One day in mid-October, however, our company was relieved from the tidal basin haul at 1900, and departed for Pusan at 0200 the following morning. We were loaded with troops and equipment and made the forced march of 350 miles in about 36 hours. Every vehicle made it under its own power. We ran into sporadic enemy fire north of Taegu several times, but all vehicles kept moving and sustained no damage.

At Pusan the company had time to do some needed maintenance work. We left our trucks loaded and ready for movement to the transports. But orders were changed. We had to unload our cargo, haul troops, then reload and drive to dockside. This kept us plenty busy for the five days at Pusan.

Once on board the transports we lay at anchor some nine or ten days before we steamed to Wonsan, in North Korea, where we landed on 1 November 1950. The trucks were transferred to LSTs by the ships' gear, and some were damaged, since the transfer was made in heavy seas.

Our first mission ashore was to deliver the cargo in our vehicles. This included 37 truckloads to the 121st Evacuation Hospital at Hamhung, some 75 miles northeast. When we applied for road clearance, X Corps directed us to keep the vehicles in the Wonsan area as the enemy had set up a roadblock fifteen miles north. Marines cleared the road, and the next day we drove to Hamhung. We returned the following day, and the Wonsan–Hamhung run became our regular route.

Just before midnight of 5 November, the company was ordered to furnish an officer, a driver, and a jeep to the transportation officer of X Corps at 0600 next morning. I received the assignment. I reported and was informed I would be the commander of a convoy assembling at 0700 to move part of the 65th Infantry from Wonsan to Yonghung, about forty miles north. I was to control forty-six vehicles assembled from various corps units. I met my vehicles and at the same time reported to the CO of the 65th Infantry. He took the vehicles, parceled them out to his battalions and companies, and I had nothing more to do than follow the convoy and return the trucks when the march was over. The convoy left Wonsan at 0930 but did not arrive at Yonghung until 1600. The movement was slow, and the convoy stopped time and again to investigate groups of civilians near the road, and occasionally to send out a patrol or engage in a small fire fight.

At Yonghung the troops were unloaded in different areas. I designated a rendezvous in Yonghung and waited for my trucks to assemble. The first trucks arriving at the rendezvous I moved out as a serial at 1700. It was 1800 before the rest were ready to go. The return trip should not have taken over two hours, but before I could clear the town I had to wait for a long Marine tank convoy. I was delayed over an hour and it was dark before my serial left Yonghung. My jeep was the last vehicle.

After we passed Kowon, about halfway to Wonsan, I noticed a fire up ahead. I doubled the stopped convoy and at the head of the column I found a 2-½-ton truck, loaded with 55-gallon drums of gasoline, on fire. The truck had been burning for some time since the drums were already beginning to explode. The flaming vehicle was in the middle of a narrow, one-lane causeway, with rice paddies on each side. My lead vehicle was halted at a fork in the road. The burning truck was on the left fork, which was the main road. I was quite sure from my previous trips that the right fork went through a village, bent to the left, crossed a bridge, and joined the main road about two miles away. I told the ser-

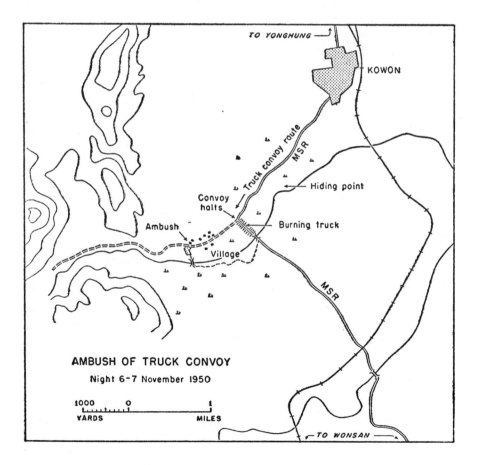

AMBUSH OF TRUCK CONVOY

Night 6-7 November 1950

geant in the lead vehicle to reconnoiter the right fork to the main road, checking especially the capacity of the bridge. He took several men with him in his jeep, and on his return said the road was wide enough and the bridge strong enough to support a 2-½-ton truck.

The convoy then proceeded by the right fork, but stopped about a mile farther on. Again I doubled the column to see what was wrong. The sergeant told me things didn't look right to him. Although the civilians were under curfew, a civilian had stood by the road as he drove through the village and waved the convoy on. Farther on, seven or eight civilians were standing in the road, but scattered when they came within the headlight beams. I told the men to remount and continue on, but at that moment we were struck by small-arms fire from both sides of the road and in front. We were forced to the rear, and I instructed the men to stay on the road and fire at anyone who approached from the fields on each side of us. This was to prevent our men from firing at one another in the dark.

Making a defense with these 25 to 30 men was virtually impossible. I didn't know them, since they were not from the 377th. Some of them had no weapons. One truck mounted a caliber .50 machine gun, and I ordered the driver to return fire with it. He got into position and pulled at the operating handle, then declared that the weapon was jammed. Later, the enemy turned this gun on us, and I believe that driver just didn't know how to use his weapon. In the circumstances I could do nothing but order the men to move to the rear of the convoy. At the tail of the column I ordered the last four trailers unhitched, the trucks turned, and the men to load up and drive out. Three vehicles were turned around, loaded, and moved out. Then I discovered I was alone with the fourth truck! All the men had left in the first three.

I got into the fourth truck, started the engine, and turned it around. As I did so a North Korean ran alongside. His white clothing stood out clearly in the night. I pointed my pistol at him and fired twice. I either hit him or scared him, because he dropped back, and I drove away.

Half a mile down the road I passed two of the trucks that had preceded me. Both were in a ditch, and one was on its side. Then I came to the third truck, which was halted and blocking the road. A hail of fire began to hit my vehicle from the left and I believe a hundred men were firing their rifles from an embankment. Bullets splintered the hood and the cab of the truck, and I felt one nick my leg. I jumped from the truck on the right side and ran through the rice paddies. I put a good mile between me and the scene of the ambush, but I saw none of the men of the convoy in that distance. Then I lay low for the night.

I heard the enemy soldiers driving the vehicles during the night, and searching everywhere for our drivers. Early in the morning I heard someone walking about, and I saw he was an American. I told him to be quiet and to join me, but he was so disgusted and tired he didn't seem to care. He said he had been captured by two North Koreans during the night, and that they had debated what to do with him. One obviously wanted to kill him, the other was for letting him go. Finally, they relieved him of his valuables, hit him over the head with his own rifle, kicked him, and let him go.

Late in the night the guerrillas burned all the vehicles, since they could not take them up into the mountains with them. During this night Kowon was recaptured, and the 65th Infantry and the 96th Field Artillery Battalion at Yonghung were both under heavy attack.

When the civilians began to come out of doors next morning I figured everything had quieted down. The enlisted man and I forced a civilian to guide us to the main road, and we started walking toward Wonsan. We hid when a jeep came along until we were sure it was carrying Americans, then we hailed it. The ride took us to X Corps headquarters, where I reported to the transportation officer, and later to G2.

I found I was not wounded in the leg as I supposed, but I had bullet holes through both trouser legs. I never learned what happened to the men of that convoy, for they came from so many different units. Those who escaped just returned "home." My jeep driver came back a day after I did, with a story that matched mine.

Two days later, the 377th moved the equipment of X Corps headquarters to Hamhung. We were billeted in that city and worked directly under the corps transportation officer until the 52d Transportation Truck Battalion and its other companies joined us. About the third week in November we were attached to the 7th Infantry Division and the company moved to Pukchong and worked directly under that division's G4.

We moved rations, ammunition, and gasoline for the 7th Division over one of the highest and most difficult mountain ranges in Korea. The main supply road was only one lane wide over a mountain that was 11 miles uphill and 9 miles downhill (going north). MPs with telephones and radios were posted on each side of the mountain and controlled the traffic. Convoys moved as quickly as they were loaded, and the south-bound trip usually carried troops, prisoners, or empty gasoline drums. A temperature of 10 below zero in the mountains did not contribute to the comfort of any trip.

On 27 November I was instructed to take my truck platoon to X Corps headquarters at Hamhung. There I was to meet a 7th Division liaison officer and receive further instructions. In Hamhung the liaison officer told me I was to shuttle parts of two infantry regiments to the Changjin Reservoir area.

On 28 November I loaded a reinforced infantry company of 325 men and headed for a small town 15 or 20 miles north of Hamhung. I unloaded the troops and went back for a second shuttle. I was met by a messenger who informed me I was to take the same reinforced company and move it to its regimental CP on the highway east of Changjin Reservoir. The instructions were rather vague as to the CP's location, but I returned and remounted the troops.

About five miles farther north, MPs stopped the convoy and delayed it for about two hours while engineers cleared the road ahead of a landslide.

While we were waiting on the road some North Korean soldiers were captured. They were walking down the road in civilian clothes but our KATUSA[1] troops spotted them. We inquired why our men were so certain, and they replied that the "civilians" had their hair cut—strictly a military operation in Korea. Interrogated, the prisoners admitted their military identities; one claimed he was from a North Korean regiment, the other said he was attached to a Chinese unit.

At 2100 we approached Koto-ri and were halted by U.S. marines. We were told the enemy had a roadblock just a thousand yards farther up the road. Our convoy pulled into the Marine perimeter for the night, and the following morning Col. Lewis B. Puller, USMC, formed all troops in the vicinity into a task force. This included a Marine company, our reinforced company, and a company of British Royal Marine Corps commandos. An artillery barrage began, and then U.S. Marine jet fighters plastered the hills on both sides of the road. I watched the show as I waited at the U.S. Marine command post.

At about 1400 I was ordered to a rendezvous point, but on arriving there found the infantry were still fighting. I stopped the convoy a few hundred yards behind the infantry and went forward on foot to the company commander. I located him in his gully CP and told him I had instructions to carry him up the road. He replied that he was still under fire and didn't see how he could possibly load up or continue through. He dispatched a messenger to inform Colonel Puller of the situation. About two hours later a message came back, again ordering the infantry to load up and proceed.

As a result of loading under fire, the infantry got all mixed up and lost its tactical unity. Other convoys began moving at the same time, and we were soon mixed with Marine and Army trucks. The British commandos were riding with our marines.

The trucks maintained a 50-to-100-yard interval. There were frequent unexplained halts, and by dark my vehicle had made only three miles. I walked forward during a halt to see the cause of the delay. At this point the road was running through a valley some 500 or 600 yards wide, flanked by sharp-rising mountains. To the right of the road was a narrow-gauge railroad in the scant fifty yards between us and the slope.

---

[1] Korean Augmentation to the United States Army.

To the left it was almost five hundred yards to the incline, but a fast-flowing mountain stream divided the distance. It was very dark except for the period when the moon was directly over the valley.

When I was some four hundred yards ahead of my vehicle, I saw five or six Chinese soldiers walking along the railroad track to our right.

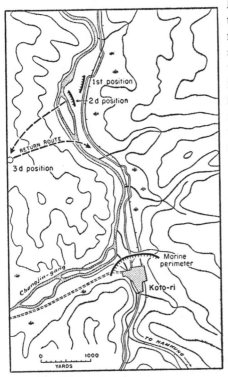

It was just light enough to identify their quilted uniforms. I warned a nearby truckload of infantrymen and they began searching the area with rifle fire. I pitched a grenade in the direction where I had last seen the enemy. This acted as a signal, and the Chinese began firing on us from the railroad and up on the mountainside to our right—all the way up and down the column. Rifles, machine guns, grenades and mortars, all east of the road, began striking the vehicles and men.

Our trucks were widely separated and there was no great concentration of men at any point. Near me were only a couple of my own men and some infantrymen. Throughout the night I did not see any of the infantry officers, but our convoy was spread over three or four miles, and they could have been anywhere in the column. Because of the confusion in loading, not even squads were together. I took command of everyone near me and directed the men to fall behind the trucks into the field west of the road. There was little cover, however, and it was impossible to dig into the frozen ground.

Casualties were mounting, and I was wounded twice. I was hit once in the back by a shell fragment, and in the shoulder by a caliber .45 slug that broke my collar bone and lodged in my neck. The pain was great. I thought I'd been hit in the neck, and an infantryman even bandaged me there. He also gave me a shot of morphine to ease the pain. I had my head propped up on my helmet and continued to give what little control was possible in the situation.

One of my men told me a truck in the middle of the valley floor had a caliber .30 machine gun strapped to its fender and a box of ammunition under the seat. After the attack had begun the driver had turned this vehicle around and had tried to make a break for it down the middle of the field, but had abandoned the attempt. As luck would have it, the truck was now in clear moonlight, in the direct line of fire, and the machine gun was strapped to the front fender on the side nearest the enemy. I called for volunteers, fearing that if we didn't get the gun the enemy would. None of the infantrymen would go, but one of my truck drivers volunteered and made the trip. He reached the truck, crawled onto the near fender and reached over the hood to pull the machine gun from its position. He could not get the tripod. Then he got the box of ammunition from under the driver's seat and returned. Throughout the night he fired the machine gun from the hip, and it was an important weapon in our defense. When he ran out of ammunition he threw the gun in a deep hole in the stream. This soldier was later awarded the Silver Star.

With our heavy casualties, and a feeling the enemy was coming in on our flanks, I decided to fall back to the stream at about 0200. At 0430 it became clear we could not remain there either. I told the men to split up, cross the stream, and head for the mountain behind. The numbing effect of the cold seemed to make it less effort just to remain where they were, and I finally decided to move on with just one of my truckers. I had to be helped to get my head up, but then I could walk. As the infantry saw me go they slowly moved out, waded the stream, and started up the hill.

As I got farther up the hill it developed that my own party would be three enlisted men and myself. One of the truckers and the infantryman with us were wounded. Only one driver was unhurt. He helped us along. After all that had gone on during the night, the infantryman still clutched a blanket, and carried it with him.

When we reached the hilltop it began to get light. I knew our feet would freeze if we did not give them attention since we had gotten them wet in wading the stream. I always carried a knife that was fashioned from an old, cut-down cavalry saber, and we used this to cut the frozen laces of our boots. I hoped to take out the heavy, inner-liner socks and warm them next to my body, but they were so frozen to the boots that I could not get them out. I threw away both socks and shoes. I used my pile-liner cap in place of one shoe and tied strips of blanket around the other foot. The men did the same.

Near daylight we became aware of another party near at hand. We were scared, but no worse than the three marines who finally challenged us. We had been within fifty yards of one another for some time without knowing it. I still laugh at the marine challenging us with his carbine. It had gotten wet when he crossed the stream and the bolt was a solid block of ice. He could no more have shot me than he could have shot his dear old grandmother back in the States.

None of the marines was wounded, so I asked them to go back the three miles to the Marine perimeter and see if they could get us some help. They agreed, but after a two-hour wait we became apprehensive. Finally, our small party began to move painfully back toward the Marine position. Soon it became apparent we would have to return to the road to make the journey. We did so and marched straight down the road to Koto-ri. It was an unusual journey, for we knew the Chinese were all about us and watching us walk. From near us they fired at a helicopter that flew up the canyon. Yet they let us hobble past.

When we reached the Marine perimeter at Koto-ri, I found that the town was surrounded. With the other wounded I was placed on a stretcher in a tent, and stayed there for three days. During the first two days rations were short and I got only one can of C rations and a couple of cups of fruit juice. Food didn't bother me much at that point, however. On the third day an airstrip was opened and the food became much better. Light planes began to fly out the more seriously wounded, and I went out by that method. From Koto-ri I flew to Hamhung, then was loaded on a C-54 for Japan. From Japan I was flown to the United States.

November 1950 was a pretty rough month on the 377th. At the end of that period we had only 21 vehicles left of our original 48. It was pretty tough on my platoons, too. In the ambush above Koto-ri, 18 of my 30 men became casualties: 3 killed, 7 wounded, 8 missing. I noticed 4 of the missing on the POW lists released by the Chinese. They were carried as "members of the 7th Infantry Division."

3. Amphibian Truck Company

Capt. Robert J. Gilroy, 3d Transportation Amphibian Truck Company

The 74th Transportation Truck Company was based on Yokohama Motor Command. On 7 July 1950 the unit was inactivated and reactivated as the 8062d Transportation Amphibian Truck Company (Provisional). There had been only 3 officers and 94 enlisted men in the 74th, and these became the nucleus of the amphibian outfit.

Immediately upon activation, the commanding officer (Capt. Robert J. Gilroy) requested additional personnel and equipment, based on the new T/O&E. The company received 100 enlisted men from commands throughout Japan, and 2 additional officers. Even so, there was only one person in the entire company—an enlisted man—who had been in an amphibian truck company before. The company did not receive any mechanics experienced in repairing amphibian trucks (DUKWs), nor did it receive additional drivers to handle the 71 vehicles the company received instead of its authorized 38.

Almost as soon as the DUKWs were issued, Captain Gilroy was informed that his company was to participate in the assault landings at Pohang-dong. The drivers were given only a short series of training talks before they were assigned the mission of loading the three field artillery battalions of the 1st Cavalry Division.

On 18 July 1950 the 8062d landed at Pohang-dong—carrying the three battalions of 105-mm howitzers, unloading them, and towing them behind the DUKWs into their battery positions. During the next twenty-four hours the company moved from ship to shore thirty thousand rounds of 105-mm ammunition, and untotaled amounts of rocket and small-arms ammunition.

On 1 August 1950 the company was redesignated the 3d Transportation Amphibian Truck Company, operating under T/O&E 55-37, augmented by one operating platoon. This called for 50 amphibian trucks, but the company continued to operate the 71 DUKWs originally assigned, still with the same number of personnel.

During 1-26 August we off-loaded approximately 26,500 tons of ammunition from nine vessels at Suyong. To handle this operation the company found it necessary to set up, staff, supervise, and operate traffic control systems used by the truck companies assisting us; unloading points in the ammunition dump, traffic nets and systems; and complete organization and control of the transfer points. Cranes were not available at the transfer points, and the A-frames organic to the DUKW company were used instead.

Concurrent with the operations at Suyong, the company sent detachments on various tactical missions. Five are of especial importance.

(1) On 8 August 1950 a detachment commanded by Sgt. Lawrence Riley was sent to operate with the 1st Marine Brigade at Masan. This detachment unloaded supplies from LSTs, then evacuated wounded from Masan under fire.

(2) On 11 August 1950 a detachment commanded by Sgt. James M. Simms was placed on detached service with KMAG for operations at Yongdok. Here the men unloaded badly needed ammunition from LSTs, then evacuated wounded to a hospital ship. All this was done under heavy fire.

(3) On 16 August 1950 another detachment under Sergeant Riley joined KMAG to unload urgently needed supplies from an LST into Pohang-dong. This mission was completed under fire while the North Koreans were attacking the town. Later these men assisted in the evacuation of the town.

(4) On 1 September 1950 a detachment under Sgt. Clifton B. Nelson was placed on detached service with the 9th Infantry to carry sup-

plies across the Naktong River. Before this could be done, attacking North Korean forces made a withdrawal necessary. This detachment helped to evacuate friendly troops under fire.

(5) On 4 September 1950 a detachment commanded by Lt. Jack W. Ley departed on LSTs for the vicinity of Pohang-dong. There the LSTs lay off shore while Lieutenant Ley's detachment evacuated 750 wounded South Korean soldiers from near the battle lines.

On 19 September 1950 two platoons were ordered to the 2d Infantry Division to assist the assault crossing of the Naktong River. One platoon, commanded by Lt. John F. Williams, reported to the 23d Infantry. This platoon made a successful crossing. In the forty hours following H-hour, it carried the 23d Infantry's three battalions and their supplies across the river. During this same period, by lashing a section of ponton bridge between two DUKWs, the platoon ferried 138 tanks across the river. The platoon remained at the site for the next eight days to operate a ferry and to assist the engineers in constructing a bridge.

A second platoon, under Lt. Claude Payne, came under exceedingly heavy fire. The crossing was made and ferry service established, but at a cost of 2 killed, 4 wounded, and 10 DUKWs damaged and sunk by enemy mortar and small-arms fire. All but one of these amphibian vehicles were salvaged and returned to service. Lieutenant Payne's operation was carried out under extremely adverse conditions. Mud—the DUKW's worst enemy—lined both river banks. Enemy fire, ground haze, and lack of information hindered the mission.

On 8 October 1950 an advance party and an operating platoon, all commanded by Lt. Carl E. Glenn, moved into Inchon and set up a bivouac at Wolmi-do. There the 3d TAT Company commenced operations. As there was no site suitable for DUKW operations, the 50th Engineer Port Construction Company was called to blast entry and exit points from almost-solid rock at the shore line.

On 18 October 1950 the entire company was engaged in a sustained cargo haul from ship to a rail transfer point. As the operation continued, wear and tear began to tell on the vehicles. In one period of twenty-four hours, three DUKWs sank as a result of rusted-out hulls. Cpl. Elmo Anderson was awarded the Soldier's Medal for saving the life of a South Korean laborer when the DUKW in which they were riding sank. Using old, rebuilt vehicles, battling a 30-foot, 5-½-knot tide, and making extremely long water hauls, the company achieved a splendid mark in tonnage hauled.

On 4 January 1951 a platoon commanded by Lt. Charles A. Boughton was dispatched with elements of the 558th TAT Company to the Han River to assist in the withdrawal of friendly troops from the far shore. That same day, the rest of the company began to evacuate Wolmi-do.

When about half of its equipment had been loaded, the company was ordered to evacuate on any ship available because of the nearness of hostile forces. The personnel and equipment were loaded aboard three different vessels. Six DUKWs that had been condemned by the Ordnance Corps were stripped of all usable parts and then sunk in Inchon harbor at 0200 hours, 5 January. The ships sailed at about 0400.

The main body of the 3d TAT Company arrived in Yokohama on 9 January 1951 and began reorganization. New equipment, including fifty new DUKWs, was received. The officer in charge of the rebuilding section of Fuchu Ordnance Center was amazed when he learned of the operation of the old vehicles formerly assigned to the company. He said that at the time those vehicles were rebuilt he had felt it would not be feasible to employ them for any purpose except training.

4. Railhead at Masan

Capt. Meade D. Wildrick, 8010th Army Unit, Transportation Military Railway Service

I arrived in Korea on 7 July 1950 in a detachment from the 8010th Army Unit, Transportation Military Railway Service. Our force consisted of 19 officers and 90 enlisted men. These were not enough to have taken over the Korean railroads—even had we wanted to, or had had the authority. Instead, our group was split into ten traffic-regulating teams. Three of these remained in Pusan, two went to Taegu, and one each went to Taejon, Yongchon, Kumchon, and Kyongju.

How well we kept things moving can be seen from our record of those early days. We were told by the U.S. military advisory group to the Republic of Korea (KMAG) and the officials of the Korean National Railroads that we would set a record if we moved more than 12 trains a day north from Pusan. Actually, we soon dispatched 24 trains daily, most of them double-headers pulling 30 cars. The trains going over the east coast single-track line could not take 30 cars, however, since the sidings were not long enough. The Koreans ran the trains; we gave the directions.

As soon as our army came to Korea we realized the importance of the railroads. Because of the long distances and the very poor roads, everyone moving in Korea wanted to go by rail. Pusan Base Section ruled that rail movement was possible only for vehicles over two and one half tons that were going farther than Taegu. Everything lighter, or going shorter distances, had to be driven.

Not long after I arrived in Korea I was assigned to establish a railhead at Masan—with only Sergeant Dennison as my assistant. Dennison was a real help, for he knew railroading and from a previous tour in Korea he could speak the language. Fortunately, the assistant stationmaster spoke English, and so did one of the switchmen.

Masan is about thirty-five miles west of Pusan, and its marshaling yard contained only eight tracks. We had a problem keeping the yard open to receive supplies for the 24th Infantry Division while its withdrawals kept forcing equipment back into our yard. Communications were so limited that we had little opportunity to plan our operations. We received advance notice whenever a train was coming from Pusan, but those from Taegu just blew their whistles as the engines entered the yards. We had to post an officer at the Samnangjin junction to halt trains and call ahead to determine whether they should be allowed to enter Masan.

The 24th Division wished to leave much of its equipment on freight cars, particularly its heavy engineer equipment. I had to explain to the division's officers that the utter lack of yard space prevented holding cars for storage purposes. The division assigned a liaison officer to work with me, and that helped. He told me where the division wanted cars spotted, and I took over from there.

In July 1950 the railroads became congested because too many persons were giving directions in Pusan. Pusan Base Section was put together hurriedly, and it did a remarkable job. However, there were a few extra—and I believe unassigned—colonels in the headquarters. They acted as expediters, and would come to dockside or to the marshaling yards and take over operations from the regularly assigned lieutenants and captains. Each had a pet mission, it seemed. They were always saying, "The men need ammunition forward," or some similar statement. Other supplies would be shunted aside and priority in unloading ships and in rail movement would be assigned. Taegu was being swamped with supplies being evacuated, and with others sent forward by the eager colonels of Pusan. The situation eventually reached the point where the port transportation officer complained to the base section commander.

A control system was established to determine daily how much tonnage could be moved to a given destination. A canvass was then made of the technical services. A train was made up to fit the requirements, and clearance was necessary before the train moved. It was not a perfect system, but it took a lot of the "hurry up and wait" out of the situation.

5. Problems in Railroad Operation

Capt. B. C. Mossman, 6th Historical Detachment. (Condensed from an article based on interviews with the following personnel of the 3d Transportation Military Railway Service: Lt. Col. Jesse M. McClellan, Commanding Officer; Lt. Col. Howard W. Martens, Assistant General Manager, Engineer; Lt. Col. Frank H. Drake, AGM, Communications; Lt. Col. Lawrence R. Anderson, Deputy AGM, Engineer; Lt. Col. Clarence E. Page, AGM, Supply; MSgt. Jack R. Spillers, Chief Clerk.)

Railroad activities in the Korean conflict have been vital to the movement of troops, equipment, and supplies. The military railway personnel have been faced constantly with problems of reconstruction, operation, maintenance, destruction, and then, again, reconstruction of the rail lines, bridges, stations, and communications facilities. All these have had to be handled along with the forward and rearward movement of supply trains as the tactical situation changed.

During the first several months, as the United Nations troops were withdrawing to the Naktong perimeter, there were few technical problems. This was a period in which traffic control and the train movements were the major considerations. When the September drive began, however, the railroads had to contend with destroyed water pumps, bridges, stations and tracks, and communications.

The locomotives of the Korean National Railroads were all steam-operated and required large amounts of water. Pumps were in poor condition originally, but in the recaptured territory they were broken or had no power. The first pumps obtained from the Corps of Engineers had a capacity of only 166 gallons per minute. Later, 480-gallon pumps were installed and found satisfactory. To provide electricity for shops, roundhouses and pumping stations, 100-kilowatt generators were installed.

Communications were also a problem. From Sindong to Seoul, communications lines were 75 per cent destroyed; from Seoul to Kaesong, 100 per cent; from Kaesong to Pyongyang, 25 per cent. U.S. signal troops and supplies were not available for repair of the lines. Until December 1950 only Korean communications men could be used, and their work was unsatisfactory.

There was no copper wire for railroad communications lines, and field wire was used in emergency circuits. These circuits would function only for a day or two. Then a second expedient was attempted—SCR-399 radios placed at each main station between Taegu and Seoul. This, too, was unsatisfactory.

By late November the telephone line between Sindong and Seoul had been pieced together and was working after a fashion. Early in December a good line was established from Kaesong to Pyongyang, but it was mid-December before the line between Seoul and Kaesong was functioning properly. The circuits between Pyongyang and Sinanju never operated.

The greatest help to the railway communications system was the Mukden cable circuits, provided by Eighth Army in late November and early December. Circuits to Pusan, Taegu, Taejon, Chonan, and Pyongyang were assigned directly to the 3d TMRS switchboard.

During the withdrawal of November–January there was no difficulty with communications. In addition to the Mukden cable circuits, the 3d TMRS now had good wayside communications from Pyongyang to Seoul.

As the troops moved north after the breakout from the Pusan perimeter, the 3d TMRS and KNR personnel repaired tracks and bridges. Such repairs made heavy demands on the engineers for timbers and tools. If the engineers had these, the 3d TMRS got them.

U.S. engineers repaired the Naktong River bridge at Waegwan, the Han River shoo-fly bridge (expedient railroad structure) at Seoul, the Imjin River shoo-fly bridge, and the high-level bridge at Hanpo-ri. Except for these, Korean bridge and track gangs repaired the rail lines during the advance. They opened the lines rapidly by using sandbags, timber trestling, and rail stringers as expedients. The Korean gangs could repair as much in three or four days as the U.S. engineers in ten. However, it was somewhat difficult to get the lightly clad Korean gangs to work during cold weather.

During the fall of 1950 the KNR had money to make repairs. However, the scale of reconstruction was so vast that in December the money ran out. It was then necessary for the United States to pay all labor, new construction, and repair charges.

By late November continuous operation as far North as the Taedong station was made possible by the completion of the bridge at Hanpo-ri over the Yesong River. On 1 December 1950 the railroad was in operation as far north as Sinanju, but there was no railroad bridge crossing the Taedong River at Pyongyang. Both bridges across the Taedong had been blown and it was necessary to unload the cars at the Taedong station, load the supplies on trucks which crossed a ponton bridge, and then reload trains going north. At the time of the Chinese Communist offensive, the Korean railroads were carrying four thousand tons daily into Taedong.

When the general withdrawal started, the technical services hurriedly evacuated large quantities of critical matériel. However, certain supplies remained in the north and others were moved northward to meet requirements. Empty cars were sent into Taedong for south-bound loading.

Successive railheads were set up at points where the division could draw POL, rations, and ammunition. As one railhead was closed, another was opened farther south. This went on for several weeks, all the way south through Chonan.

The locomotives and rolling stock north of the unbridged Taedong River were destroyed because they could not be evacuated. South of Pyongyang, every effort was made to save as much as possible. Rail yards were stripped. Inoperative locomotives were destroyed. Bridges, switches, control towers, and other equipment were dynamited.

A typical closing of the rail line was the operation at Yongdungpo. On 4 January, 23 trains (462 cars) moved south-bound between 0001 and 2030 hours. One of the last trains contained machinery and equipment from the KNR shops and yards. The movement control personnel rode the last train, while the engineer and transportation representatives who demolished the yards withdrew by jeep. By 0200, 5 January, Yongdungpo was cleared, and trains were moving south on both tracks of the main line.

Similar operations took place at Ascom City and Inchon. Heavy traffic moved out by rail over the main line, but much was moved by rail to Inchon and placed on ships. Rail yards at these two cities were blown on the night of 4 January; the railroaders, including the KNR employees, were moved to Pusan by water. Only the last two switch engines working at the docks were destroyed.

During the withdrawal, thousands of Korean refugees streamed south. Railroad yards became so crowded that the refugees had to be driven away before the trains could be made up. This was particularly true at Seoul and Yongdungpo. All south-bound trains carried refugees —as long as one more could hang on.

Screening points for the north-bound cars were set up along the main line. Items not needed, or intended for units that had moved, were cut out. But even with this system, the consignee unit was often gone when a car arrived at its destination. If possible, a re-routing or re-consignment was made.

The urgency of the tactical situation brought much disorganized loading. Some cars were not marked, others were marked inadequately, and on some the marks were obliterated. The railroads moved all cars. Screening was carried out along the line, but it allowed many unmarked cars to be brought all the way to the Pusan area.

Early in January, 20 to 30 trains were coming into Pusan area daily. The rail lines could not handle this volume. About 50 per cent of the cars arriving were unmarked. Screening teams, which opened the cars, often found items for three or four different services loaded into one car. It took months to clear the Pusan yards of the retrograde tonnage.

The men of the Korean National Railroads showed great loyalty and courage during the withdrawal. In several instances train and engine crews moved their trains from a city as the infantry withdrew. At Sojong-ni the infantry had taken up positions south of the town while the KNR crews were still making up the last train.

6. Railroading in Korea

Capt. Max N. Brown, 714th Transportation Railway Operating Battalion

An American can teach a Korean to run a railroad by our standards, but it takes patience. There are many things we can do in fifteen minutes that take Koreans two hours. This wouldn't make much difference if combat didn't make all operations urgent. But when you realize that the Korean railroads moved approximately 95 per cent of all tonnage to the front, you know the Koreans (and the Americans who assisted them) gave a pretty fair account of themselves.

I commanded Company C, 714th (later 724th) Transportation Railway Operating Battalion. Company C is the operating company—it furnishes the men who run the trains. In Korea we had to tailor our operations to the situation, and many changes were made.

The Koreans provided full crews for their trains, and their hands were on the throttles. In late 1951 we began to bring some diesel engines into Korea, and we placed our own men in the cabs of these—plus a Korean pilot engineer.

Except for this late development, it would appear that we had no job. This was not true. We provided about a hundred conductors. The Korean conductor on each train was in command and, in a sense, our man was an advisor. But on one thing our conductor had absolute control: dropping cars. To prevent wholesale pilferage we insisted that no car could be cut out of a train at a way station unless our conductor approved. He had to check each claim of a hotbox or other failure.

Beginning at Pusan, the 714th Battalion operated beyond Wonju on the eastern railroad and to Taejon on the double-track main line. Normally, an operating battalion controls 90 to 125 miles of track, but we covered 500 to 600 miles. In this situation Company C was assigned 400 of the 511 men in our battalion, even though the T/O&E gave us only 289. To get the conductors we needed for our operation we used our unassigned steam engineers and gave others on-the-job training.

The shortage of freight cars placed a severe strain on the railroad system. We had approximately 7,000 cars, but 500 of these were in very bad shape. Estimating a seven-day turnaround between Pusan and the front, we figured 8,500 cars were the minimum to handle the load. We received a one-day advance notice of our requirements, and that kept us jumping to have cars on hand. More than once the cars were not in our yards and we could not meet the demand.

The shortage of cars and their constant use led to several problems. We could not take cars out of circulation to repair them as often as we should have. Also, we could not allow cars to remain on the sidings—something that had to be drilled into commanders in the forward areas.

Looking back at our operations in Korea, I believe our biggest problem was keeping the tracks open. We had an unbelievable number of derailments—I recall six in one day—and we had only one car with a hook on it. The derailments were caused most frequently by the worn-out equipment, but sabotage did occur. We were fortunate in having a group of experienced Koreans clearing the tracks. I marvelled at the ingenuity of the Koreans as they put freight cars back onto the rails with little or no equipment. Everything considered, the Korean railroad personnel have done extremely well.

7. Transportation Corps Operations at K-27

Capt. James B. Reed, Headquarters, X Corps

I landed at Inchon with the 7th Infantry Division. At the time I was doing a two-year tour with a combat arm. In October 1950 I reverted to the Transportation Corps, and was assigned to X Corps headquarters. When I was asked if I knew anything about air-terminal operations, I replied, "No." It made no difference.

I was ordered to K-27 Airstrip at Yonpo, several miles south of Hungnam. The Army personnel at the field consisted of one second lieutenant (myself) and an enlisted man. Soon we were assigned a jeep, a trailer, and a driver, and later we were augmented by a truck platoon. After several weeks I was replaced for several days by a captain; then I returned to K-27 and again ran the operation.

My mission at K-27 was to document Army cargo and passengers. The combat-cargo officer was glad to have us because the Air Force was not equipped to handle the job. We received a great deal of cooperation and good accommodations.

It was my duty to see that Army passengers were received at the terminal and given transportation to headquarters, or that they were placed on a plane. We gave maximum assistance. Then we checked passenger manifests to see that the lists were correct.

Medical evacuees were handled differently. Their flight was arranged between the surgeon of X Corps and the Air Force base surgeon. The wounded were moved from ambulances to planes, and the Air Force nurses and specialists took over from our medics. I received an extract of the manifest, however, so I could count the evacuees as passengers through the port.

The cargo operation was different. As soon as a plane arrived, an Air Force cargo checker went over the manifest to see what was aboard. The allocation number on each crate showed the service to which it belonged and its general contents. A platoon of marines stationed on the field unloaded the cargo from the planes into our trucks, and the checker indicated the proper section of the in-transit storage area to which each item should go.

We rarely knew in advance what was coming, but sometimes we were told to be on the lookout for a particular item. A small shipment might have the address stenciled on the box. In such cases we quickly notified the consignee, but most shipments did not list the name of the consignee. Every day we reported what was in the in-transit storage area and the consignment number to G4 of X Corps. At corps it was a matter of matching the requests with the receipts. This was done rather haphazardly at first and we had some errors. Once an American hospital requested a shipment, and a ROK hospital made a similar request at the same time. The ROKs inquired and we surrendered a medical shipment to them. We found later that they got the shipment due the American hospital. Many of the supplies were now consumed, and it was necessary to reorder for the U.S. group. It was not always easy to unscramble the shipments, but in time the operation worked more smoothly.

The picture changed greatly during the evacuation of Hungnam. Instead of documenting cargos that arrived, we just loaded and moved cargo and passengers as fast as we could outload them. We forgot about safety limits and carried maximum loads. Still, in the midst of the confusion and evacuation, the Air Force did a peculiar thing. While we were trying to get rid of supplies, planes coming from rear areas brought us drums of gasoline we did not want. It took a lot of time to unload those 55-gallon drums, and then we had to haul the gasoline to Hungnam to get it evacuated. We got the Air Force to stop once, but then the shipments began again. Don't ask me what it was all about. I never figured it out.

Neither the Air Force nor the Army had sufficient personnel at K-27 to carry out terminal operations as completely or efficiently as in

Pusan. There the Transportation Corps loaded and unloaded the planes and controlled the ground operation completely.

8.   Breakage En Route

> Major Lawrence Dobson, Observer for The Quartermaster General. (Excerpt from an oral report of 25 April 1951.)

All food going into Korea had to pass through the port of Pusan. I was utterly amazed when I visited the port on the first of March, for I saw an operation that, had anyone told me existed, I would have said, "No, they can't do it."

Cargo ships were block-loaded; in other words, similar components were segregated within the ship. But they were not being unloaded that way. The stevedores were Koreans, and with no supervision in the holds, everything was thrown into the cargo net. The loaded nets were not lowered, but were dropped. The cases of food were picked up, carried over, and thrown into piles, and segregated later.

Every time a case was broken, something was stolen. When they did not break a case open, the Koreans had small knives with which they were very adept. They cut the cases open—especially the post exchange packs. It was estimated that we were taking a 10 per cent complete loss on all subsistence items passing through the port. My estimate was that 90 per cent of the cases had some damage. This might be only a dented can, but we were still absorbing a loss before it came into the hands of the quartermaster.

I discussed the situation with the commanding officer of the 55th Quartermaster Depot (Col. Louis E. Cotulla). He said he was aware of the situation but had done everything he could with the port command. I later discussed it with the Eighth Army quartermaster (Col. James M. Lamont), and wanted to talk to G4. I was told, however, that there was a change in command coming into Pusan and that the new CG had previously commanded the New York Port of Embarkation. He knew how to unload ships, and he appreciated the cost of supplies.

I went back to Pusan on 30 March and was as astonished as on the first trip. I will not say the condition had been completely corrected, but it had improved so much that the loss was cut to normal.

Now, how did the port situation affect our rations? The 55th Depot would requisition two million balanced B rations. They would arrive by ship, and then the damage would take place. Of course, the damage was not proportionate throughout. Instead of two million balanced rations, it might be that only a million and a half balanced rations and a half million unbalanced rations were received.

I said that at the time of my second visit that handling was very good. It was, with two exceptions. Some ready-to-use dough mixture, procured in 1947, was packaged in corrugated boxes, and these were falling to pieces. The second exception, hams and poultry, are packed in wire-bound boxes. If the rope of the cargo net hits the space between two hams, the box is immediately crushed and stacking is then difficult. But worse than that, the contents are stolen. I feel we should discontinue the use of wire-bound boxes, unless we are packing something solid.

Not all of our losses occur in Pusan. Between Pusan and the forward elements the loss was near 10 to 15 per cent until about the first of January. Then corrective action was taken. These corrections were minor, but they reduced the loss.

One trick is to use a heavy wire to close the boxcar door, cutting it off short so that pliers are required to open it. Better than anything else, the quartermaster stopped marking the contents on the outside of the car.

There is still a loss in the supply dumps because we have to employ Korean labor, but the loss is greatly reduced. I feel now that the over-all loss from Japan to the forward element does not exceed 10 per cent.

PART III

Chemical Corps

1. The 2d Chemical Mortar Battalion

Major Cleo M. Willoughby, 2d Chemical Mortar Battalion

The 2d Chemical Mortar Battalion consisted of a headquarters, a headquarters company, and three mortar companies.[1] At full strength each mortar company had 171 officers and men, twelve M2 4.2-inch mortars, three 2-½-ton trucks, five ¾-ton trucks, and thirty-five jeeps. Communications equipment included both radio and wire. The battalion headquarters and each company maintained a fire direction center.

The 2d Chemical Mortar Battalion was part of IX Corps Artillery during the ten months I served in it. The battalion was attached to the 2d, 7th, and 24th Infantry Divisions, the 1st Cavalry Division, the ROK 6th Division, and the British 27th Commonwealth Brigade. When attached to the 7th Division we were further sub-attached to its infantry regiments. In most other divisions we reinforced the fires of the field artillery battalions. But no matter where we were assigned, we always looked to the 24th Division for logistical support.

We worked for a considerable time with the British 27th Brigade and found it a very pleasant relationship, although the large number of units in the brigade made it difficult for us to provide enough observers and liaison officers. But this was a minor problem compared with the language obstacle we met in supporting South Korean troops.

More important than language was the difference between South Korean methods and our own. The ROK units normally sent small detachments about two thousand yards forward of the main line of resistance. This greatly restricted our ability to fire. If we set up our mortar tubes on the MLR so we could reach beyond the outpost line, we were caught when the detachment pulled back. If we went into position a normal distance behind the MLR, we were out of range.

The ROKs attached us to their division artillery. Partly from pride,

---

[1] The chemical mortar battalions of the United States Army were transferred to the infantry in October 1952.

and partly from lack of effective communications, they seldom assigned us a fire mission. Our men disliked being so far forward, where they attracted considerable fire, if they didn't have an opportunity to shoot. In time, however, understanding between the ROK units and our battalion improved.

The 2d Chemical Mortar Battalion was not once pulled out of the line between October 1950 and October 1951. The only time we were not firing was when we were moving from one unit to another. The infantry mortar companies normally rested whenever their regiment was relieved, or went into reserve. The artillery was back far enough to set up tents and build shelters for their men. But this was not true for us. Our companies went into position from 500 to 1,500 yards behind the MLR. Here our men were always under tension, and had to be very careful to maintain local security.

Although a chemical mortar battalion is designed to deliver massed fire, in Korea the rough terrain, the broad fronts, and the regimental combat team type of fighting made this impossible. Still, we had organizational advantages over the infantry mortar companies. Our battalion commander was in a position to ask for a sector, guarantee fires, and then insist on being left alone. The commander of the infantry mortar company seldom had so much freedom. Our T/O&E gave us enough officers for observation and liaison assignments, while the infantry mortar companies had only privates first class for those jobs. Our officers were better trained, and their higher rank made it easier for them to advise battalion and company commanders.

We had another advantage in that we used artillery firing methods, while the infantry continued to use the procedures of the smaller infantry mortars. We used grid-target computing, and the artillery FDC gave us a flexibility that the infantry did not have.

One of our worst problems in Korea was the shortage of spare parts. Medium ordnance repair companies of IX Corps did not have base plates, elevating screws, and traverse nuts in stock, and they had trouble getting them. Often it took five to six weeks to get a replacement part. Once I had to go to Japan to get parts so that we could continue firing.

Heavy vehicles to haul ammunition and supplies were always short. We had enough jeeps, but our heavy rate of fire forced us to haul ammunition tonnages beyond our capacity. Battalion did its best to stretch the limited transportation by adding trucks directly to the mortar companies and by maintaining forward ammunition dumps, but these moves were inadequate when all three companies were firing for sustained periods.

Thinking back about my experience with the chemical mortar battalions, both in World War II and in Korea, I cannot help but rate the

M2 4.2-inch mortar a fine weapon. It packs a terrific wallop, can give accurate support, and has all-around value for close support when given proper logistical support.

2. Letters from a Commander

Lt.Col. Edgar V. H. Bell, 2d Chemical Mortar Battalion. (Letters to Maj.Gen. E. F. Bullene, Chief Chemical Officer, U.S. Army.)

13 November 1950

I wrote to Colonel Efnor [Lt.Col. Sam Efnor, Jr.] the other day and told him of the activities of the battalion. I asked him to pass this information on to you. There is not much to add at present. We are now with U.S. troops on the offensive again, and the battalion is doing very well.

I have been promised some new mortars, and when we get them the entire battalion will be in action. We have had a great deal of breakage of mortar parts—elevating screws and traverse nuts are the principal ones. Replacement parts that we brought from Edgewood Arsenal are nearly exhausted and there are no other 4.2-inch mortar parts in Korea.

I have not permitted fire over four thousand yards. It has been extremely difficult to keep the mortars in range. There are no roads as we know them, only narrow cart trails barely passable (one way) by jeep—and then only in dry weather. These cart tracks are nearly always raised well above the surface of adjacent rice paddies. Once a vehicle is off the trail it is nearly always bogged down for good. Tremendous frontages assigned to infantry units require us to do a great deal of rapid movement, so hand-carry is entirely out of the question.

Ammunition has been a terrific problem, but so far we have never had less than one hundred rounds per mortar on position. This requires great effort and much truck movement as supply lines are very long in point of hours of travel.

I am operating a very small forward command post. I have with me the S3, the assistant S3, the S2, communications officer, and surgeon—together with 22 enlisted men. The rest of headquarters company, under Major [Merritt W.] Briggs, is about twenty miles to the rear where they can work in comparative calm and comfort. This has many advantages, as the administrative personnel can settle down in one spot and stay there for a week or more while we move nearly every day. The small detachment up here can move quickly and does not further clutter up congested trails. For security we tie in to some nearby infantry battalion or regimental command post when we stop for the night.

If any other chemical units come over here they should bring additional tentage. We have very little and there is no shelter available. The few buildings are preempted by higher commands, leaving only open fields for people like us. It is bitter cold and, though the battalion has drawn special winter clothing, the men still suffer because there is no shelter. A couple of squad tents in each company rear would be worth their weight in gold.

I keep the company rear echelons near to me. These consist of the mess trucks, supply trucks, and motor maintenance trucks—with the personnel from those sections. The battalion sees to all supply of rations, ammunition and POL. We feed two hot meals and one C-ration meal to the forward units. However, a few of us who are constantly on the move rarely have anything but C rations. The kitchen crews must be able to bake good bread, for there are no bakeries over here.

Personal cleanliness is difficult, as there are no laundries or shower points. The country is crawling with lice and fleas. I require frequent foot inspection, as I am most fearful of trench foot.

We are fighting mostly against the Chinese now, as the North Korean units are broken badly and fight principally as guerrillas. The Chinese are well equipped with small arms, automatic weapons, and mortars. The Chinese usually attack down draws and bottoms, and in covering these approaches our mortars have done their best work. The Chinese take terrific losses, but they keep on coming. Our mortar men get into frequent small-arms fights.

We certainly need the new M30 mortar badly and have hopes of receiving it one of these days. If I had only one in each company it would be useful in reaching the 120-mm mortar used by the Chinese. Their mortar has a range of 6,500 yards and they can sit back and plaster hell out of us while we are out of range. The best antimortar weapon is another mortar.

There is much more that I could tell you, but I have so little time. The morale of the battalion is very high and the men are full of fight, wishing to avenge our losses at Unsan. We do not really need anything here except 36 mortars and three or four more mortar battalions equipped with this new weapon.

16 December 1950

Following the withdrawal of all United Nations forces to the Chongchon River in November, the battalion was attached to the 5th Infantry (24th Infantry Division) and rushed to Kunu-ri. The 24th Division was relieved by the 2d Division, and we shifted to that outfit.

Since the withdrawal from Unsan, the battalion has been committed and shooting every day. We had Company C intact with all three platoons, and Company B with two platoons. Company A, having lost or destroyed all of its mortars and nearly all of its other equipment, was out of action.

Early in November, as things were not too rosy, I sent our administrative section back to Sukchon. I reinforced Companies B and C with officers and men from Company A. Refitting Company A was a terrific task as we had to go all the way back to Pusan for the vehicles and most of the equipment. Efforts made to have corps or army re-equip us were unsuccessful. Only aggressive and hard-driving action on the part of Capt. [Clair L.] George (battalion S4) and his assistants got us our equipment. They went to Pusan, drew the trucks, loaded supplies, and then drove them more than 450 miles over the world's worst roads.

We were able to replace only half of our losses in vehicles and even less of the communications equipment. I completely reorganized the battalion while in the lines and redistributed personnel and equipment to have Companies A and B each with three platoons. We had Company A back and shooting just two weeks to the day after they were knocked out.

When the drive started about Thanksgiving, we were attached to the 9th Infantry (2d Infantry Division). We had pushed northeast to a point a few miles north of the town of Kujang-dong when the Chinese hit us again. The 9th RCT was badly cut up as was part of the 38th RCT. Company C was overrun and initially we got only four jeeps, an officer and 24 enlisted men out of the mess. Later most of our personnel either drifted back or were located in clearing stations. I sent the survivors back to our rear, which I had just moved to Kunu-ri. We kept Companies A and B in the fighting, and it was hot.

The next day the Chinese hit again and the big withdrawal started. We pulled out with what was left of the 2d Battalion, 9th RCT, the last to leave. They had a total of 274 officers and men, and we loaded them on our vehicles. We retreated to Won-ni, where we put up a roadblock which lasted just two hours. It was about 0330 when the infantry battalion commander reported to me that he had only 30 men left of his 274, so we all pulled back to Kunu-ri. We went into position there and the following night, at about 1900, received an order to pull out—saving what we could but destroying any equipment we could not get out. At the time we received our march order, we were firing at a range of seven hundred yards. We lost only one jeep trailer which upset and was burned.

After a rough night, I gathered up the pieces and re-formed the battalion. We were immediately attached to the British 27th Commonwealth Brigade, this making our fifth attachment in twenty-five days. That's enough, in itself, to drive a battalion commander stark mad.

We joined the British and have been with them ever since. I am happy with this attachment. These people know their business; they know heavy mortars.

We have been the covering force for IX Corps since early in the withdrawal, and the battalion constitutes the light artillery for the brigade. We have not yet been able to obtain any replacement of our equipment losses at Kujang-dong by legal means, but as we are the rear guard of a withdrawing army, we have picked up some gear. Our S4 with a party of thirty-five men is now in Pusan, and I hope to see them back here tomorrow with enough equipment to place Company C back into action with two platoons.

We could not operate more than eight mortars per company no matter how much equipment we had, for our strength is down to 23 officers and 352 enlisted men. I have cut headquarters company down hard so as to have about 100 officers and enlisted men in each of the lettered companies. But even to operate only eight mortars "the bread is sliced mighty thin," and most men have two jobs to do.

While I feel horrible over the loss of so many fine officers and men, it is a little comforting to know that we lost them while fighting, not while withdrawing. Company C, for example, knew they were being swamped, but they fired defensive fires at six hundred yards and had only ten rounds left in the company when the last rush hit. They were able to destroy eleven of their twelve mortars. The Chinese got to the vehicles first, as usual.

31 December 1950

We are still attached to the British 27th Brigade and have 24 mortars in action with a total strength of 338 enlisted men and 23 officers. Of the 33 chemical officers who left Edgewood Arsenal with us, only 19 are still here. Of the 14 who have left, 5 are missing in action, 2 are wounded in action, 4 hospitalized for noncombat causes, and 3 have been transferred. None of the hospital cases will be returned within ninety days. This leaves us pretty short-handed both for officers and enlisted men, but we are doing all right.

You will be interested to know that we have never been withdrawn for reorganization nor have we received any enlisted replacements. We have received four officers since we were committed. Unfortunately, these officers knew nothing of mortars and very damned little about combat troops. We lost one officer within three weeks, and it was a shame —like sending a lamb to slaughter.

I feel very strongly that if the Chemical Corps is to continue to have chemical mortar battalions, it should procure and train the correct type of combat officers for this duty. I would not give a tinker's damn if such an officer did not know one end of a test tube from another, but I would insist that he have a thorough knowledge of infantry organization, tactics and weapons. I would not care about a college degree if the officer had the will to fight.

I also feel that chemical mortar battalions should not be sent to any theater *as* chemical mortar battalions unless the use of toxics is contemplated. The personnel may be sent as filler replacements or the mortar companies may be sent out as heavy-mortar units, but there just is no slot for a chemical battalion except where chemical munitions are to be used.

This present attachment is by far the best one that we have had. The 27th Brigade has no heavy mortars and we fill the gap between their own 3-inch mortars and the direct-support artillery, thus bringing the brigade's fire power to nearly that of one of our regimental combat teams. We have an important slot to fill, but when we are attached to an American division (and we have supported four of them), we are used only to reinforce the fires of their own heavy-mortar companies. I have had to fight hard to keep our companies from being attached to the organic mortar companies. This is a waste of fire power, and worse still, a waste of man power. A separate mortar battalion has no role in the present army organization except in the case of gas warfare.

We are in pretty good shape. Morale is high, and while the weather is bitter cold, our men are well equipped for it and can get along.

12 January 1951

We are still in support of the British 27th Brigade. With them we were the last troops out of Seoul.

I do hope that one more effort will be made to award our people the Combat Infantryman Badge. It seems to me to be rank discrimination to keep this badge from our men simply because of the one word, "chemical," in our unit designation. The men in the heavy-mortar companies of infantry regiments serve the same piece, fire the same ammunition, and are subject to the same hazards as are the men of our battalion. Frequently in Korea, the infantry heavy-mortar companies have been attached to my battalion for operational control. Of course, when this was done, the more dangerous assignments were given by me to our own companies.

It is common practice for us to operate jointly with the forward observers of the infantry heavy-mortar companies, their fire direction centers, communications and ammunition resupply. Occasionally we perform the security missions for an infantry mortar platoon, and once we manned their mortars for them. It is interesting to note that we are able to keep eight mortars per company in action with present-for-duty strengths averaging less than 80 enlisted men per company. The infantry companies usually run 120 to 155 enlisted men and only attempt to keep five or six mortars in action. . . .

We have very little left of headquarters company, as I have transferred every possible man to the mortar companies. The personnel section and most of the motor section are kept well to the rear, while I operate the forward command post with 3 other officers and 18 enlisted men. It is amazing how much can be done by so few people, but it is quite difficult and the strain is beginning to tell. I rotate both officers and enlisted men as much as possible. A couple of weeks of eating and sleeping back in our rear echelon restores a man a great deal.

3. Smoke Generating

> Lt. Freddy B. Parish and Lt. George D. Sisson, Jr., 68th Chemical Smoke Generating Company. (Lieutenant Parish interviewed in Korea by Capt. William J. Fox, 7th Historical Detachment.)

The 68th Chemical Smoke Generating Company arrived in Pusan in October 1950. Its early assignments varied from unloading and guarding cargo on the piers to working at the airfields.

During November 1950, the company was stationed at an airfield near Ascom City. Part of our men were arming planes, and the rest were mixing napalm and loading fire bombs. The company field-tested the E3R2 incendiary-oil mixing and transfer unit (for mixing and pouring napalm) and found it most satisfactory. The bombs were attached to the planes, and the napalm gel was then blown into the bombs under pressure. It was an around-the-clock operation with fighters being serviced during the day and bombers at night.

In March 1951, the company began its normal mission of generating smoke. It would be difficult to say that the company was successful during the next six months. The mountains of Korea produce variable and unpredictable wind currents. Besides, military units worked close together, and smoke which helped one often hurt another.

The unpredictability of the wind was illustrated many times. On 4 March 1951 the 68th Smoke Company was called upon to generate smoke as a part of a feint in Operation WELLSEND. A short test period proved that the wind was from the wrong direction. On 13 March smoke was again used, but this time the winds changed so frequently that the smoke was not effective.

From April to August 1951, part of the company remained on alert to screen Seoul in case of air attack. Many alerts occurred when "Bed Check Charlie" roamed around at night. On a red alert one night, smoke was generated. The following morning the Air Force claimed that the smoke limited the vision on a nearby field to such an extent planes could not take off. Thereafter the smoke was generated near Seoul only on clearance from the joint operations center.

On 1 June, the 68th smoked a bridge construction site. Soon an artillery colonel arrived, complaining bitterly that his observers were unable to see. When smoke was used on a river crossing, the Filipino troops were frightened by the smoke and wore handkerchiefs as masks. Even a training mission for the 25th Division failed. Haze was created to simulate darkness, but the training was unrealistic when the machine-gun tracers could not be seen.

The only successful smoke mission occurred in July. The 27th RCT was making an attack near Kumhwa, supported by part of the 89th Tank Battalion and some quad .50s of the 21st Antiaircraft Artillery Battalion. We were to give a smoke screen, but were prevented by the wind. In the attack two light (M24) tanks and a halftrack were disabled by land mines. Efforts to recover these vehicles were thwarted by accurate enemy artillery fire.

On the following morning our 2d Platoon began generating smoke at 0700. Conditions were ideal. There was a heavy moisture in the air and gentle breezes blowing toward the disabled vehicles. It took twenty minutes for the wind to carry the smoke eight hundred yards to the tanks, and a strong haze soon built up. Recovery units removed the tanks and halftrack within two hours, and no artillery fire struck the area.

On a basis of number of missions performed and number of men employed, our smoke operations in Korea were not justifiable. But had enemy aircraft often attacked our supply installations, then the smoke company would have been invaluable for passive defense. The mountains and winds, however, made close support of ground troops impossible.

4. Napalm Bombs in Korea

Col. Donald D. Bode, Chemical Officer, Eighth Army. (Interview by Historical Office, Office of Chief Chemical Officer, U.S. Army, 1 March 1951.)

Our napalm-filled bombs are made in Japan. They are made of plastic, cost forty dollars each, and hold 100 gallons. New ones are now being made which hold 90 gallons.

The Navy uses Corsairs and dive-bombers to carry their bombs; the Air Force uses F-51s, F-80s, F-86s and B-26s. They experimented at one time with carrying six tanks of napalm on an F-80, but the normal load is two tanks of gasoline and two tanks of napalm. On an average good day, the expenditures of napalm are: Air Force, 45,000 gallons; Navy, 10,000 to 12,000 gallons; Marines, 4,000 to 5,000 gallons.

At one time there was considerable difficulty in getting a good mix because there were no thermometers to test the temperature of the gasoline. The personnel mixing the gel would get the current temperature from the weather report, but the gasoline would be from 10 to 15 degrees colder than the air temperature from sitting out in the cold overnight. That problem has been solved by using thermometers and the E3R2 mixing unit. The E3R2 is very efficient, and when standardized will alleviate mixing problems. In a letter to me, one chemical officer stated that his men formerly worked a 24-hour day on mixing napalm. Since they have received the E3R2 units, and have been checking temperature more closely, his man-power needs have been so reduced that his men spend much of their time helping Air Force personnel in jobs such as loading bombs.

After the first few months of World War II, napalm was mixed in England and shipped in 55-gallon drums to the Continent, where it was handled by air chemical companies. In Korea two smoke-generating companies are used to mix the napalm.

Often, fire-bomb tanks are only half-filled with napalm to lighten the load so that jets can take off from a short runway without difficulty. This requires the expenditure of more tanks, but is necessary at times.

The tactics are much the same as those used during World War II. Napalm fire bombs have been dropped from high-altitude bombers, but with little success. Dive-bombing at very low levels (25 feet) is satisfactory, but the effectiveness of the bomb is reduced to some extent by its skipping when it hits.

Napalm is very effective against enemy personnel and as an antitank weapon. A hit anywhere within fifty feet of a tank is effective. It is used widely and successfully against dug-in enemy personnel. When the bomb lands, the burning napalm spreads out and drops down into foxholes. It is especially effective against trenches and improvised protections such as drainage and irrigation ditches where enemy soldiers are spread out along a wide front.

The lack of enemy ground fire allows low-level bombing, even as low as 25 feet. However, a number of duds result from drops as low as that. There are three main reasons for duds: extremely low altitudes, failure to arm the bomb, and broken arming wires.

The value of napalm is indicated by the great number of requests for its use.

5. Flame Throwers

Major Charles H. Barclay, Chemical Officer, 1st Cavalry Division

The flame thrower is an extremely effective weapon, but it has its limitations. In Korea the steepness of the hills and the weight of the weapon were particularly important. Then, too, we found that few men were trained to use it.

During Operation COMMANDO in October–November 1951, the 1st Cavalry Division planned to use the flame thrower extensively to clean out enemy bunkers. To do this we first had to qualify operators. For this training, we generally selected replacements who had recently arrived from the U.S. training camps. Although Army Field Forces has a requirement that all recruits be trained in the flame thrower, we made a survey of 85 men and learned that only 2 had fired the flame thrower, 12 had seen demonstrations of its operation, and the others had never even seen the weapon. These men came from seven or eight different replacement training centers.

Battalion commanders were urged to use the flame thrower during COMMANDO. As the attack progressed, we had 97 flame-thrower missions. The problem was to get the operator within effective range. Too often the Chinese would let the operator get near, and then drop hand grenades down on him. Of the 97 attempts, about 90 operators reached a point where they could use the weapon.

Once the flame was discharged, the operator was a sure target. Of the 97 flame throwers sent out, 65 were lost through enemy action or were abandoned so the operator could escape. Six operators were killed.

The 1st Cavalry Division also employed the flame thrower in defensive positions, mostly at night. In the 8th Cavalry Regiment a company using two flame throwers burned twenty enemy on their defensive wire. An examination of the bodies the next morning showed that none of these men had been shot. Another night advantage is the three or four minutes of battlefield illumination afforded by the flame thrower.

In setting up Defense Line WYOMING, the 1st Cavalry Division placed one thousand drums of napalm in front of the infantry positions, but these were never used. The drums were filled, set in the ground at a 45-degree angle with the opening facing the enemy. A block of tetryl and an 81-mm white phosphorus mortar shell were set underneath the drum, and the whole apparatus fuzed with detonators. This was a defensive weapon, but it would also provide ten minutes of illumination.

PART IV

Signal Corps

1. Developing a Signal Organization

Lt.Col. George Lieberberg, Signal Section, Headquarters Eighth Army

The organization of communications in Korea developed on a logical, common-sense basis within the urgency of the situation. The conflict was not anticipated, and so the troop list of Far East Command was not prepared.

Communications were vital. There wasn't enough time to plan troop assignments in detail. It was a matter of moving from Japan to Korea those units which were most needed. At first, signal troops would be necessary to handle communications from Japan to Korea and maintain the Mukden cable. After Eighth Army was in Korea, tactical communications would become essential.

Eighth Army signal troops on duty in Japan consisted of a signal operation battalion, two signal construction companies, two radio relay companies, a signal depot organization, and various signal service detachments. FEC signal troops consisted primarily of a signal service battalion. Because this was also a critical period for communications in Japan, withdrawal of signal troops from their tasks had to be handled carefully.

The 8052d Post Signal-Detachment was activated during the first week of July 1950, and sailed immediately for Pusan. Within a matter of days, half of the 304th Signal Operation Battalion, the 522d Signal Construction Company, and the 8035th Signal Service Company (Very High Frequency) arrived in Korea. These units established Eighth Army's communications system, and tied in with Far East Command's signal troops who were operating in the vicinity of the 24th Division. By the time the 25th Division was committed (approximately 12 July 1950), Eighth Army was supplying communications to its subordinate major commands. Just before Taejon fell, the FEC signal unit returned to Pusan. This unit was later organized into the 8226th GHQ Long Lines Service Group, and furnished communications between FEC and Eighth Army. Personnel of the 8226th operated side by side with Eighth Army troops.

In the first days the troop assignments to Korea were primarily the responsibility of Col. Thomas A. Pitcher. So accurately did he judge future signal needs that these detachments formed in miniature the structure later established. Col. Emil Lenzner joined Eighth Army as signal officer in September 1950. Under his guidance, the section became an efficient operating unit.

As Eighth Army moved to Korea, its headquarters split. The forward echelon advanced with the troops while the rear command post remained in Yokohama. This Yokohama headquarters acted variously as a communications zone agency and an over-all troops and logistical planning headquarters. Col. Paul Neal, the senior Signal Corps officer remaining in Yokohama, planned the requisition of signal units after comparing the troops in a type field army with those currently at hand. Adjustments were made for the unique elements of the Korean situation and a priority established, but the troops arrived in the order of their availability. So much of the high-level planning was done in Yokohama during the first month that Eighth Army's signal section was able to limit its activities to planning and constructing combat communications, and carrying on such routine operations as the preparation of signal operating instructions.

The signal troops requisitioned in early July began to arrive from the States in August and September. It was soon realized that a signal group headquarters was required to administer and support these units. A provisional group was activated early in 1951. This provisional group was later reorganized under an authorization by the Department of the Army. All Eighth Army signal troops were attached to the signal headquarters.

Other problems of signal organization arose from local conditions. One factor was the structural peculiarities of Eighth Army itself. Until August 1950, Eighth Army had no corps. This forced us (under signal doctrine of supporting to supported) to provide communications to each division, and to each regiment in army reserve. This required more terminals and, therefore, more strength, than were anticipated in the establishment of a signal section for a type field army.

2.   Answers Not in Textbooks

Capt. John W. Pierce, 24th Signal Company

Although U.S. Army doctrine teaches that wire is the primary method of signal communication, I did not find this so in Korea. Here we had to depend more often on very high frequency radio. Distance, speed, terrain, and road nets limited the use of wire.

Road nets in Korea were so limited that sometimes three divisions would have to depend upon a single two-lane road for their main supply road. As a result, so many lines were laid along the road that the wires became jumbled. They were difficult to identify, follow, or repair. The poplar trees, which closely bordered most roads, made it difficult to get a hastily laid line off the road. Even the use of an improvised wire boom did not help much.

When the communications lines were long we had real difficulties. Even spiral 4 cable (4 wires wound to form a single cable) has an operational limit of twenty-five miles unless the wave is amplified, but division signal companies do not have repeater equipment for amplification.

Most often when the 24th Signal Company (24th Infantry Division) was called upon to provide dependable communications, we turned to VHF radio. VHF is not problem-free, but we were able to solve most of our problems. Location of terminals is the major difficulty. Since VHF operates on the line-of-sight principle we had to install our equipment on high, and often isolated, areas. The isolation of our stations was normal when the distance between our terminals was great or a large hill mass was in our way, but the sites were often extremely difficult to establish and maintain. Some parts of a VHF station cannot be broken down for hand-carry to less than 330 pounds, and an entire station weighs two tons. Resupply of food and fuel was a continuing problem.

The isolation also brought a serious security problem. When a terminal station was located near a headquarters, that headquarters normally maintained the security. This was often done even when the terminal was not inside the security perimeter. But with no headquarters nearby, we sometimes requested help from the Korean National Police. I did not have much faith in the personnel of this force, and in some cases it was better to use our signalmen as guards.

The 24th Signal Company did not have any of its terminals attacked by guerrillas, but one terminal was hit by enemy troops in July 1950. We were new in the Taejon area, the situation was confused, and the station had not established adequate security. The North Koreans hit so fast that no one actually knows what happened. One man was killed and two wounded, and the terminal had to be destroyed to keep it from falling into enemy hands.

We learned that we had considerable leeway in the location of our stations. When we couldn't get line-of-sight we tried expedients before we went to the trouble of establishing relay stations. One solution was to try a change of frequency. Lower frequencies would bend easier than the higher ones. We learned to locate our VHF stations in river beds or valleys that had steep banks. So long as the path did not make an acute turn, and so long as both stations were located some distance from the first obstacle, we could expect that the signal would bank off one hill after another. The Signal Corps manuals don't tell you how to make bank shots with VHF radios, but we used them frequently in Korea.

3. Flexibility of VHF

Capt. Frank D. Secan, 304th Signal Operation Battalion

The VHF radio communications in Korea exceeded all expectations. The 304th Signal Operation Battalion used sets AN/GRC-3 and -4, and operated them at ranges far beyond their 25-mile line-of-sight specifications. This was especially valuable to us during the rapid advance after the breakout of the Naktong perimeter—and until the Mukden cable could be rehabilitated.

The longest leg of a VHF radio circuit that I ever made was 90 miles. We were transmitting messages 140 air miles from Seoul to Taegu. The first leg crossed two mountain ranges and came to a relay station on a peak in a third range. The distance was so great that we couldn't even see the mountain our terminal was located on. We just sighted from a roof-top in Seoul toward a white-capped mountain in the first range. How the wave got beyond that mountain I don't know. Ninety miles was an extreme range, however. We got some dimming and blurring right at sunrise and sunset, but we used the arrangement successfully for a month.

The first maps we had of Korea were especially poor in the vertical scale. When a signal officer made a map reconnaissance for a VHF circuit, he could seldom rely on the result. I once planned a relay station on a mountain between Pyongyang and Anju. When my installation party reached the map location of the relay site they encountered a slight difficulty: there was no mountain. The nearest real elevation was fifteen miles away.

In teaching about VHF radio, instructors often place more emphasis on the difficulties of line-of-sight than is necessary. VHF waves bend, bounce, and do many other tricks. I have aimed such waves up valleys, through mountain passes, and once directed my beam directly at a large mountain—yet had the signal clearly received.

This last case occurred during the Naktong perimeter fighting, when my signal platoon was called on to provide communication between Eighth Army headquarters and the 19th Infantry. This was an unusual arrangement, but at that time the 19th was one of the major reserves of Eighth Army. The distance was twelve air miles, but there was a mountain between us.

We would not have thought of trying VHF radio except that someone near the 19th Infantry turned on his VHF set and heard Eighth Army. We knew that if one person could get the signal we could too. I had a radio team at the CP of the 19th, but they had difficulties. The regimental communications officer refused to allow the team to place their radio on any high point because it might attract attention. The men were ordered to establish their station in a creek bed which had steep banks. The antenna reached no higher than the top of the bank. No reception was possible. I took the matter directly to the army signal officer, and our radio men were directed to select their own site.

Eighth Army's terminal was established at 300 feet, the 19th Infantry's at 600. The mountain between us was 2,100 feet. We picked a low wave length. Our technical calculations told us that our circuit couldn't work—but reception was perfect.

As a result of worry about line-of-sight, I have seen a number of VHF stations located on the topographical crests of hills and mountains. Sometimes this is necessary. Most often, though, you can accomplish line-of-sight without sitting on the summit. On the slope you can get out of the wind, with its consequent technical troubles and personal discomforts. It is more accessible and makes installation, supply, and displacement much easier. It is less likely that the enemy will find you. Whenever you can avoid the crest, do so.

4. The Provost Marshal's Transmitter

Major Dale H. Shick, 2d Logistical Command

The provost marshal section in Pusan was extremely busy in August 1950. Aside from normal duties, it had to run five POW camps, control refugees, and protect communications at the critical period of the perimeter fighting. Inadequate communications hindered effective handling of these missions.

In Pusan it is difficult to use frequency-modulated radio because of its line-of-sight characteristic. Military police vehicles mounted FM radios, and sometimes, though they operated close to one another, they still could not communicate with one another or their headquarters because of the intervening hills.

The provost marshal turned to the signal officer of Pusan (later 2d) Logistical Command for a solution. The signal officer (Lt.Col. George Callahan) ordered me to install a central radio transmitter that would give the provost marshal section continuous contact with its vehicles and installations.

A map reconnaissance of the Pusan area seemed at first to indicate that the transmitter must be set up on the harbor island of Mokto. This location would be ideal for line-of-sight, for the island formed an apex to the V-shaped Pusan valley, but Mokto's sharply rising 1,300-foot hill has no road to its summit. All equipment, housing, food and fuel would have to be laboriously carried to the summit. Further, the distance to the transmitter site would rule out the use of remote control from the provost marshal headquarters. All messages would have to be relayed. Enough personnel to operate around the clock would be required, and gasoline and rations would have to be packed to the summit of Mokto indefinitely.

I made a reconnaissance which took half a day. From the crest I could see the entire panorama of Pusan. But I was more impressed with the difficulties that Mokto would present than with its advantages.

Next day I surveyed the low hills inside Pusan, and on the Kumgang Temple Hill I found a site that I believed might work. A road led up the slope, and on the eastern side I found a 90-foot pole. It seemed to me that communications could be established if we placed a whip antenna on the top of this pole, even though our antenna would not reach the crest of the hill.

I borrowed two jeeps which mounted SCR-610 radio sets. If an SCR-610 at our proposed transmitter site could communicate with another SCR-610 going about the Pusan area, then surely the more powerful SCR-608 with a high antenna would do even better. Trials showed that contact could be maintained, and I knew I had the site I was looking for.

I reported my decision to establish a transmitter on Kumgang Temple Hill and pointed out the many advantages of the site. Colonel Callahan doubted that this would work, but he did not give me a direct order to stop—only a strong indication that I had better be right.

It took a full day of preparation, and then a day of work, to set up the transmitter. We took power from a nearby electric line, and ran a remote control the two miles from the provost marshal's office using a combination of spiral 4 cable and two metallic cable pairs. This gave us a radio circuit and a telephone circuit. A large crate from which we had recently unloaded an AN/GRC-26 was easily made into an operator's shack.

Everything worked perfectly when we turned on the power switch. One night I happened to tune in and picked up a military police jeep patrol. This patrol had a roving assignment, and the operator was describing the women he saw as the patrol moved from one area to another.

Looking back on that job, I realize I was lucky. I know there was a great deal of wave bending to get our signal all the way out to the airport. I know it was stretching our luck to install that remote over a two-mile circuit, when specifications list a remote as being good only for half a mile. But all the equipment worked better than performance schedules list. It surprised Colonel Callahan when the radio worked—and I got more and more relieved that night each time that operator described another woman.

5. Relay Station on Hill 1157

Lt. Jasper Lupo, 101st Signal Operation Battalion. (Interview by Capt. Pierce W. Briscoe, 2d Historical Team.)

The divisions of IX Corps were advancing rapidly, and it was obvious that they would soon be out of radio range. Therefore, on 23 May 1951, the Radio Relay Platoon of the 101st Signal Operation Battalion was ordered to erect four VHF relays on Hill 1157.

Next day, at 0500, the detachment moved out with two 2-½-ton trucks of radio equipment; a 2-½-ton truck carrying twenty-five Korean laborers, their A-frames, and rations; and a ¾-ton truck carrying Lt. Jasper Lupo and a six-man relay team. Leaving the MSR, the detachment drove over a narrow, rocky trail. This trail crossed a stream five times, but led to the western slopes of Hill 1157. Four miles from the MSR, the vehicles could go no farther. A base camp was established.

It took an hour to divide the equipment and to load everything needed for the first two VHF relays on the Koreans' A-frames. On each trip they carried 3 power units, 6 transmitters, 6 receivers, and other supplies. The loads averaged over 300 pounds!

Lieutenant Lupo and his Korean interpreter moved ahead of the bearers during the climb. Because the group might run into enemy stragglers, a warning signal was agreed upon. Three miles up the trail, scattered small-arms fire came close to the lieutenant, but the march was not delayed.

After an eight-hour climb, the bearers reached the mountain top at 1730. Lieutenant Lupo had already selected the radio relay site. The Koreans immediately began their return march, laying field wire along the trail to the base camp as they descended.

Eight 25-foot antennas were erected and oriented by compass. Locations for eight more were selected. Equipment was unpacked, assembled, checked, and by 1900 the first two relays were ready for operation.

Meanwhile, the Koreans had reached the base camp and had loaded the remaining equipment. They returned to the crest of the mountain at 0200, 25 May. The signalmen worked throughout the night and assembled the second two relays. The VHF station was completed and all four relays were operating by 0600. Eight tons of Signal Corps equipment and other supplies had been carried to the top and assembled on Hill 1157.

6. Everyone Wants a Telephone

Lt. David S. Howard, 532d Signal Construction Company

From the moment the 532d Signal Construction Company arrived in Korea on 10 July 1950, we got calls for telephones. It seemed at first as though there were more staff officers in Eighth Army headquarters than troops in the field—and every one of them wanted a phone. We put in phones as fast as requests came in and laid lines from them to the switchboards. But we didn't have enough drops (spaces) on our boards to tie in all these local lines. It was so bad we just had to throw the unconnected lines on the floor. And whenever some officer did fight through a priority for his phone, we had to pull someone else's line off the board.

This wasn't because we didn't try. Our officers and men worked with absolutely no regard for shifts. When you were finally exhausted, you slept for a couple of hours and then came back. Even the signal officer of Eighth Army (Lt.Col. Thomas A. Pitcher) went out with the wire crews and helped string the lines.

Our wires, equipment, and methods were the same as those we had used in World War II. But we did make far more use of spiral 4 wire; even the divisions were using it. This soon put spiral 4 in very short supply, but it greatly reduced our signal maintenance.

As the Naktong perimeter became smaller, the number of telephone lines in each unit rapidly increased. This usually happens in a stable defense. But in the perimeter this "defensive stability" only applied to certain units. Others shifted very often. The 24th Infantry Division, it seemed to me, was the one that moved the most, and we had a hard time keeping wire in to them. At one time the 24th was west of Kochang and we were ordered to tie them into the Mukden cable at Miryang, about forty road miles away. So we sent out two crews and started laying two spiral 4 cables from each end toward the middle. But by the time these crews met and ran their test calls, the 24th had moved.

The Mukden cable was of great use to us, but unfortunately it was not located centrally. From Taegu to Yusong the cable runs west-northwest; then it turns north along the western edge of Korea. To get communications to the central and eastern sectors we used every open wire line we could find. The wires above ground suffered more from combat and needed far more work than the Mukden cable did, and even when repaired they were of poor quality.

Rather than patch the old open wire circuits indefinitely, Eighth Army started to build new lines in February 1951, when our troops began their second drive to the north. We connected with Mukden cable at what was then the closest point (Chochiwon), then went northeast to Chungju, and on to Wonju. From there, the open wire line followed close behind the troops. Eventually this line was made a center-of-peninsula trunk, tapping the Mukden cable at Taegu and moving north through Hamchang for a connection with the older open wire line at Chunju.

Communication wires went up everywhere in Korea. Today it isn't like it was in those early days when we had to throw the local lines on the floor of the switching central. Everybody has a telephone now.

7. The Mukden Cable

Capt. Wayne A. Striley, 71st Signal Service Battalion

I flew from Tokyo to Korea with 3 other officers and 19 enlisted men of the 71st Signal Service Battalion. We landed on 4 July 1950.

Our mission was to keep in operation the Mukden cable—Korea's key telephone-telegraph system. The cable and repeater stations were of Japanese construction, now run by the Ministry of Communications of the Republic of Korea. The cable contained ten quads, each consisting of two twisted-pairs of wires. It was buried one meter into, and one meter under, the Pusan–Seoul–Pyongyang–Mukden highway. In South Korea there were repeater stations at Miryang, Taegu, Kumchon, Yusong, Chonan, and Osan.

When we arrived at Pusan the cable was operating as far as the front lines. My job was to learn as much as I could about it and to service it in the forward area. I left Pusan on 5 July with a wire foreman and a cable splicer. At Yusong we halted and I decided to go no farther. The military situation was too uncertain.

As U.S. and ROK forces fell back we had less and less cable to maintain. We did not destroy the cable or its repeater stations during the withdrawal that summer. We figured we would return and need that cable.

In September 1950 we were prepared for the breakout from the Naktong perimeter. Several communications groups worked on sections of the cable during the advance. My detachment kept right behind the infantry, and until we reached Yusong we were able to operate the cable within several days after an area was captured. After Yusong the infantry outdistanced us—especially after they linked up with the forces moving south from Inchon and Seoul.

The cable was now in pretty bad condition, especially in those areas where the fighting had been heavy. Since it was buried right under the main supply road, and only one meter deep, it was cut at numerous places. Bomb explosions, artillery fire, and even mortar fire had cut it. Our operators could tell us within two miles where to look for a break, and we would search the road. Sometimes the North Koreans had tapped the cable and used a pair for local communications. When they withdrew in the fall of 1950, they did not repair the cable. Short circuits were frequent. Generally, some pairs of the cable were good most of the way, but often they were not strong enough to work a carrier wave. When the entire cable was cut we made a hasty splice and returned later to do a finished job. This procedure was different from that of World War II, but in Korea the destruction of signal equipment was greater.

Cable splicing is a technical job, and we never had enough specialists. Many of the trained men had lost their skill during prolonged assignments as cooks or mess personnel. Eventually we had to import civilians from the United States—and pay them fancy wages.

The repeater stations were in good shape when we reached them, except at Kumchon, where the station had been destroyed by artillery fire. But all stations were without electric power and were as effectively out of action as if they had been destroyed.

However, this situation had been anticipated. In Japan the signal section built a number of mobile repeater stations in large trailers. These stations were a combination of CF-1, -2, and -3. In other words, they contained telephone terminals, telegraph terminals, and repeaters. The repeater vans were shipped to Pusan and followed the infantry closely, although the vans were difficult to maneuver on the Korean roads.

The mobile repeater stations were built of American equipment, but they functioned well in the Japanese circuits. I understand we could get only four circuits from each quad instead of six, but that was because of the different design of our equipment. When a van reached the approximate location of the repeater station, the construction men quickly tied both ends of the cable into it.

The Mukden cable advanced and withdrew with our forces. It was a great artery of communication—and a godsend to the Signal Corps. I don't know what we'd have done without it.

8. Signal Operations in Korea

Col. Thomas A. Pitcher, Signal Section, Eighth Army

From the signalman's point of view, three things stand out in Korea.

First, the VHF radio companies provided the backbone of our communications system. This method of transmission was so flexible that it could keep up with the infantry in the rapid moves that characterized the fighting in 1950-51. VHF provided communication over mountains, across rivers, and even from ship to shore. It carried teletype. It gave clear reception at all times—even when it was used at twice its rated range. After a headquarters was hooked up by wire, VHF remained as a secondary method of communication.

Second, the Korean campaign was an outstanding example of cooperation. Personnel and equipment of all units were pooled. Although the long-lines group in Pusan came under Far East Command for operations, they lent us cable splicers and other personnel. When Eighth Army began building an open-wire line trunk from Chochiwon to Wonju, the long-lines people provided almost as many construction men as we did. On the Mukden cable the long-lines group took over the repair of some sectors while Eighth Army worked on others. FEC made several of the cable repeater station vans. We never competed over personnel or services.

Third, the destruction of signal facilities in Korea was extreme. The open-wire circuits were so badly damaged that Eighth Army had to build its own lines. The Mukden cable was not damaged by the U.S. forces as they withdrew in the summer of 1950, but it was seriously damaged by combat near Kumchon and between Osan and Suwon. The cable was so close to the surface of the Pusan–Seoul road that it was cut by bomb explosions and mortar and artillery fire. Only the Kumchon repeater station was destroyed, but many other repeater stations were rendered unserviceable when soldiers and civilians stripped them. To prevent this, the signalmen made every effort to get to the repeater stations before our own troops ruined them. We got to the Sariwon station before the infantry—and took seven prisoners.

The destruction of signal equipment was systematic during the withdrawal during the winter of 1950-51. We didn't know whether we were leaving Korea, but we took no chance of leaving anything behind which could aid the enemy. We did a thorough job of destroying the repeater stations, cable, and open-wire lines.

There has never been a U.S. theater of operations that taxed our signal resources more. We were assigned many difficult jobs, and we got them all done.

9. Division Artillery Message Center

SFC Richard L. Albrecht, Headquarters, 24th Division Artillery

The bane of our message center was the M209 code converter. It was slow to operate and mistakes could be made very easily. Every day it had to be set up carefully, but a number of times a unit of the division was overrun and the signal operating instructions were compromised. Then we had to get a new code setting, and start our work all over again.

In their enthusiasm to get messages delivered, a number of message centers sent communications by several methods. All classified messages —even those labeled RESTRICTED—had to be encoded before they could be transmitted by radio. It always seemed we got our coded messages at night. It was normal most evenings for the code clerk to work several hours on messages, only to find that the same messages had already been received by courier and distributed.

Our artillery battalion agents were very conscientious men. They always got their messages through. If one route was cut by the enemy, they would try another. While we operated in South Korea the agent always carried a shotgun guard, but when we were in North Korea the commanding general ordered that only in an emergency would a vehicle travel alone at night. Usually we dispatched at least three vehicles along the same route at the same time.

When an artillery battalion displaced and division artillery did not, the agents made the move with their battalions. When both division artillery and the battalions moved simultaneously, the agents accompanied division artillery headquarters. Then the first trip an agent made to his battalion was especially hazardous because of the possibility of getting lost. Fortunately, we never lost an agent during the time I worked with message center.

10. Code

Lt. Arthur J. Cramer, 7th Signal Company

I ran an excellent message center, and I was especially proud of my cryptographers. They worked under great difficulty, but they were excellent at encoding, decoding, and security. When we saw the lax handling of highly classified messages after we had guarded their security, we sometimes got a little discouraged. I saw so many security violations and made so many reports I finally turned my eyes the other way.

The entire cryptography system is cumbersome under the best conditions, but it is intolerable when it is not working properly. Typical of the conditions that slow up the system were the overclassified messages. We received so many five-day-old FLASH (highest priority) messages from X Corps that they became a joke.

Our cryptographers were overburdened with long messages that were also forwarded by some other (and often faster) method. Many times at night I would awaken my whole crew to get them working on a number of long messages—only to find they had previously been received by telephone in the clear, or had been brought by courier.

Another difficulty was the lack of experienced cryptographers in several of the headquarters with which we communicated. The worst instance occurred in connection with the aerial resupply of one of our regiments. On 2 January 1951, the 7th Infantry Division's forward CP was located at Yongju, while its 17th Infantry occupied positions near Chechon. Between these towns the road winds through several long mountain passes. In one of these defiles the enemy established a roadblock. A decision was made to send an airdrop of food, ammunition, and medical supplies to the 17th Infantry.

A FLASH message to Eighth Army (through X Corps) was delivered to my code room at about 2300. My men gave the message their fastest handling and delivered the encoded message to the radio operator in ten minutes. From our headquarters the message was sent to X Corps headquarters. As we normally did in such cases, we asked for an acknowledgment from the addressee when the message was understood. Because of the importance of the message I violated channels and radioed it to our division's rear CP. From there it was to be delivered by courier to Eighth Army at Taegu.

By 0230 we still had not received an acknowledgment from either X Corps or Eighth Army, so we again requested an acknowledgment. Back came word that the message was still being decoded. They couldn't break the coded message. At 0500 we received an acknowledgment from Eighth Army, which had received the message through our secondary channel at 0130. Early the next morning (3 January) the airdrop was carried out on order of Eighth Army. Four hours after the supplies were received I got an acknowledgment from X Corps headquarters that our message had been decoded. An investigation followed that incident.

11. The World's Biggest Little Airline

From *Signal*, November-December 1951. (Copyright by and re-produced by permission of Armed Forces Communications Association, publishers of *Signal*.)

Events in Korea have just completed a strange cycle in military history. The Army Signal Corps, which hatched the Air Force by buying the first American military airplane from the Wright brothers before World War I, is now hatching a new but smaller air service. Today over the dusty, arid hills of Korea it is operating one of the world's biggest little airlines.

The midget airline performs an important job which is as old as warfare: getting the messages through. While most people think of battlefield messages flitting back and forth via telegraph, telephone, or radio, there is still a great bulk of documents, maps and photographs which must travel by messenger. In one recent month the airline hauled 34,000 pounds of messages between Eighth Army and its corps head-quarters.

Carrying messages by plane is nothing new, but in Korea it has become important. Jeep, or motor messenger service, had always received more use until the Korean campaign made getting messages from one battlefield to another more difficult. There are few roads there, and all of them are rough. It doesn't take many miles of bouncing over Korean roads to ruin a vehicle even as tough as the Army jeep and with so many other military vehicles on the narrow, dusty roads it takes too much time to get from one point to another.

The answer to the bad roads was the light airplane, the L-5, or "mos-quito." While it took a jeep two days to make a run from army field headquarters and back, the light airplane does it in four hours or less. In fact, the first plane the Signal Corps recruited for this kind of work put fifteen to twenty jeeps out of work.

Today with five planes, five pilots and a ground crew of seven, the Air Section of the 304th Signal Operation Battalion is a busy outfit. Since September, when it got into operation, it has hauled a total of 82,000 pounds in payloads. Charts in the operations hut show its planes are making eighty flights a month. Each pilot puts in about seventy-five hours of flying time a month, which means he has to make a flight every day of the week with few exceptions.

There is nothing fancy about the way the airline operates. Each day before noon a jeep brings out the messages in mail sacks and tosses them inside the door of the operations hut alongside the dusty airstrip. A clerk inside tallies them in and marks them for different corps headquarters. Sometimes there is a passenger, but the maximum payload is limited to four hundred pounds. At 1300 the pilots walk back from the little mess hall and climb into their planes. The ground crew—one mechanic to a plane—has already given the planes a final check and squared away the baggage in the rear compartments. With a wave from the pilots the planes waddle out to the end of the strip and take off.

If nothing unusual happens they will be back before sundown. They follow routes carefully plotted on the map in the operations hut. Each pilot picks his route from the weather information given him before taking off, tells the clerk which route he will use, and when he arrives at his destination he sends word back by telephone which route he will use on the return trip. These precautions are always taken so that if a pilot gets into trouble a search plane will know where to look for him.

Except for these measures, the Mosquito pilot is left on his own to get from one temporary landing strip to another with his cargo. There is no radio beam to guide him, and though he carries a radio its range is too short to be of much help and, even if it were longer in range, there is no one to listen for his distress signal.

He travels like an Indian scout, checking his position with known landmarks along the way. Rivers, mountains, roads, lakes and villages spread out below him in a great map. Usually he flies within view of main supply roads where he could get help if he had to make a forced landing. And, if he is forced to land, the broad, flat banks of the Korean rivers make good places to bring down a light plane in an emergency.

The little airline has an excellent record for both safety and faithful service. So far no plane or pilot has been lost. Yet, in a country notorious for poor flying weather, the pilots have admitted only ten times in eight months of operations that it was too dangerous to fly.

The light-plane messenger service fills a gap between jeep messengers and big-plane courier service. Most division and corps headquarters manage to clear a landing strip nearby, but there isn't always room enough for the big planes or the improvised fields may be too soggy after a rain. That's where the light plane "brings in the bacon."

In World War II light planes did a similar kind of job, but it was not recognized until recently that what was needed was genuine operate-it-yourself, light-plane messenger service. Pilots and planes were recruited from the infantry and artillery, where the light plane has been in use as an observation and spotter plane. The world's biggest little airline has been born and the Signal Corps has its early wings back again.

12. Division Aerial Photography

Capt. Cass J. Joswiak, 2d Signal Company

The inclusion of a photo section in the division signal company is a post-World War II innovation. One officer and 15 men are assigned and their mission is to take both tactical and publicity photographs. The men have both still and movie cameras, and there are three K-20 cameras for aerial work. The section has enough laboratory equipment to develop and print all its own still shots.

In Korea, under orders from General Headquarters, Far East Command, film processing was denied the division signal companies except in emergencies. It was understood that an emergency occurred when a VIP visited the division and publicity photographs were desired immediately. But our interpretation of this order provided an opening wedge for aerial photograph at the division level.

The main problem with aerial photography through the normal Army-Air Force channels was that eight days elapsed between the time the 2d Infantry Division requested a photo and the time the prints were delivered. Usually the situation changed so radically during this period that the division either had no interest in the terrain photographed, or the enemy had changed his position.

Soon after the 2d Division arrived in Korea I told the G2 about the possibility of aerial photography by our photo section, but he was not very interested. Our first aerial shots were made in August 1950 on request of the division engineer. He wanted aerial photos of the Naktong River to use in planning river crossings. The pictures we produced were obliques, and they gave a clear view of the bridges, approaches, and far shore. In addition to terrain, they showed a considerable number of enemy installations.

From this time on we had many calls from G2 and others for aerial photos. Right after our first Naktong River shots we were asked for photos of Hill 409—all the way around. This hill was between the 2d Infantry Division and the 1st Cavalry Division, and we anticipated that our 2d Division would have to reduce it before we could cross the Naktong. The photos were taken one afternoon and handed to the photo interpreter team the next morning. They located enemy dugouts, bunkers, and foxholes on the photos.

Still later in August, we were called upon to help find out if any enemy build-up was taking place along the front of our division and that of the 25th Infantry Division. The PI team designated an area for us to search and for two days we made four daily photo runs over it. The results showed the arrival of a North Korean armored division just in front of us. In this way we were able to anticipate the thrust and limit the penetration by the enemy.

During the fighting along the perimeter, the 9th Infantry had a particularly difficult time with Hill 201. The regiment captured and lost that hill so many times there was a great deal of comment about the regiment and its abilities. The division commander (Maj. Gen. Laurence B. Keiser) ordered me to get complete aerial still and movie coverage of Hill 201—"for posterity." Those pictures really showed what the regiment had been up against in the way of rough terrain and vicious close-in fighting. You could see the camouflaged enemy approaches, positions never discovered or captured, destroyed equipment, and the many dead littering the area.

In September, as the division was preparing to break out of the Pusan perimeter, the photo section was ordered to photograph the winding road the troops were to travel. We flew ten miles beyond the Naktong River to Chogye, shooting pictures all the way. These photos showed where to expect trouble from the enemy and the terrain. As soon as the attack got under way we photographed the road to Hyopchon, and we continued to photograph the route of the 2d Division until we were pinched off by other divisions.

The 2d Infantry Division did not get back into action again until November 1950. Because of the nature of the Chinese fighting methods— hiding by day, fighting by night—we could not help much with our photography. In January and February 1951, as we began to attack again, we were able to get very good spot photos for use by our commanders in their limited attacks. In addition, we made a daily photo sweep of the division's front.

We had several problems in our aerial photography. One was the demand for better photos than we could produce. We were frequently asked for mosaics with grid coordinates superimposed on the photo. This was far beyond our capability. We just took good obliques and pinpoint shots. Their value was in speed of delivery.

The second problem was getting the liaison pilots to fly close to what we wanted to photograph. At times we urged the pilots to bring the plane down within a thousand feet of the ground or lower, but it was no use. They flew no lower than three thousand feet over enemy territory, and then complained that they could hear bullets coming close. I never heard any, but I have seen holes in the wings after we got down.

From this account it should not be assumed that all our photos were aerials. The photo section continued to take movies and stills of combat operations. We photographed our full share of VIPs, but we were especially proud of our aerial photographs.

13. Combat Cameraman

Lt. Robert L. Strickland, 71st Signal Service Battalion. (Extracts from a letter written while Lieutenant Strickland accompanied the 1st Marine Division into Seoul in September 1950.)

We got across the Han River and caught an ambulance going up to the front. Almost from the time we left the river we were under sniper fire—not just occasional shots, but heavy fire. And most of the roads were under mortar fire, which made the going rough.

When the ambulance turned off I got out and started walking. We went a few yards and got pinned down with a group of marines by mortar and small-arms fire. I got a few shots of jeeps running under fire.

From here we went up, one at a time, toward the real front. I hooked up with one outfit that was moving up and shot some scenes of them moving past a knocked-out North Korean tank. Then I got some shots of our tanks with flame throwers moving up with marines in the background.

The next shot was a lulu. I am afraid that silent film can't do it justice. The tanks started moving through an opening in the sandbag barrier. There was one marine lying near the opening with his rifle pointed down the road. As the tanks moved through, all hell broke loose from the enemy antitank guns and rifles. The marine by the opening jumped almost straight up and ran like a bat out of Hades. The spot he had been lying in had just got plastered, but I don't think he was hit.

After that I shot some scenes over the sandbag barrier at the burning building in the background. It was exploding periodically. I didn't get a good explosion shot but I caught one section of the building falling with a terrific roar amid clouds of smoke and dust.

In one of these scenes I really missed a bet. There was an old Korean woman sitting right in the middle of things, standing guard over an old man who had been wounded. It was impossible for me to get across the street for a close-up. The air was whipping with everything from flying stones to big antitank shells. When the sound boys get to this part they can dub in all the battle noises they can get and they still won't be realistic enough.

I shot my next stuff at a road junction where some marines were running across the open toward a small, triangular building. There was a tank and a lot of buildings burning in the background. I finished shooting and ran across after them, stopping at the corner of the building to shoot again. About four men passed me from behind as I stood there shooting up the street. All of them ran right into a mortar shell and got hit, one of them seriously. He got the one that was intended for me.

I kept shooting while a couple of them picked up the seriously wounded man and helped him to hobble to cover. A few minutes later an antitank shell came close enough to my left arm to ripple the sleeve on my jacket. I stepped back and looked around. By now there was a wounded marine and a wounded North Korean lying back of the burning building. Another marine with an automatic rifle was guarding them. I framed my picture so that they were in the bottom of the frame with the burning walls in the background. Then, right on cue, the wounded marine with his two buddies helping him along came hobbling into the frame for a great shot.

Right after this we got so much fire of all kinds that I lost count. There were more mortar shells, more antitank stuff and more small-arms fire and then it started all over again. In a few minutes the little area back of the burning building which gave us cover was crowded with wounded men. They lay there in pain among burning debris and hot embers, hugging the ground to keep from getting hit again.

There was only one medic—a Navy corpsman—so I put my camera aside and gave him a hand. I missed a lot of good pictures but there is no need to say the pictures were not that important. I have seen a lot of men get hit both in this war and in World War II, but I think I have never seen so many get hit so fast in such a small area.

I finally got free to start shooting again. By the time the corpsman and I got the first men fixed up the other corpsmen had run the gantlet of fire to help us. Those corpsmen really have the guts to go in any time and place to help a wounded man.

I started to get a low-angle shot of some marines coming across the road toward us. While I was getting down to shoot a mortar landed right in the middle of them. I missed the burst but I got the camera going again as the smoke cleared. The guys in the street were running like mad. They headed for our little area, running all over me, but giving me a nice "fade" by blocking the camera lens. I hung around long enough to get a shot of the litter bearers running for cover with one of the wounded men.

For the next half hour or so, I couldn't seem to get back to shooting again. I guess I was a little shaky. The fighting had moved on up the road from me, and once you get out of it you find it awfully hard to force yourself back again.

After fooling around for a while I worked down the road and stopped off in a kind of alley with a bunch of marines. I heard a tank coming up the road and I got ready to shoot. Just as the tank got in the frame, one of the marines fired a carbine about six inches from my nose. The camera lens went straight up and I was madder than a wet hen until I saw a sniper fall out of a tree behind me.

I took some final shots up at the sandbag barricade. There wasn't much to shoot at, just marines moving up and some shots of tanks firing into a concentration of North Koreans who were trying to encircle us. They were in front of us, on the right of us, and only about a hundred yards away on the left of us in a little village.

About that time the tanks started firing their 90s right over our heads. The blast was so terrible that I still can't hear well today. It was getting late and I had to get to the airport at 1700 to send back my film. I got one more long shot looking back toward where the marines were still fighting, and then left.

PART V

Medical Corps

1. Battalion Forward Aid Station

Lt. Rudolph A. Sarka, Medical Company, 7th Infantry

In December 1950 the 7th Infantry (3d Infantry Division) had one doctor in each aid station and two at each collecting station. Some divisions were critically short of doctors but we had enough because we had just arrived in Korea.

To permit the doctors to work more freely, the Medical Service Corps officers normally established battalion forward aid stations. Such an aid station was set up on a ridge west of Hamhung in December 1950.

The 1st Battalion, 7th Infantry, was withdrawing eastward from Sachang-ni toward Hamhung. When we reached the crest of the last mountain before Hamhung we were much relieved. We knew that the enemy could not cut us off from evacuation at the port. But then we were ordered to hold on this ridge.

Our infantry lines were along the forward slope, the battalion command post was four or five miles back of us, and the trains were two miles beyond that. This deployment kept our vehicles off the mountain where they might be caught if we had to pull out in a hurry.

The battalion aid station, the surgeon, and the box ambulances were with the battalion trains. The jeep ambulances were near the command post. I established the forward aid station along the road, only a few yards behind the infantry companies. The ridge was so sharp that I could be only a few yards behind the riflemen and still have both concealment and cover. At one time I requested two box ambulances, and they drove within thirty yards of the foxholes without being observed.

An enlisted medic is qualified to apply a tourniquet, to bandage wounds, and to give sedatives. In addition, as a Medical Service Corps officer, I was authorized to administer plasma and blood. I could tell when a patient needed immediate attention and could alert the doctor to be ready to treat the man when he was evacuated. I was authorized to request helicopter evacuation from my forward aid station when this service was available. My job, then, was to fill the gap between the aid man with his small kit, and the professional physician in an aid station, working with more extensive equipment. On the front lines a doctor could have done little more than I.

In any case, no one can complain that our forward aid station didn't give immediate service to the infantry. I was so close that when I needed to make a phone call, I just picked up the rifle platoon leader's sound-powered phone.

2. Evacuation at Soksa-ri

Lt. Rudolph A. Sarka, Medical Company, 7th Infantry

On 19 May 1951 the 7th Infantry Regiment left Seoul and moved east to the vicinity of Ami-dong. One battalion went into a blocking position that night and the other battalions closed in assembly areas. The next day an attached platoon of the division's reconnaissance company made contact with the enemy near Soksa-ri. On the 21st all three battalions were committed in an attack.

The terrain where the 3d Battalion fought was rough. Litter evacuation of the wounded was necessary, so the battalion surgeon (Capt. Gilbert S. Campbell) and his medical assistants followed close behind the assault companies. It was impossible to bring the aid-station equipment forward, and Captain Campbell worked with the supplies from his aid kit. The battalion aid station, manned only by two medics, was three miles to the rear.

Normally, litter jeeps from our medical company collecting station pick up their patients at the battalion aid station. In this operation, however, the litter jeeps passed the aid station and came up the road to a point only fifty yards from the base of the mountain on which the 3d Battalion was fighting. Between the road and the mountain were four channels of the Soksa River. The main channel gave the litter bearers a great deal of trouble because the stream was fast-flowing, waist-deep, and had large boulders in the stream bed.

A man wounded on the firing line was immediately treated by Captain Campbell. Then he was carried down the mountain by a five-man litter team led by an American or ROK soldier and using four Korean bearers. The trip took an hour and a half.

Once the patient reached the jeep evacuation point his bandages were checked and adjusted, and his general condition observed. Seriously wounded were loaded two to a jeep; lightly wounded were often loaded seven to a vehicle—one in the front seat, four in the back, two on the hood.

The jeeps bypassed the battalion aid station and took the patients to the advanced clearing station. Here the seriously wounded were evacuated by helicopter and the others by box ambulance.

Although this arrangement departed from the normal evacuation procedure, it worked well.

3.   Helicopter Evacuation

Lt. Martin Blumenson, in *Special Problems in the Korean Conflict,* published by Eighth Army headquarters. (Based on interviews of Col. Thomas N. Page, Surgeon, Eighth Army; Lt.Col. Arne D. Smith, Medical Section, Eighth Army; Major Sydney L. Fouts, Liaison Rescue Officer to Fifth Air Force; Capt. M. A. Mecca, Rescue Controller, Fifth Air Force; Capt. James E. Childers, 8193d Helicopter Unit.)

In the past, the tendency has been to move surgery as close to the patient as possible. In Korea this was undesirable because of the fluid tactical situation, the limited highway net, the rough roads, and the mountainous terrain. If they used helicopter evacuation, the hospitals could stay longer in each location and allow four or five days of postoperative care for a patient before further evacuation.

Helicopter evacuation in Korea evolved out of circumstances. A detachment of the 3d Air Rescue Squadron, whose mission was to retrieve downed pilots, began to receive occasional requests from Army units to evacuate wounded from mountainous positions. Whenever its helicopters were not busy, the detachment responded. During the rapid advance of the ground troops in the fall of 1950, the helicopters were especially helpful in speeding evacuation over the lengthened routes.

In January 1951 three Army helicopter detachments arrived in Korea with the mission of evacuating seriously wounded from the front lines. Each detachment consisted of 4 helicopters, 4 pilots, and 4 mechanics. Two detachments were equipped with Bell H-13 helicopters; one had Hiller H-23s. Each craft carried only a pilot and was equipped with two baskets or pods for litter patients. Under exceptionally good flight conditions, one walking patient could be carried at the same time.

The Eighth Army surgeon placed the first two detachments to arrive under the control of the IX Corps surgeon. Since IX Corps was in the center of Korea, the helicopters were also able to serve the other corps.

The first problem that arose was the necessity of teaching the helicopter pilots what their aircraft could do in front-line evacuation. The pilots could learn only by trial and error.

The ground forces then had to learn the limitations of helicopter evacuation. In the popular conception, helicopters landed on mountain peaks, lifted straight up into the air, and operated in all types of weather. It was necessary to understand that helicopters could not fly at night, operate in bad weather, or land on sloping terrain. They needed take-off space; they could not fly in heavy winds; they had limitations of range and altitude. They also had less lifting power in the thin, warm air of summer.

Ground troops had to understand the importance of reporting accurate coordinates to locate the patient. They had to be taught the necessity of marking the landing site with panels and of using colored smoke grenades to indicate proper location and wind direction.

Combat elements sometimes requested helicopter evacuation as a convenience. By the fall of 1951, ground units had learned to request a helicopter only for cases involving head, chest, and abdominal wounds, multiple fractures, and great loss of blood. Even then, evacuation was available only if an ambulance could not reach the patient, if a rough ambulance ride would seriously injure him, or if it was necessary to get him to a medical installation quickly. As a working premise, the local surgeon decided whether the patient needed helicopter evacuation and the helicopter detachment commander decided whether the helicopters could reach the patient.

Ground forces generally did not realize the extreme vulnerability of helicopters. Their lack of speed and inability to fly at high altitude increased the hazard of enemy ground fire. Furthermore, helicopters were extremely sensitive to damage. Lack of the gliding characteristics of a conventional plane and the increased problem of pilot control meant that almost any damage from enemy fire was fatal to the craft. Pilots did not wear parachutes because of the danger of falling into the blades if they jumped from a disabled craft. When an area was under enemy observation the patient had to be prepared for quick loading.

Because there was always a shortage of helicopters in Korea, Eighth Army ordered that these craft not be used on missions involving danger from enemy action. This did not prevent pilots from evacuating patients from units surrounded by the enemy; nor did it prevent the evacuation of casualties sustained by patrols operating forward of friendly front lines.

The first two Army helicopter detachments to arrive in Korea were attached to the 8076th Mobile Army Surgical Hospital (MASH). At that time IX Corps headquarters was at Chungju; the hospital was forty miles to the rear. This arrangement left long distances between the helicopters and the combat lines. It was then decided to dispatch the helicopters from corps headquarters. Later, all the helicopters moved into the division areas. Normally, one helicopter was stationed at each division clearing station. From there it was but a few miles to the front lines.

Certain expedients adapted the helicopters for evacuation. Plastic bags were used to keep the patients warm. Flexible tubes were fitted from the engine to heat the patients in flight. Covers for the pods were devised to keep the wind off their faces. The fact that the patients in the pods could not receive medical care while in flight remained one of the serious limitations of the helicopter, even though a mechanical device permitted them to be given plasma. The limitation on medical care and the short fuel-range of the craft make it necessary to keep helicopter flights short.

Helicopters in Korea had evacuated eight thousand casualties by 1 November 1951. Many of these men would not have survived without this transportation. The smooth ride and the rapid arrival at a clearing station or hospital possibly caused a lower rate of shock fatalities than in World War II. The treatment of head injuries was expedited because helicopters carried patients swiftly to neurosurgical teams.

The presence of helicopters in Korea helped morale. Although much experimentation in the use of helicopters for evacuation remains to be done, this "ambulance of the air" has proved its usefulness in the Korean conflict.

4. Optical Treatment in the Field

> Capt. Daniel B. Sullivan, 24th Medical Battalion. (Interview by Lt. Martin Blumenson, 3d Historical Detachment.)

Before May 1951 there was no medical officer in the 24th Infantry Division qualified to do refracting and no equipment for adequate eye examination. Men needing glasses were evacuated through medical channels, often as far as Taegu and Pusan. This wasted a great deal of time and sometimes caused individuals to be permanently lost to the division because they were returned to duty through replacement channels.

Early in 1951 the Eighth Army surgeon recommended that refracting be done in the division medical battalions. The 24th Medical Battalion (24th Infantry Division) received a trial lens set, but there was no other equipment.

In April 1951, the commanding officer of the Clearing Company (Major Samuel Rothermel) determined to implement Eighth Army's recommendation. He sent Capt. Daniel B. Sullivan to the 4th Field Hospital at Taegu for a refresher course in refracting. All medical officers know the theory of refracting, and the refresher course provided a review of theory and a chance to develop skill in practice.

Returning to the battalion with eye charts, eye drops, and a retinascope obtained from the 4th Field Hospital, Captain Sullivan arranged for space for an optical shop, and then trained an enlisted assistant. Units were told of the new service and on 9 May optical examinations began.

Each refraction took only a few minutes. If glasses were needed the prescription was recorded in the soldier's immunization record (his Form 66-1) and in the records of the medical battalion. The soldier was sent to the 8076th MASH, where his prescription for glasses was filled immediately. The hospital maintained a stock of lenses and ground special ones when needed. The entire process took less than a day.

Whenever the division went into reserve, the 6th Army Mobile Optical Unit, operating from an optical van, moved into the medical battalion's area and filled a prescription for glasses within a matter of minutes. It was not unusual for a soldier to have his eyes examined and be fitted with glasses within an hour.

After the optical section began its work, the enlisted assistant gained enough training and experience to do the refracting himself. Examination of the eyes for pathology remained the duty of a medical officer, however.

From 9 May to 16 September, 897 men were examined and 768 had glasses prescribed and fitted. Only 34—those with pathology or needing other treatment—had to be evacuated. These figures include not just men of the 24th Division, but soldiers of the 7th Division, Eighth Army and its corps units, as well as British Commonwealth units.

The saving of man-hours within the 24th Division has been tremendous. The increase in speed has led to an increase in the number of soldiers seeking treatment and, therefore, to an improvement in health and morale.

5. Dental Treatment in the Field

Major Peter M. Margetis, Dental Surgeon, 24th Infantry Division. (Interview by Lt. Martin Blumenson, 3d Historical Detachment.)

The division dental surgeon has authority to distribute his dental officers as he wishes. Each division is authorized 18 dentists, but in January 1951 the 24th Division had only 15—enough for combat, but not enough for garrison duty. When Major Peter M. Margetis arrived at the 24th Medical Battalion, all of the 24th Division's dentists were on duty at a central clinic except one at division rear and another at the advanced clearing station.

Major Margetis saw no advantage in keeping the dentists centralized away from the troops. A man needing dental treatment might have to spend a whole day traveling from his unit to the dental clinic. Under this system of distribution, only one thousand dental operations (fillings, extractions, and prosthetic work) were performed each month.

Major Margetis distributed the dental officers one to each regiment, division headquarters forward, division headquarters rear; two each to the replacement company and division artillery; and three each to the clearing company and the medical battalion (including the division dental surgeon).

Each dental officer has an enlisted assistant and a No. 60 dental chest. The chest is only slightly larger than a foot locker, but it contains a folding dental chair, electric motor, instruments, lights, trays, and medications. Mobility is no problem and definitive dental treatment can be performed.

Although it had been the practice to send all impaction cases to rear medical installations (usually the 8076th MASH), Major Margetis insisted that all such work be done by the division's dental officers. Only four patients were evacuated as dental cases (gunshot wounds are considered medical cases) in six months.

As a result of the new distribution of dental officers, dental operations increased from 1,000 to 8,000 a month. More dental work has been accomplished and less time has been lost by soldiers seeking dental work.

6. Changing the Mission

Capt. John M. McGuire, 1st Mobile Army Surgical Hospital

Early in November 1950 the 1st MASH landed at Iwon, on the northeast coast of Korea, and moved inland to Pukchon. Here we worked for thirty days attached to the 7th Infantry Division. This month was unlike any other period for us. Our hospital "followed the book" in both organization and operation at Pukchon.

We were set up in a two-story school building which we shared with the 7th Medical Battalion. Although the 7th Division had infantry regiments near the Yalu River and Changjin Reservoir, relatively few casualties were evacuated to Pukchon. The 7th Medical Battalion was able to receive and care for the nonsurgical casualties. This allowed the 1st MASH to limit its admissions to patients requiring surgery. During November we received a total of 171 surgical cases and were successful in treating them without a single death. We gave each case maximum attention.

At Pukchon, although we were more than a hundred miles from many of the units we were serving, only two patients—both extremely serious cases—were air-evacuated to us. Shortage of airfields near the infantry regiments was the major reason for limiting air evacuation.

After our withdrawal from North Korea we moved near Kyungju. We were assigned to X Corps and our responsibilities were increased. Instead of operating as a mobile army surgical hospital—that is, a small, sixty-bed hospital assigned to one division—we were called upon to care for the casualties from the 1st Marine Division, the 2d and 7th Infantry Divisions, and the 187th Regimental Combat Team.

We rapidly expanded from a 60-bed to a 200-bed hospital, but our personnel increased from only 16 medical officers, 16 nurses, and 100 enlisted men, to 20 medical officers, 20 nurses, and 120 enlisted men.

The expansion of the hospital meant that our primary mission was enlarged. Instead of handling only surgical cases, we began to receive medical cases as well. Because the increased work load had not been accompanied by a corresponding increase in personnel, it occasionally became necessary for us to evacuate some patients without operating. In no case, however, did this jeopardize a patient's chance of survival or return to duty, for air and hospital-train evacuation to the next medical installation was always available.

7.   Operation of the 8076th MASH

Lt.Col. John L. Mothershead and Capt. Samuel L. Crook. (Interviews by Lt. Martin Blumenson, 3d Historical Detachment.)

The primary function of a mobile army surgical hospital is to do emergency, life-saving surgery and to make the patient transportable to rear medical installations. The MASH was originally a 60-bed hospital with the mission of supporting one division. Because there were not enough evacuation hospitals in Korea, the surgical hospitals were expanded to 200-bed capacity. With the increased patient load, personnel, services, and tentage, there has been a decrease of mobility.

To improve the mobility of the 8076th MASH, the officers designed a new tent plan. Hospital tents are formed of detachable sections. Using 41 main sections and 16 end sections, the 8076th designed a unique hospital which was especially adaptable to displacement. The core of the hospital is shaped in a **U.** Around this basic center, tents are added and subtracted as the situation changes.

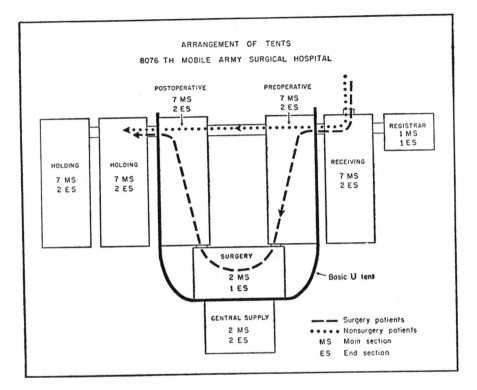

The hospital is moved in two phases. In Phase I, the tents housing the registrar and receiving-and-holding are taken down. The laboratory, the pharmacy, and the admitting functions of receiving are moved into the preoperative ward. The tentage that has been struck is then moved to a new location with half of the personnel of preoperative, postoperative, surgical, and central supply, plus one receiving clerk. At the new location a second basic **U** is formed, consisting of preoperative, postoperative and surgical. Central supply functions of sterilizing instruments and dressings are carried out in the surgical tent.

At one point, therefore, there are two functioning hospitals. The hospital in the rear continues to admit patients until the forward installation is complete. When the advance unit begins to receive patients, the rear installation stops all admissions. When its patients have been evacuated, the rear unit moves up and joins the advance hospital as Phase

II of the move. The tentage of Phase II is added externally to the basic U in its new location. The medical officers and enlisted men who have not yet moved come with Phase II. All nurses move with the rear element.

Moving from Chunchon to Hwachon, the 8076th relocated its installations in this manner:

19 September

0900 Capt. Samuel L. Crook left Chunchon to check several sites in the vicinity of Hwachon.

1000 Lt.Col. John L. Mothershead received final orders to move to the vicinity of Hwachon. Key personnel notified of impending move.

1200 Captain Crook notified that the move would be that day.

1300 Tentage at Chunchon began to be struck.

1330 Captain Crook notified Colonel Mothershead of new site and its location.

1530 Phase I convoy left Chunchon.

1730 Convoy arrived at Hwachon.

2230 Basic U set up at Hwachon. Ready to receive patients.

2400 Advance unit opened; rear unit closed.

20 September

0800 Patients at rear unit transferred to 629th Clearing Company, which moved into Chunchon to assume the function of evacuating patients to the Chunchon railhead and airstrip.

1300 Phase II convoy left Chunchon.

1500 Rear unit arrived at Hwachon. Basic U expanded to form complete MASH.

Several modifications have been made to equipment to adapt it for local conditions. To increase the hauling capacity of the hospital vehicles, trailer hitches were taken from abandoned trucks along the road. The hospital had Ordnance weld these hitches to a butt plate on the rear of each 1-ton trailer. Each 2-½-ton truck now safely hauls two trailers, thereby doubling its hauling capacity.

The tents have been made warmer by the use of Air Force gasoline-burning heaters which blow hot air to the tents through ducts. A sliding light system has been devised so that illumination can be moved to the best advantage in surgery. A sprinkler system has been developed to keep down dust. A food box has been developed to keep flies off food carried from the kitchen to the ward. The hospital has had no diarrhea attributable to fly contamination.

In the medical field, one of the expedients developed by the 8076th is the upright which has been welded on the bar holding the Thomas splint to the litter. This modification permits giving intravenous fluids while the patient is being moved. Because some type of holder for litters was needed to support them at a higher level than the cot, an iron-pipe tripod was improvised. This improved the hydrostatic pressure in certain types of lung surgery cases where drainage was needed.

PART VI

Ordnance Corps

1. Mobile ASP

Lt.Col. Walter W. Gerken, Ordnance Officer, 1st Cavalry Division

The 1st Cavalry Division was serving in Japan when it was alerted for movement to Korea. We planned an amphibious assault at Pohang-dong, but it was actually an unopposed administrative landing on 18 July 1950.

Before it left Japan, the division was warned it could not count on ordnance support for at least thirty days after landing. Therefore, we were instructed to carry a thirty-day supply of ordnance spare parts and replacement items. In addition, the division ammunition officer (Capt. Charles Russell) was told to carry a minimum of two extra basic loads of 155-mm. ammunition and five extra loads of 105-mm. ammunition.

This requirement was not only in contradiction to U.S. Army ammunition doctrine, but was well beyond our capability. The division ammunition officer's job normally is to allocate—but not handle—the division's ammunition. The infantry and artillery units clear their requisitions with the DAO on the way to the army dumps to pick up the rounds. But in this operation the division's ordnance company was to carry ammunition.

The problem of spare parts and replacement items involved considerable planning. We took only those things we figured we would need most. Even so, we had to stuff every inch of the machine-shop trucks, and use the M24 tank transporters to carry spare parts. There was no space for the additional ammunition. Captain Russell just loaded it on the landing craft and we figured to handle it as the situation in Korea allowed.

In Korea the G4 of our division and the G4 of Eighth Army coordinated activities right on the Pohang-dong docks. It was understood we would need railroad locomotives and cars, and G4 of Eighth Army simply asked our requirements. The engineer, quartermaster and other units made their requests, and we asked for 2 engines and about 25 cars. There was no railroad transportation officer at Pohang-dong, so Captain Russell performed this function.

From Pohang-dong, elements of the division moved west and relieved the 24th Infantry Division as it withdrew from Taejon. All our vehicles traveled by road, but we moved the twenty-five cars of ammunition by rail.

We handled the ammunition by moving the train to a railroad siding a safe distance behind the front—perhaps twenty-five miles. Then an engine and five cars of ammunition would run forward to establish a division ammunition supply point as close to the infantry regiments as possible. The ammunition was never dumped on the ground, but was kept completely mobile.

The closeness of the ASP to the guns was such that at both Hwaggan and Kwan-ni the artillery was grouped around the area where the forward ammunition train halted. At Kwan-ni one battery was within a hundred feet of the car. Rounds were carried directly from the flatcars to the guns.

We were shelled at Kwan-ni. Artillery fire fell in the area of the ASP and, while it did not hurt anyone, it scared the train crew. The Korean engineer uncoupled the locomotive and was about to take off for safer parts. Had he gotten started he probably wouldn't have stopped short of Pusan. His departure would have forced us to abandon the cars and ammunition. But the engine didn't leave because we kept the engineer in his cab at gunpoint until it was time to displace. We had some difficulty in getting the train crew to move forward with the ammunition again.

After this incident we held the ammunition in three echelons rather than two. The main train was kept well to the rear, a second echelon of four cars was two or three miles behind the ASP, and only one car was run forward. Even so, we had an irate Transportation Corps officer complain that we were destroying the morale of the Korean trainmen.

Labor was easy to obtain for this operation. We recruited as many civilians as we needed and kept them with us by issuing rice three times a day. We normally had a car of rice and other provisions with us at all times.

Our operation grew rapidly. We got ammunition from a number of sources. In the hurried evacuation of Seoul and Ascom City the South Koreans had apparently shipped out everything they could, and the 24th Division got hold of much of the miscellaneous ammunition. When we relieved the 24th they gave us their supply. This ammunition was further mixed by receipt of stocks from the 25th Division and other units. Whenever we heard some unit couldn't evacuate its ammunition, we picked it up. After we had been pushed back to Taegu we turned in 106 cars of ammunition to Eighth Army! We lost no ammunition or railroad equipment in the entire operation.

This was one occasion when the DAO was more than a pencil-pusher.

2.   Artillery and Hand Grenades

Lt.Col. John E. Harbert, 314th Ordnance Ammunition Group

Commanders of tactical units have repeatedly emphasized the fact that the Korean conflict has been essentially a contest between enemy manpower and U.S. fire power. Communist forces in Korea have been employed against us on an 8-to-1 ratio. We have countered with a ratio of more than 100 to 1 in fire power. The pitting of fire power against manpower has led to unprecedented logistical problems.

During a sixty-day period (19 August to 18 October 1951), 158,303 tons of ammunition were delivered to regiments and battalions of U.S. I, IX, and X Corps from 17 forward ammunition points operated by the 314th Ordnance Ammunition Group. This represents 27 Liberty-ship loads, or 3,332 rail-car loads, or 39,527 2-½-ton-truck loads (100 per cent overloaded). The 314th has had over 900 rail cars of ammunition moving forward from Pusan and Inchon at one time.

Paradoxically, the enemy's "human-wave" tactics and the mountainous terrain have made Korea a battleground of artillery and hand grenades. As a result, in this sixty-day period, we delivered across the front 3,092 rounds to each 105-mm howitzer; 2,579 rounds to each 155-mm howitzer; 1,830 rounds to each 155-mm gun; 1,631 rounds to each 8-inch howitzer—but only 391 rounds to each 60-mm mortar and 546 rounds to each M1 rifle. Over 400,000 hand grenades were used by Eighth Army. One infantry regiment used over 900 in one night.

Such ammunition expenditures are not for the Ordnance field commander to question. His job is to supply the demand. However, I have often wondered whether we could maintain such a rate of fire during a global war.

Ammunition supply problems are never present during training. Therefore, when the fighting starts, organization and methods of providing this combat essential are too often left to be developed by inexperienced and untrained men. This causes waste, hoarding, confusion, and sometimes panic at the critical periods of battle. When logistics meet the demands of tactics, there is little inquiry into the miracle of ammunition delivery. But the instant a shortage hampers operations, we can expect inquiries into the most minute details of ammunition movement along the pipeline. Fear of an ammunition shortage has often led to runs on ASPs—like runs on banks.

Ammunition requirements cannot be measured by bulk tonnages alone, for there are more than five hundred different types of ammunition and their components. Substitutions can often be made within classes I, II, III, and IV items.[1] This is not so with ammunition. The key to successful ammunition supply is the delivery of correct type and amount of ammunition to the right place at the right time. Requirements fluctuate greatly with the type of combat.

The 314th Ordnance Group developed a unique stock control and reporting system. Accurate, timely information vital to all commanders was forwarded daily. The ammunition picture for the entire peninsula was in the morning ammunition brief. This form analyzed graphically, in nontechnical terms, the ammunition by type, location, and availability. It greatly helped us control the flow of ammunition, and it dispelled the fear of shortages displayed by commanders of tactical units.

3. The Van Fleet Rate of Fire

Capt. David L. Mathews, 69th Ordnance Ammunition Company. (Condensed from an interview by Lt. John Mewha, 8th Historical Detachment.)

During the defensive Battle of the Soyang River (10 May to 7 June 1951), X Corps exceeded all previous ammunition expenditures. The fighting was close and the divisions used "walls of steel" to halt the Communist drive.

The artillery made the greatest demand on ammunition because of the weight and bulk of their rounds. In this engagement the artillery often fired for long periods at five times the normal rate. On 22 May the artillery fired 49,986 rounds on the corps front. Artillerymen, firing at a rate of 250 rounds per gun per day, came to speak of "the Van Fleet rate of fire."

A normal build-up of ammunition in the forward areas had taken place before the attack. Units carried their basic loads, and the ammuni-

---

[1] Supplies are divided into five classes: *class I*, articles consumed at approximately uniform rates, such as rations; *class II*, articles authorized by tables of basic allowances, such as radio sets, tools, and arms; *class III*, engine fuels and lubricants; *class IV*, articles not authorized by tables of basic allowances but needed for operations contemplated or in progress, such as barbed wire and construction materials; *class V*, ammunition, pyrotechnics, antitank mines, and chemicals.

tion supply points at Hongchon and Wonju were well stocked. But in 28 days the corps expended 25,000 tons of ammunition, and fired more than 1,800 tons in one day. The supply level became low at Hongchon and trucks often had to make the longer drive to the supply point at Wonju. Airlift was used to bring hand grenades and ammunition to Hoengsong, but this never exceeded 300 tons a day.

During the entire battle, the 2d Magazine Platoon, 69th Ordnance Ammunition Company, remained in position at Hongchon—even though many other division and corps supply units had been withdrawn. At one point in the battle the enemy approached to within eight miles of the ammunition dump, so an infantry company was sent to guard that installation.

The ammunition platoon continued to supply ammunition without interruption. While a 500-ton capacity is its rated maximum, the platoon maintained a 1,163-tons-per-day level at the height of the battle. During a six-hour period in the middle of the night of 20-21 May, the platoon loaded 540 trucks with 4 tons of ammunition each.

4. Division Ordnance Work

Lt.Col. Barton O. Baker, Ordnance Officer, 25th Infantry Division

I get tired of hearing people say that the first soldiers going to Korea were not properly trained. The 25th Infantry Division, under Maj.Gen. William B. Kean, received excellent training. I have seen our men in Japan going through mud and grime, and actually using thoroughly realistic time-and-space factors. What we needed was more men.

Our technical troops were as efficient as the infantry. In the Ordnance Corps we not only trained our own men but carefully pushed instruction in first- and second-echelon maintenance and repair as far forward as we could. In Korea our company did not need corps ordnance support until the division received a great many attachments. Counting the attachments, the 25th Division at times included thirty thousand troops!

At least 20 per cent of our repairs were accomplished in the area of the using unit. We took the parts and tools to the job and used the tank crews and gunners to help us. It gave them training, let them see the functioning of their weapons, and, if there had been negligence, they saw the results of it. Sharing in the repair reduced the amount of carelessness.

Nothing was so outstanding about my company as the high desire of the men to produce. Two examples occurred about a month apart.

After the fighting reached the 38th parallel, the bulk of our division was held near the line, but the tank battalion and the 155-mm howitzer battalion were attached to divisions moving toward the Yalu River. At Anju, about 1 November 1950, our units were relieved from their attachments so they could perform their maintenance and wait for the 25th Division to move north.

Both the tank battalion and the artillery battalions needed a great deal of servicing after the hard fighting. The shop officer from the ordnance company flew north to learn what they needed. He returned, got the parts, and took half of the ordnance company north to begin work at once. Ten days later, when the division arrived at Anju, these battalions were in excellent condition.

Early in December the 25th Division was forced to withdraw by the Chinese offensive. Our SOP provided the following order of march: division trains; service companies; two infantry regiments; ordnance armored maintenance platoon; tank battalion; the third infantry regiment; demolitions experts. The role of the ordnance armored maintenance platoon was to repair or evacuate any equipment that failed and, on call, to move back through the armor and last infantry regiment to service or evacuate equipment.

When we reached the small village of Chunghwa we had about twenty trucks we could evacuate no farther. These were placed near a crossroads and persons passing were invited to cannibalize them. A more serious problem, though, was the need to change eight tank engines. This had to be done before the platoon could proceed.

The temperature was 10 degrees below zero that night. We pulled the eight tanks into an area near the crossroads of the town, erected tents, started bonfires, and went to work. We started at about 1800, and by 0600 all eight tanks had new engines and were on the road. It was a hard, cold night, but Ordnance did its job. Before noon of that day the enemy was in Chunghwa.

5. Close Ordnance Support

Lt.Col. Joseph M. Heiser, Ordnance Officer, 7th Infantry Division

On my way north to become ordnance officer of the 7th Infantry Division in January 1951, I stopped to talk with the ordnance officer of X Corps. He told me frankly that ordnance conditions in the 7th Division were not what they should be, and that I was going into a situation where my career was at stake. The commander of X Corps (Lt.Gen. Edward M. Almond) has asked two of the regimental commanders of the division about their ordnance support and they had told him that the company might as well have stayed in Japan: the units of their regiments never saw it and they did not feel it was supporting them. Feeling had reached such a point that ordnance men along the road were refused food by units of their own division!

When I reached the division I concluded that the ordnance resources had not been fully utilized. The 707th Ordnance Maintenance Company was located near Yongchon, 120 miles south of the division's CP at Tanyang. A turnaround between the company and the division took twenty-four hours.

There were several reasons for the distance between the company and the division. Part of the division had suffered heavy casualties in the action near Changjin Reservoir. After evacuation from the port of Hungnam the division had assembled and hurriedly moved off to fight in a new sector. January 1951 was a month of uncertainty in the division, and it hesitated to move its heavy equipment forward as it advanced.

The ordnance company was weighted down by a backlog of two hundred trucks waiting for third-echelon repairs. In addition, the company was carrying three hundred tons of ordnance parts above its authorized allowance. It would take sixty 2-½-ton trucks to carry the three hundred tons even with the normal 100 per cent overload! The extra parts were being carried because the former ordnance officer feared he'd sometime want a part that the ordnance depot company wouldn't be able to supply him. However, there was no selection in the parts. Many of them were nonmoving items, and a check of the stock-record card showed eighteen thousand items. By April this had been reduced to about six thousand, and I am convinced that it could have been cut further.

The backlog of vehicles and the excess parts kept the ordnance company from joining the division. Companies and regiments were so far from ordnance that they had little choice but to run their vehicles until they quit. Then the vehicles had to be towed back.

Our division had at its disposal the support of the 7th Ordnance Medium Maintenance Company, yet it failed to use it properly. This support company was only five miles away, but vehicles were sent there only when the division's company did not have, or could not get, parts to make a repair. It was ironic that the support company did not overload itself with parts, yet it more frequently could get what it needed because the supply sergeant worked more closely with the depot company.

Shortly after I came into the 7th Division, Maj.Gen. Claude B. Ferenbaugh assumed command. He was vitally concerned with the problems of the technical services and gave us much of his attention. I knew he expected aggressive action, and I meant to deliver it.

I turned over our surplus parts and backlog of vehicles to the supporting ordnance company. Then I moved the division's ordnance company to Yongju—only twenty miles behind the division. Within ten days the supporting ordnance company had cleared the backlog, absorbed or returned the extra parts, and had moved near us. From this time on the two ordnance companies worked closely with each other and, on an informal understanding, under my direction. The supporting company leapfrogged to provide support. Sometimes it sent out detachments to assist our using units, and it was always available to take over our backlog when we had to move quickly. In those days we were very careful to maintain our mobility.

Before I took over, the division's ordnance company had sent detachments to the using units only a few times. Immediately after I took command I sent one third of the ordnance men out in detachments to the regimental combat teams. The men lived and worked right in the service companies. They taught first- and second-echelon maintenance and repair, and gave on-the-job training. In an emergency they even did first- and second-echelon maintenance themselves to get a unit on its feet. At the same time, the service company trainees did a good deal of the third-echelon work under our supervision. It was a turn-about proposition, and we were less worried about echelons than giving training and repairing vehicles.

For the next six months the close contact between the ordnance men and the using units was marked. By June, two thirds of the ordnance company was with the service companies. During this month our regiments were called upon to make a series of probing attacks. Commanders felt, as they had during the January action, that they needed ordnance support, but they were reluctant to burden the forward areas with heavy equipment. Here the well-developed cooperation between the ordnance men and the service companies paid off. The 7th Ordnance Medium Maintenance Company and one third of the division's company stayed well to the rear at Chunchon, while the ordnance service was still being maintained as far north as Hwachon by our attachments to the service companies. Anyway, preventive maintenance and careful repair had so cut down the third-echelon repair that we never had more than 35 vehicles in our shops at one time. Actually, the company was begging for work!

Another vital service that the ordnance company provided was to supply qualified mechanics and drivers to the division. Our on-the-job training was building up a creditable maintenance force, but rotation meant that our trained men would be leaving. The replacement pipeline did not bring us adequately trained drivers or mechanics, so we set up a division mechanical school.

The division's G1 screened all of the replacements for mechanics and men whose civilian experience indicated mechanical ability. Every man he found was brought to our ordnance school. We set up our own staff, consisting of a captain, a warrant officer, and eight ordnance technicians, and we normally had from eighty to a hundred in training. We had close coordination with the using units and every feature of the school was tailored to their needs. If the artillery needed a gun mechanic, we trained one. If a gun mechanic came to us needing refresher training, we gave it to him. The captain and two NCOs did the planning, the others checked the progress. As the training was primarily on-the-job in nature, we really had as many instructors as there were mechanics in the company.

As soon as the automotive mechanics and others were trained, we formed them into detachments and moved them out to the using units. We maintained control over each man, checking to see that he kept our standards. We transferred the trainee to a regiment when he seemed ready. A gauge of the success of our school was that we never had a single complaint about a man we trained.

The key to the close support we furnished the 7th Division was the close liaison. I spent 90 per cent of my time visiting the using units, and my staff was constantly doing the same. Command liaison was most important, though, for the commanders wanted to talk with the man who actually made the decisions.

Our coordination was not limited to the division. The strengthened ties with our support maintenance company made for greater mobility and flexibility. In March 1951 the 7th Division made a hurried move from Hajinbu-ri to Hangye—a distance of a hundred miles. Two RCTs were to swing south while the third was to take a calculated risk and travel a road through country whose status we did not know. The lone RCT was accompanied by a strong detachment from our ordnance to assist it in case of breakdowns. The supporting ordnance company split into three detachments and established maintenance points (garages) along the southern route. The bulk of the division's ordnance company made an administrative move. It was, therefore, able to begin operations in the new position immediately.

In April 1951 another important move was ordered, but the final destination of the division was not known. We transferred all of our repair backlog to the supporting ordnance company and it moved straight south. In this way it was able to support the division regardless of the direction the division shift might take.

Close support is, and must be, the aim of every division's ordnance company.

6. Attempted Tank Evacuation

> Lt.Col. Herbert W. Wurtzler, Ordnance Officer, I Corps; Capt. Gentle S. Banks, Lt. Leroy Ingram, MSgt. William T. Wilson, Sgt. Richard L. White, and Cpl. Earl M. Friday, 57th Ordnance Recovery Company. (Narrative by Capt. Edward C. Williamson, 4th Historical Detachment.)

In the latter part of November 1950, a withdrawal was taking place along the whole front of the United Nations forces. The bitter fighting and the casualties are well known. Something of the cost in equipment and matériel should also be mentioned.

The 44th Ordnance Depot Company had occupied the buildings of the military academy of North Korea in Pyongyang for some weeks before the withdrawal. The fifteen- to twenty-acre drill field was used as a collecting point for disabled ordnance equipment. Here were massed for repair 30 to 40 tanks, 500 vehicles, an 8-inch howitzer, and three or four 105-mm howitzers. All were reparable, but none operational. Stored here also were 2,000 boxes of truck engines, transmissions, differentials, and transfer cases.

The 44th Ordnance Depot Company began its evacuation without enough transportation to move even its organic equipment. The collecting point was closed, nothing more was accepted, and every unit had to get its disabled equipment to safety as best it could. There was now little hope of evacuating anything disabled in Pyongyang. On 2 December the gates of the collecting point were thrown open and cannibalization invited. Demolition crews later destroyed what was left.

The withdrawal brought the 57th Ordnance Recovery Company (Capt. Willard Baker) of I Corps to Pyongyang and it, too, settled at the military academy. The normal mission of the company was to handle battlefield recovery of tanks and to augment the recovery facilities and corps and divisional ordnance units.

In spite of the improbability of evacuating the equipment already in Pyongyang, the 57th Ordnance Recovery Company still tried to help units that were having trouble. At 1600, 29 November, the motor officer of the 6th Heavy Tank Battalion (Captain Lawrence) rushed into Captain Baker's CP and excitedly told him that nine of the 6th's tanks were limping down the Sukchon and Sunchon roads.

Captain Baker turned to his operations officer (Lt. Gentle S. Banks) and asked, "Do you think we can help them?"

Banks replied, "I think so, sir."

While Baker and the mess sergeant got Lawrence some food, Banks called Lt. Robert L. Brown and Lt. Leroy Ingram to the motor pool. After the three officers had checked the recovery equipment, Banks assigned Ingram to the Sunchon MSR and Brown to the Sukchon road.

Brown and Ingram moved north with five tractors from the M26A1 tank transporters. Their greatest problem was the south-bound traffic. The tractors crowded the road as they moved along. At 1900 a colonel of the 5th RCT stopped Lieutenant Ingram. Although the road at this point was 17 feet wide, the colonel informed Ingram: "This is a tactical withdrawal. Pull over and give the traffic going south the right of way." Ingram halted his tractors for about twenty minutes, but at a convenient break in the traffic he moved on. On the way he continually received slurring remarks from individual drivers, but was not stopped again. At 2300, nine miles north of Pyongyang, he discovered some of the ailing tanks. The drivers—cold, tired, and dispirited—had pulled off the road and had started a fire.

On the Sukchon MSR, Lieutenant Brown made one halt because of a traffic jam. At 2130, thirteen miles north of Pyongyang, he met the crippled tanks.

As long as possible the lieutenants let the tanks limp along, then towed them when they could go no farther. At Pyongyang the tanks crossed the Taedong River and moved to the Taedong marshaling yards. Their crews remained there with them. Both tank groups reached the railroad yards by 2400.

It was imperative that the tanks not fall into enemy hands. To get the tanks loaded and dispatched, the 57th called the 8046th Ordnance Field Group and requested that coordination and details be arranged. The next morning (30 November) Ingram and Banks went to the railroad transportation officer to check the availability of flatcars for the evacuation of the tanks of the 6th Heavy Tank Battalion. Banks learned that no arrangements had been made, that loading facilities and cars were not available at the Taedong station, and that the transportation personnel didn't care much what happened to the tanks. As a result, Banks decided to move the tanks to Sadon station—a small marshaling yard five miles east. On the way the lead tank damaged a small bridge, and the convoy had to halt until the engineers made some hasty repairs. The march was completed by 1130, and the ordnance tractors returned to the military academy and brought their organic trailers across the Taedong River. It was now essential to get the 57th's own evacuation under way because the class 50 bridge was soon to be removed.

At Sadon station the RTO informed Lieutenant Banks that Eighth Army had given the Air Force priority in loading. The Air Force had an assortment of equipment at the yards: some vehicles, but a lot of items like mess tables, Korean chairs, and office equipment. Banks pointed out that most of the Air Force equipment was boxed and could be loaded without tying up the only ramp. The transportation officer replied, "In spite of the fact that you need the ramp to load the tanks, you don't have any cars anyway." Banks answered that if he could get some cars he would be able to start loading at once, but once the Air Force began they probably would not give up the use of the ramp. The RTO agreed to confer with the Air Force lieutenant colonel in charge of loading to see if he was willing to leave the ramp open for loading tanks. Banks heard the lieutenant colonel state flatly that he had a priority and that he wanted both the ramp and all the cars. From the tone of the conversation Banks figured that it would not be worth while to speak to the lieutenant colonel personally. The Air Force used the ramp.

Nothing more in the way of loading could be done at this time, but at 2000, 1 December, a switch engine arrived with six cars of tanks consigned to the 6th and the 70th Tank Battalions. The ramp was available since the Air Force had pulled out—abandoning much of its equipment in the rail yard. The ordnance company helped unload the replacement tanks because it planned to reuse the flatcars to evacuate disabled tanks. But two of the replacement tanks could not be started. They too had to be reloaded for evacuation. These, with five other tanks that had been brought to the Sadon yards from the collecting point, made a total of fifteen M46 tanks and an M26 tank to be loaded.

After the replacement tanks had been unloaded, the ordnance company began loading. The night was dark and cold, and only two tanks were loaded during the entire night. The next morning (2 December) the loading went faster, especially since some of the tanks helped others. A tank that could be started would pull another up the ramp and onto a flatcar. The operating tank then moved forward to a second car and two tanks were loaded in one operation. Even so, it was slow work finding cars and moving them to the ramp. In this operation flatcars were used that normally would have been considered too light. All paper work was dispensed with and the sixteen tanks were loaded by 1130, 3 December. This was fortunate, because the 57th Ordnance Recovery Company was under strict orders to leave the Pyongyang area not later than 1200.

Banks notified the RTO when the tanks were loaded. At the same time he stressed the importance of getting the tanks out. Banks, however, got the impression that the tanks would not receive a sufficiently high priority, and he then attempted to telephone the I Corps ordnance officer (Lt.Col. Herbert W. Wurtzler).

Though Colonel Wurtzler was not at his office, the message was relayed to him. He notified Eighth Army headquarters that the tanks were loaded and ready to go. They assured him that every effort would be made to get a locomotive to move the tanks south. The RTO at Sariwon personally informed Colonel Wurtzler that he would send a locomotive to Sadon station. Three engines were dispatched on 4 December, but on 4 December, as the last train went south, the tanks were still at Sadon.

On 6 December, the ordnance section of I Corps received a report from the Air Force that it had destroyed sixteen U.S. tanks near Pyongyang. This was the fate of the tanks the 57th had tried so gallantly to save.

7. Operation Failure

Anonymous

Many truck companies and battalions in Korea did not establish adequate preventive maintenance programs. The result of this was frequent truck failures, expensive repairs, and threatened failure of their transportation mission.

The primary equipment of a truck company is the GMC 2-½-ton truck—the Army's work horse—one of our finest pieces of equipment. I believe every maintenance officer will agree that the "Gimmy" is a rugged vehicle, but even the most rugged piece of mechanical equipment must have maintenance or it will not operate long.

The truck companies had a difficult, demanding job hauling supplies over long, rough, mountain roads. On their shoulders often rested the responsibility for the success or failure of an operation. It was most important that each truck be so maintained that it could deliver its critical load of supplies at its destination at the proper time.

One would expect that personnel of the truck companies and battalions, knowing the importance of their mission, would realize the need of sound operating procedures and scheduled maintenance. Actually, the story was just the reverse. Neither at the battalion nor at the company level was there any evidence of a definite preventive maintenance program.

There are many examples to illustrate this disregard for preventive maintenance.[1] A company commander was heard to say: "How can I do any preventive maintenance on my vehicles? I never see them until they have broken down." Another said, "We are too busy; we just can't take time." Still another, "There isn't much use doing anything with these vehicles; they were worn out before we came over."

In November 1950 a transportation battalion commander came to his corps headquarters complaining that almost all the vehicles in one of his companies were deadlined, and he wondered "how in hell" he was going to do his job if Ordnance didn't keep his vehicles running. An ordnance officer was present and asked the battalion commander to go with him immediately to the truck company to inspect the trucks and find out what was necessary to put them back in shape. The battalion commander declined, but he did agree to telephone a list of parts needed for repair. The ordnance officer promised that the parts and ordnance mechanics would be in the company motor pool next morning.

The parts requirement was received and the mechanics, parts and tools were on the job next morning. The mechanics promptly discovered that the vehicles in question did not need the engines, axles, and transmissions that had been ordered. What was needed was a thorough check, adjustment, and general tightening—normal first- and second-echelon maintenance.

When the Ordnance representative tried to find what organizational spare parts were needed, he could find no stock records or any semblance of a company motor pool. No one knew who needed which parts. Later, he discovered a large box of jumbled parts and assemblies. Many of the parts duplicated the ones ordered by phone, and the stock was far in excess of authorized allowances.

In another instance a battalion commander was quite proud of a maintenance program he put into operation. In his plan all vehicles of his battalion would receive their semiannual maintenance check at the battalion motor pool. The plan was fine as far as it went, but there was no adequate plan for the daily, weekly, and monthly maintenance inspections. He made no provision for the vehicles while they were on long trips, traveling in convoy over exceptionally dusty roads. Poor road conditions often necessitate daily attention to filters, bearings, and bushings that ordinarily would be serviced on a monthly schedule.

It is interesting to note that this battalion had to have sixty engines replaced in one week! Inspection of the original engines showed that the engine failures were caused by lack of preventive maintenance and improper operation. On a second occasion this battalion brought forty-eight vehicles into an ordnance company one day for field maintenance repair. The same day the battalion's personnel complained to

---

[1] See "Equipment Without Operators," pages 42-44.

the army transportation officer that they would not operate efficiently because so many of their vehicles were deadlined in Ordnance! Seventy-five per cent of the shop work could have been avoided if preventive maintenance had been done.

PART VII

Quartermaster Corps

1. Division Supply Operations

Lt.Col. Marcus E. Cooper, Quartermaster, 1st Cavalry Division

Throughout the first six months of 1950, the 1st Cavalry Division was so scattered that it was difficult for its 15th Quartermaster Company to support it. I recall that division headquarters, the 2d Battalion of the 7th Cavalry, and service troops were at Camp Drake; the 8th Cavalry and the 1st Battalion of the 7th were in Tokyo; the 5th Cavalry was at Camp McGill; Division Artillery was at Camp Drew. Early in May the 8th Cavalry was shifted with elements going to Camp Zama and Camp King.

About 25 January 1950, post quartermasters were assigned and army service units began supplying each of those camps. This left the division quartermaster with technical responsibility but no operational control of the division's supply operations. The extent to which this separation of functions took place is illustrated in the case of the quartermaster of Camp Drake. When the executive officer of the 15th QM Company was assigned this task, he was transferred to the 8013th Army Unit.

In 1950 the 1st Cavalry Division was emphasizing combat training of its units. The 15th QM Company, relieved of most of its operational responsibilities, spent most of its time learning combat principles. Little practical training was possible for the class II and class IV supply sections, but the class I and III groups were able to work in the maneuver area at Camp McNair. My company commander (Capt. Jenis C. McMillan) and I were working on a plan to train the quartermaster personnel by attaching them to the army service units when the Korean action broke out.

I believe it was 1 July 1950 that the division was alerted for an amphibious landing in Korea. Our original landing site was described only as "somewhere along the west coast of Korea." The assault wave was to outload by 14 July, the second wave on the 16th or 17th, and the third wave several days later.

I had been taught at the Command and General Staff College that it required sixty to ninety days to plan and outload a division for an assault landing. As this operation was to be accomplished in eight to twelve days, it seemed to be a tremendous task. It was.

The 1st Cavalry Division's strength was only 13,000 or 14,000, with a T/O&E in proportion. Quartermaster requirements for the landing were 22 days of class I (7 days operational, 15 days class B rations); 30 days maintenance factor of class II and class IV supplies; and 30 days of class III.

Although there was short supply of the operational rations, class I presented few problems. There were plenty of B rations available. Class II and class IV were more difficult, but class III gave us the most trouble. There were two problems: how many trucks we would have, and how far they would go. First our tank company was taken from us, then our vehicle strength was changed from day to day. We guessed that ten gallons per vehicle per day would be normal at first and, fortunately, we guessed fairly accurately.

I was charged with transporting class II and the operational rations of class I to shipside in the outloading. Army delivered the B rations. Class II and class IV were to be loaded by my personnel coming in with the third wave.

I was allotted space for 65 officers and men and 28 vehicles in the assault wave. I elected to go, and chose the purchasing and contract officer (Lt. Charles Lambert) and 4 men from the division quartermaster's office; the 2d Truck Platoon (Lt. James Evans); 28 men from the Supply Platoon (Lt. Albert N. Abelson); and the Field Service Platoon officer (Lt. George M. Gibbs). In the second wave my executive (Lt. Francis P. Cancelliere) and Captain McMillan were to bring the bulk of the quartermaster troops, while the remainder were to come in the third wave on D plus 5.

Space for class I and class III supplies was authorized on each of the three waves, but class II and class IV supplies were all to come in the third wave. Each individual was to carry two operational rations, two suits of fatigues, two pairs of combat boots, and necessary underwear and toilet articles. Other clothing was to be carried in duffel bags. Vehicles were fueled and carried extra cans of gasoline.

On the morning of 18 July the first landings were made without opposition, not on the west but on the east coast of Korea—near Pohang-dong. The shore party received class I and class III supplies and our supply section began to issue them on D plus 1. All units were issued B rations to maintain the two-day level per individual. Instructions were also given to use the B ration whenever possible.

I anticipated that the division would remain in the beachhead area until the second wave arrived. The urgent need for troops near Taejon, however, made necessary the immediate commitment of our first wave. A typhoon delayed the second wave, and the third was still in Japan waiting for ships.

On the afternoon of the 20th, the 5th Cavalry Regiment started for Taejon. At about 2000 my truck platoon and a supply detachment followed. The trucks carried 90 per cent class III and 10 per cent class I supplies, since we were less concerned with going hungry than with losing our mobility. I instructed Lieutenant Lambert, who commanded this force, to establish a supply point in the vicinity of Kumchon or Kwan-ni, the situation to determine which was the most desirable. That night the supply platoon began loading class I and class III in rail cars for shipment forward. I left the Pohang-dong area on the morning of the 21st with division headquarters. Lieutenant Abelson kept a detachment to finish the loading. At Kumchon I learned that Lieutenant Lambert had opened our supply point at Kwan-ni, and I sent this information back to Abelson. By the 23d we were receiving and issuing rations carried by rail from Pohang-dong.

On the 21st I placed my first order for class I and class III supplies directly with the quartermaster of Eighth Army (Col. James M. Lamont). Although we had fifteen days' B rations coming over the beach at Pohang-dong, these were divided among the different waves and we dared not chance a shortage. Army told me I could get B rations as I needed them, but few operational rations were available. I made every effort to have our operational rations forwarded from Pohang-dong in full-car lots. These shipments were issued only to units whose patrols, drivers, and men were normally away from their kitchens at mealtime. We also had a heavy demand for the C ration because its greater variety of meat items made it popular.

The quartermaster of Eighth Army told me I would receive little in class II and class IV supplies, for his stocks were almost depleted. I didn't worry about this because I knew I had a thirty-day maintenance factor coming in the third wave, and I knew each man had been well equipped when he left Japan. I would not have been so unconcerned had I known that the thirty-day supply would not arrive, and that, because of confusion in shipment, 70 to 80 per cent of the personnel of the regiments would not receive their duffel bags. The rocky hills cut up a pair of boots in twelve to fourteen days, while the rain took its toll of boots, fatigues, and ponchos. It was 1 August before we received much class II and class IV assistance, and by then we needed clothing, shoes, stove parts, and cleaning and preserving materials.

On the 22d, at Kwan-ni, we opened the first cemetery for the division. We had no graves registration section or trained personnel, and our few graves registration supplies were with the second wave. Eighth Army could not evacuate bodies, and we had to provide for our own dead. Not only were we short of experience in graves registration, but I had no manual covering the subject. Fortunately, the division G1 had a manual with some information and the division chaplain had a pamphlet. I sent Lieutenant Evans to Eighth Army headquarters at Taegu and there he obtained a supply of burial bottles, personal-effects bags, mattress covers, and burial forms.

I searched the Kwan-ni area for a cemetery site but most of the flat ground consisted of unsuitable rice paddies. The most likely place for a cemetery was 400 or 500 yards from our class I and class II supply point, which was not ideal. G4 approved our location, and the first interments occurred on 23 July. We had no fingerprint kit, but we soon found that a regular stamp pad would work. Every man buried in our cemeteries was fingerprinted, regardless of whether he was identified or not. We made a careful note of all identifying marks, scars, and tattoos. Some 32 or 33 bodies were interred at Kwan-ni, only 2 of which were unidentified. Some bodies were returned by the regiments, some by the companies, others evacuated through medical channels, and occasionally a driver would find a body along the road and bring it to us.

We had trouble with the personal effects. If the effects were still on the body, we inventoried them. If the effects had already been inventoried, we checked to see that all were present and then forwarded them to Eighth Army. But army began to notice that our inventory of money sometimes did not tally with the amounts it received. Several times there were shortages of five or ten dollars, though never was the complete sum missing. We could not account for this. After I left the division I heard that some of the men in the graves registration section had been caught stealing.

We also had a case where a ring had been removed from the finger of a British major, but this occurred before the body reached us. I had heard that the body was being evacuated through medical channels, and was present when it arrived. That night a friend inquired whether a signet ring was among the effects, for he knew the major's family attached great sentimental value to it. The inventory did not list the ring, so we disinterred the body to make sure it had not been overlooked. It was obvious that the major had worn a ring a short time before, but it was not on his body when it reached our cemetery.

It was in Kwan-ni that our ration first included fresh meat. By mistake a carload of rations consigned to the 25th Division had been placed on our siding. The car, containing frozen ground beef, was not refrigerated, and it was obvious some spoilage had already occurred. I called army and received permission to utilize whatever I could. Mr. Kummer and his food service personnel checked each box, discarding all meat about which there was the least doubt. The over-all loss was about 35 per cent. The remainder would not feed the entire division, so we got in touch with the units' S4s and told them, "first come, first served." We had no trouble clearing the shipment.

The bulk of the quartermaster company, coming in the second wave, joined us in Kwan-ni during the night of the 24th. We selected a school building as a billet but never occupied it. The order came to displace our class I and class III supply points to Kumchon because the infantry was being pushed back.

Our evacuation was somewhat confused in this, our first experience in withdrawal. We issued two days of B rations to every unit that would accept them. This cut our load and at the same time insured against need if there were any delay in opening our new supply point. We loaded both the railroad cars and the trucks. There wasn't enough transportation, so we had to shuttle with the trucks. We got all of the supplies out, but the last two trucks were still being loaded after the infantry had cleared the area. Several rounds of mortar fire landed nearby but caused no damage.

We opened our new supply point in Kumchon without delay. Everything at Kumchon was kept mobile and, as much as we could, we left supplies in boxcars until we actually issued them. Rations were coming to us direct from Pusan, but carloads of supplies from Pohang-dong, which had been delayed or misshipped, were still arriving.

In Kumchon I found that the quartermaster of the 25th Division (Major John Pachomski) had his distribution point in the marshaling area. The desirability of our companies working together was obvious, and my company moved next to his. The 25th QM Company helped tremendously by giving us cleaning and preserving materials, soaps, mops, brooms, and a few items of clothing.

While we were in Kumchon we began to receive our first shipments of fresh vegetables. These were airlifted from the hydroponic farms in Japan. The vegetables came in limited quantity every second day. Rather than issue a little to each unit, we rotated the delivery and gave enough for an ample serving. We had a standing priority on fresh foods for the hospital, then for the front-line troops. These vegetables were a real morale-builder.

We opened our second cemetery in Kumchon on the 26th. It was our smallest, for by now it was nearly impossible for the infantry to recover its dead as it fell back. It was in Kumchon that the 1st Cavalry Division received Eighth Army's famous "last stand" order which forbade us to fall back. This order was rescinded, however, and on the 31st we moved to Poksong-dong for two days.

In late August, division ordered 100 men and 4 officers of the quartermaster company to be held on five-minute alert. These men were part of Task Force Allen—our last reserve. Fortunately, this force was never needed.

The Eighth Army supply points in Taegu were located in the railroad area. We got permission to locate our class I point nearby, and obtained the use of a siding and shed area for our class III supplies. The II and IV area was six or eight blocks away from the marshaling yards. Eighth Army had five large warehouses for class II and class IV supplies, and it turned two of these over to us. In these warehouses we stored PX supplies and beer—when they were available. To save needless handling, our supplies came directly from Pusan by rail instead of stopping off in the army depots.

The fighting came close to Taegu and several nights enemy tanks ineffectively lobbed shells into town. It was a real convenience to have our warehouses near those of army. Army moved its depot troops out of Taegu several times, and turned its dumps directly over to me. In turn, I issued supplies to everyone in the area. At one time or another I supplied the 9th Infantry (2d Infantry Division), the 27th Infantry (25th Infantry Division), the 21st Infantry (24th Infantry Division), and numerous nondivisional units.

Each time the depot troops pulled out of Taegu they would tell me approximately how many troops I would be expected to supply. When I submitted requisitions to Pusan they were honored without question—even when I drew for 35,000 instead of 13,000. Class III items were usually in good supply except for an occasional shortage of 80-octane aviation gasoline. Some components of the B ration would build up and I returned flour and meat to Pusan whenever I feared the surplus was great enough to embarrass me if we had to move quickly.

At Taegu we received our first bath trailers. The third wave leaving Japan received these, though not in time to test them. We found that two of the four did not work, and the diaphragms and other parts could be repaired only in Japan. So back they went.

We used the civilian laundries in Taegu, but their capacity was insufficient. We hired men, women, and children, furnished them soap, and had them washing clothing by hand in the Sin-chon River. In September our first laundry unit was in operation under the control of Capt. Carl D. Hennessy, who had recently joined us. We continued to use the Taegu laundry, but now dispensed with the hand-washing.

Soon we received six ice-cream machines. These were much too bulky; two 2-½-ton trucks were required to move each machine. We turned them back to army immediately. In 1951, the division received improved, portable machines which supplied ice cream to the entire division on a once-a-week basis.

Eighth Army took over operation of the Taegu ice plant. The medics approved the plant for sanitation and the engineers chlorinated the water. Ice was issued daily to every unit. An unusual use of the ice came when the enemy surrounded a company of the British 27th Brigade (attached to the 1st Cavalry Division for logistical support as well as operations). The isolated troops suffered from a water shortage. Attempts were made to airdrop water in one-gallon canvas bags, but these split and the water ran out. One of my officers (Lt. McGail C. Baker) suggested that we drop ice. We placed 15- to 20-pound blocks in barrack bags and dropped them with great success.

The truck platoon I had brought with me in the first wave was now strengthened by the arrival of the other two. One platoon I did not control, however, for it was attached to the 2d Battalion, 7th Cavalry. This battalion was kept mobile as a part of the Eighth Army "fire brigade" system. Although we were short of trucks, we were not hampered since we depended on rail to bring us our supplies.

Early in August I discussed with the Eighth Army quartermaster the need for winter clothing. Already it was cool at night in the hills where our infantry was fighting. Eighth Army was aware of the need and had established a three-phase program for issuing winter uniforms—contingent upon delivery of clothing from the United States on the dates requested. The first phase included the delivery of winter underwear, M43 jackets, and gloves by 15 September. The second phase was to bring wool clothing by 1 October. The last phase would deliver sleeping bags, pile-lined jackets, overcoats, and wet-cold climate clothing by 15 October.

The underwear, jackets, and gloves arrived about the middle of September and we issued them as fast as possible. Unfortunately, before all our clothing could be issued to the units, the breakout from the Pusan perimeter took place and we had no chance to complete delivery for some weeks.

By 24 September, the 1st Cavalry Division's progress was such that we believed it was time to push out class I and class III distribution points. Lieutenant Cancelliere and one of our new arrivals (Lt. Earl W. Gallert) located these at Chongju on the 25th. Our three truck platoons were with the infantry, and army furnished us two truck companies to move supplies. I stayed with the company in Taegu until 2 October.

It was about 130 miles to Chongju and bad roads made it a full-day trip each way. On the 26th, the division advanced more than a hundred miles to make a junction at Osan with the 7th Infantry Division, which had landed at Inchon. On the 29th, Cancelliere established another class I and class III point at Ansong to receive supplies that had been airlifted to Kimpo. I sent some B rations to Ansong by truck, but army stopped this.

Division supply points were located at Taegu, Chongju, and Ansong, with supplies furnished from both the north and south ends. I had no communications faster than messenger, and I soon lost touch with the situation. I hoped that class I and class III supplies were being issued, and I learned later that they were. One of our truck platoons returned on 2 October, and I moved the company to Suwon. I left enough personnel in Taegu to operate the class II and class IV points, for I wanted to be sure these items got forward to us. Small class I and class III distribution points remained in Taegu to supply the division's rear-echelon troops, but had I known the situation forward I would have arranged for the rear echelon to use army supply points in Taegu.

Driving north we carried enough winter underwear, M43 jackets, and gloves to supply the units that had not drawn them in Taegu. We did not get to issue the clothing until the troops were in Kaesong on 9 October. I found that on the rapid march of the division those men who had received underwear and jackets took care to hold on to them.

Our Suwon distribution points opened on 3 October. For about a week we were issuing everything on hand and replacing nothing. Then we closed the I and III points in Taegu but left the II and IV supply personnel there until they could get the clothing forward. The shortage of both rail facilities and trucks kept us from moving the clothing at this time, even though the weather was getting cold.

In late September, 3d Logistical Command opened at Ascom City— between Inchon and Seoul. I opened a class III distribution point at Yongdungpo on 5 October. On the 9th we started an all-class supply point at Kaesong, and here we opened our fifth cemetery. When we moved from Kaesong on the 15th we began a series of class I and class III supply operations that were little more than one-night stands. Nothing was dumped on the ground, and we loaded from tail gate onto tail gate. We opened at Hanpo-ri on the 15th and closed on the 18th. We opened at Sinmak on the 18th and closed on the 21st. Hwangju opened on the 19th and closed on the 20th. On the 21st we opened a distribution point at Pyongyang and it remained open until 4 December. On 30 October we were to establish a dump just south of Unsan, but the men found the town in enemy hands, so they set up some eight or ten miles to the south. On 31 October, we opened a dump at Anju to receive airlifted supplies landed at Sinanju for I Corps. We later turned this operation over to Eighth Army. On 2 November we opened a supply point at Pakchon but we had to evacuate it hurriedly the next day. The quartermaster company did not lose anything there. However, part of the 8th Cavalry, one company of the tank battalion, and one company of the engineers came out light and fast. We had to replace a thousand sleeping bags, two or three kitchens, most of the mess gear, and a lot of clothing.

The bulk of the division's winter clothing was still in the Taegu warehouses—400 to 500 miles away. As soon as the railroads began operating as far north as Seoul, we moved several carloads of winter clothing to that point. That meant the clothing was still 170 miles from us, but division G4 began to canvass all units for trucks we could borrow to make the trip to Seoul. It was very cold now and everyone supplied trucks until it hurt. We sent 180 from Pyongyang to Seoul in convoys of 30 and 40. The roads were so bad that there was about a 30 per cent truck casualty rate from broken springs.

Our boxcars had not been guarded on the railroad, and some pilfering had taken place. But we had anticipated a strength of 18,000 U.S. and 8,500 KATUSA personnel in our requisitions, whereas we now had 18,000 U.S. and only 3,500 KATUSA personnel. An officer in Pyongyang separated the clothing and issued it in the priority: infantry, engineers, artillery, other units. In no case did a service unit or headquarters draw anything out of sequence, but a fast-talking division headquarters supply sergeant almost succeeded until I learned about it. We outfitted U.S. and KATUSA personnel alike except that the OD7 overcoats went to the U.S. soldiers and the men of KATUSA drew wool overcoats.

After the rail lines were open to South Pyongyang, we received the rest of our own clothing from Taegu and also some from other sources. Soon we had an overage in certain types of winter clothing. Instead of moving this clothing to Eighth Army dumps we issued it to nondivisional units when directed by army. We also issued some clothing to British and other UN troops.

In September a wet-cold climate instruction team arrived from the United States. It consisted of Lt.Col. James P. Streetman and an enlisted man. We were in Pyongyang before they were able to instruct the troops, but fortunately this coincided with the issue of winter clothing. I believe their opportune lectures did much to prevent nonbattle casualties.

In Pyongyang an attached platoon of the 549th Laundry Company (Lt. Upshaw Sams) gave the division more laundry service than it could use. The tactical situation was so fluid that regiments often could not return their dirty clothing. In their free time we let the laundry platoon work for anyone—after they took care of the needs of the hospitals.

We opened class I and class III supply points at Sapyong-ni on 27 November and closed them on the 29th. The 29th was the day Lieutenant Evans's truck platoon got caught in a roadblock while carrying troops of the 5th Cavalry, and the day we began our long withdrawal. On the 29th, we opened a supply point at Sunchon, and hurriedly withdrew before we issued anything. At 1800 of that day we were returning to Sainjang, and on 1 December our most advanced supply point was Pyongyang.

On 2 December we began to clear our class II and class IV supplies out of the Pyongyang area. I got in touch with the assistant G4 of

Eighth Army and requested ten or twelve boxcars to evacuate supplies, but he was unable to furnish them. I had two partly loaded boxcars at my siding, so I filled them as quickly as I could and they were moved that night.

On the morning of the 3d, Colonel Streetman and Lt. W. T. Niedermeyer found 4 empty boxcars and 2 gondolas of empty gasoline drums on the freight yard. The rail transportation officer agreed to let us unload the drums and use the cars and gondolas. We loaded them with class II and class IV supplies.

At 2045, before our cars were removed, an ammunition dump several blocks from our warehouse caught fire. When the shells began to explode, the locomotives left our area. One or two of our warehouses burned and so did our gondolas. The boxcars were spared.

On the morning of the 4th, the locomotives came to pull out our loaded cars. Unfortunately, the ties had burned under the track and our cars were derailed. We loaded all available trucks with class II and class IV supplies and I put a man out on the road to offer units anything they would take. The only II and IV supplies we lost were those that burned in the fire.

On the night of the 3d, and during the 4th, we hauled class I and class III supplies from Pyongyang across the river. Again we stopped vehicles and offered gasoline and food. At 1800 on 4 December we destroyed the surplus gasoline and rations that we could not evacuate. This amounted to 15,000 to 30,000 gallons of gas—all in drums. That was the first time in Korea our company had to destroy anything to keep it out of enemy hands.

On the 5th we opened a supply point at Namchonjon; we closed it on the 8th. On the morning of the 8th we moved to Kumchon (in North Korea) and sent all our class II and class IV supplies to Ascom City.

On 8 December 1950 I was relieved of my assignment and returned to the United States on emergency leave. Colonel Streetman was assigned in my place. After I returned to Korea from my leave I spent eight months in the operations division of Eighth Army's quartermaster section.

2.　Quartermaster Problems and Services

Lt.Col. Homer P. Harris, Quartermaster, 2d Infantry Division

Korea is a paradise for the artilleryman, but not for the quartermaster. I've served with armored divisions and there the quartermaster component is a battalion. I feel that an infantry division needs more than a quartermaster company. The infantry division has been beefed up by the addition of numerous automatic weapons, recoilless rifles, bazookas, and a tank company for each regiment plus a tank battalion for the division. Our present ammunition requirements are beyond the hauling capacity of the using organizations, even when they are augmented by the trucks of the division's quartermaster company. Artillery battalions are firing twelve thousand rounds a day, and the infantry is firing mortars and recoilless rifles at a prodigious rate.

In the spring and summer of 1951, to meet the overload placed upon the 2d Quartermaster Company, we had to have an overstrength unit. Instead of the authorized 11 officers, 2 warrant officers and 216 enlisted men, the division G1 knowingly let me accumulate a strength of 19 officers, 3 warrant officers and 311 men. By this method we approached battalion strength.

Another way to support the division was to overload the equipment and overwork the men. Overloading has to be supervised, for while a 2-½-ton truck will easily carry a 100 per cent overload without injury, it does have limitations. I caught people at an ammunition supply point trying to load 14 tons on a 2-½-ton truck! After that I made out a weight chart for various types of truck loads, and made the drivers responsible for seeing that extreme overloading did not occur.

The overworking of men also occurred in Korea. In spite of an occasional movie or band concert, there was little release for the men, and no place to go. As a result, the tendency was for soldiers to work around the clock. Even now that I have returned, I find it difficult to break away from the habit of sleeping three hours and then working eight or nine. But, under the stress of operations like these at Heartbreak Ridge, we had to work our truck drivers so constantly hauling ammunition that three or four accidents occurred in the mountains when the drivers fell asleep. The overloading of equipment and the overworking of men will not pay off in sustained operations. I have reported this many times when I have recommended a quartermaster battalion for the infantry division.

In addition to hauling huge quantities of ammunition in Korea, we were responsible logistically for too many persons. Normally I drew rations for 35,000 troops and petroleum products for 44,000. Any way you figure it, that's an army-size job. We supplied our own division, men of KATUSA, Korean laborers, UN battalions of French, Dutch and Thailanders, and we were even saddled with the job of drawing rations for the indigenous laborers of a Marine division located fifty miles away. At one time, we supported two Marine artillery battalions with class I and class III supplies. The marines liked our support and were disappointed when they had to return to their own supply channels.

The problem of supplying bulk rations was further complicated by the special rations and supplements we had to furnish the other UN troops. This varied from additional bread and potatoes for the French and Dutch to special spice supplements for the Thailanders.

Our food was the best any army in the field has ever received. One actually got tired of so much steak, chicken, and turkey, and I occasionally longed for stew. Fresh eggs, when on the menu, were issued 225 per 100 servings, with 5 per cent allowance for breakage.

We served ice cream weekly to the troops. When the paper-container supply was exhausted, we distributed the ice cream in the regular insulated food containers. I was always worried about the possibility of sickness should the ice cream get contaminated, but we never had a case of this. My ice-cream man improvised a device to sterilize our serving containers by using live steam, and it was by this method that we eliminated bacteria. I steered VIPs away from the ice-cream plant to avoid contamination and to avoid serving samples of our work. News of that kind might cause a "run on the bank."

In the fall of 1951, Maj.Gen. Robert N. Young replaced Maj.Gen. Clark L. Ruffner as commander of the 2d Infantry Division. General Young soon showed evidence of his airborne training. We began experiments in airdropping supplies and equipment to small detachments or units that had special needs. The flame thrower is one example. It is very useful to the infantry in certain operations, but is most often left behind because of its weight. General Young figured that if we could airdrop a flame thrower to the right men at the right time, it would be used. In addition, there was the need to air-supply patrols, outposts, and other groups in mountains too steep to be reached any other way.

The division air officer (Major Linton S. Boatwright) worked with me on a series of experimental drops. I soon realized that the problem was complicated, so I suggested to General Young that two officers be sent to the 187th Airborne RCT to learn about airdrop. This was done. We received fifty parachutes, and after each drop we repacked them ourselves. Our cargo planes were the division's own L-19s, and using six different packs, we loaded as much as 120 pounds under each wing. At the division airstrip we maintained a quartermaster detachment and a ready line consisting of priority supplies. When Eighth Army's air section learned of what we were doing, it ordered us to stop, since our L-19s were not properly braced to carry such a weight. When we received a group of new L-19s, this prohibition was lifted. So far as I know, we pioneered this division airdrop, but other divisions are using it now.

Along with General Young's airdrop idea came his plan for a daily laundering of socks. Here the division's policy of performing the maximum service for the individual soldier applied. Each company sent to the laundry a barrack bag containing all the socks worn the previous day. We gave bundle service, returning the same socks to the unit that delivered them. I know that full use was not always made of this service, but General Young insisted on a daily sock inspection and close attention to the men's feet. We had only sixteen cases of frostbite in the division during the winter of 1951-52—and most of those cases didn't involve feet. Every report of a frostbite case was followed by an inspector general's investigation, and the blame determined.

Our quartermaster company set up a fix-it shop along with its other services. Weather, dust, and mistreatment took a heavy toll of typewriters, office machines, fire units in field ranges, and Coleman stoves. We repaired all these items and centralized all replacement parts at division for that purpose. Unfortunately, we were often out of parts because our kits did not seem to contain the parts we needed. Several investigations of this were made, but the situation did not change. I did not evacuate any of our office machines, for generally if we didn't have a spare part, neither did the army service center which supported us.

We did call on the service centers for covers for typewriters and office machines. When a machine came to us for repair it was returned with a cover—and a strong suggestion that the cover be used. We pointed out that all machines should be covered, even during the short period when operators knocked off for lunch.

The 2d Quartermaster Company in Korea gave an outstanding performance. It supplied more men with more items and more service than our doctrine ever anticipated.

3.   Delivery by Air

Capt. William J. Dawson, Jr., 8081st Quartermaster Airborne Air Supply and Packaging Company

The 8081st Quartermaster Airborne Air Supply and Packaging Company is the most-decorated quartermaster company in the U.S. Army, and the only Army unit in Japan to earn combat credit. But if you ever saw these men at work, with their tails hanging out of the rear of a C-119 while they got their cargo ready to drop, you'd know they earn their points, decorations, renown, and jump pay. We drilled into our men this motto: "Lives of individuals in combat depend on the supplies we deliver. Risk yours, if necessary, to get them there."

I reported to Ashiya Air Base, on Kyushu, on 14 February 1951. At that time the company had 4 officers and approximately 88 men. Capt. Cecil W. Hospelhorn, who organized the company, was in the United

States presenting his packaging and airdrop experiences in lectures and demonstrations. The operational procedures I mention are sometimes modifications of the methods he initiated.

At this time the company was commanded by Lt. Claude A. Jones, and I became his executive officer. We had a company headquarters, a parachute maintenance section, an air-supply section, a manifest section, and two air-delivery platoons.

The air-delivery platoons were responsible for loading the planes and dropping the cargo. The 1st Air Delivery Platoon (Lt. Paul E. Smith), in addition to its general duties, was responsible for all heavy drops. These men were all old-timers and persons Captain Hospelhorn had known for a long time.

The 2d Platoon (Lt. Billy G. Bishop) repacked all parachutes as its secondary job. Ashiya Air Base is on the beaches of the Sea of Japan, and the humidity there is high. For this reason personnel chutes had to be repacked every thirty days and cargo chutes every sixty days. We used Japanese employees to repack the cargo chutes, but the personnel chutes were never turned over to anyone outside the company.

When I arrived at Ashiya the company was working full-time. The men were loading and dropping an average of 35 planes every day. That is beyond the normal expected capability of an air-delivery company, but this rate continued for six weeks. In February 1951, X Corps turned to airdrop to build a stockpile of gasoline and rations, since land transportation was inadequate. We were pushed to operate at this level and could not have maintained it had we not been assisted by several hundred Japanese civilians. Later our load leveled off at five to ten planes a day, four or five days a week.

The air-delivery platoons worked in shifts. One platoon would do all the loading for a week while the other platoon had its men ride the planes and discharge the cargo. Assignments changed every Sunday. During the time our work was so heavy it was normal for our officers to spend their evenings in the orderly room, where they could play cards while waiting for the loading orders to arrive. We rarely bothered to go to the movies since we expected to be pulled out before the first show was over.

Orders for an operation normally came to us between 2000 and 2400. Requests came through G4 of Eighth Army, to 8247th Army Headquarters, Troop Movement Section, and then to us. Our first alert would tell us the number of planes to be loaded and the type of cargo. Our manifest section, which operated on a 24-hour basis, would receive the serial number of each plane, its capacity, the amount and type of cargo it would carry, and the on-station time (an hour before take-off). The capacity of planes varied greatly—largely because of fuel loads. The manifest section worked with these data, broke down the loads, and make a working manifest for each plane. They followed a few simple rules. For example, gasoline and rations were not to be loaded in the same plane, but gasoline and ammunition could go together.

While the manifest section was working, the commander of the loading platoon would send out his alert squad to the planes to check the tie-down bolts and put in the rollers. Either the company commander or the executive officer called the motor pool and ordered the vehicles for hauling the cargo from the ready line to the planes. We had available, on thirty-minute call, ten semitrailers and ninety 2-½-ton trucks. The drivers were Japanese who worked on an around-the-clock schedule. We always preferred the semis because they would carry more cargo, and their higher beds made it possible to slide the cargo straight into the rear of the plane. With the trucks we had about an 18-inch lift. It took four 2-½-ton trucks to carry the cargo to one plane, while it took one and a half semis to do the same job. We never placed cargos for more than one plane on a truck for fear of confusion. At the ready line the trucks were loaded by Japanese laborers according to the working manifests.

While the trucks were being loaded and the alerted squad was placing the rollers in the planes, the loading platoon was assembling. The loaders reported to the hangars at the same time that the cargos arrived. From a central point the loading officer (platoon leader) ordered two American soldiers and four Japanese laborers to each plane, with the trucks and cargo. As each truck was unloaded it was released. Before the loaders left the plane they made up a white loading card giving all pertinent facts. They then returned to the hangar with the last vehicle and reported to the loading officer to be assigned other trucks and cargo for another plane. The loading officer sent his platoon sergeant to inspect each loading job, and before leaving the field he personally checked each plane. No one left the area until all inspections were finished. Normally a platoon could load five or six planes an hour.

It was informally understood that if the loading crews finished their work before 2400 they would not be called for training until 1300 the next day. If they finished after 2400 they were off all day. Actually, however, it meant very little to give them the day off, for most of their loading was done at night. Finally, under the pressure of work the training schedule broke down anyway.

Shortly after we received an operations order we notified the consolidated Air Force-Army mess of the number of in-flight lunches our men would need. The hour of assembly for the platoon assigned to fly depended on the length of the flight. The normal time from Japan to drop zone in Korea varied between two and three hours. An hour before take-off all crews and quartermaster flight personnel were due at the planes. An hour before on-station time the flight platoon began drawing their parachutes, pistols, in-flight lunches, emergency rations, and equipment. For example, if the drop were scheduled for 0800 and the flying time consumed two hours, then take-off was at 0700, on-stations at 0500, and assembly at 0400.

On arrival at their plane the quartermaster crew obtained the white loading card, checked the cargo to be sure it was safe, and then notified the crew chief they were ready. A copy of the manifest was turned over to the pilot, who had the final responsibility for proper loading. By the time I arrived at Ashiya the pilots had so much confidence in our men they rarely checked our work. I would say the best pilots still checked and never took our word for it, but usually the check was omitted. Our pilots were first-rate.

After take-off the dropmaster and his assistant continued to check the cargo. While the plane was climbing they checked the front cables. When the plane leveled off they checked the rear cables. Periodic checks were made if there was any unusual motion while in flight.

Usually the flight was monotonous and often uncomfortable. The turnaround time was four to six hours. The cabin of a C-119 contains only four seats, and those are occupied by the crew. If the Army men moved forward, they had to sit on the floor with their legs out straight —and that is uncomfortable over a period of time. Lots of times there wasn't room up front because of cameramen, passengers, or flyers riding to get in their flight time. In the winter, or when the planes flew at high altitude, it was cold in the back of the plane. And looking out the open end of the plane always made me nervous in spite of my being called "Ace" Dawson.

Twenty minutes before we came over the drop zone the crew chief gave us a signal and our men moved to the rear of the plane to remove cables. The ties between bundles were removed; then the forward cable safeties were severed but remained taut against the bundles. When everything was ready the dropmaster and his assistant moved to the front of the cargo compartment and waited for the two-minute warning. At two minutes the bomb-shackle-release safety (a little red disc) was removed, and the men returned forward to await the signal to drop.

Over the drop zone the plane came in at an altitude of about 800 feet and at a speed of only 110 miles an hour. This is dangerous flying because of the low altitude and near-stalling speed. When dropping right on the front lines the plane makes an excellent target for small-arms fire. The planes approaching the drop zone came in trail at about 1,000 feet apart. This increased their accuracy but it also added to the danger of collision or other accident.

At the instant the bell rings the pilot pulls up the nose of the plane and jams the throttle open. This lurch causes the load to move down the rollers in the floor and out the open end of the plane. The dropmaster and his assistant run to the rear of the plane and count the bundles as they open, so they can figure the number of malfunctions. The rate normally ran to about 3 per cent. After the count it was necessary to reach out of the open end of the plane and pull in the static lines. If any of the cargo failed to clear from the plane the dropmaster informed the crew chief, who told the pilot to make another run. Then it was just a matter of flying home, checking in the equipment, and waiting for the next day—unless there was a second flight.

These are the broad outlines of the air-delivery system, but of course there were many ramifications and problems. To speed up operations we normally kept all classes of supplies packaged and ready to drop on our ready line. The ready line was actually a small dump with the supplies on skids and the ropes tied. We ran out of containers and used rope to hold the items together. In fact, we used nine million feet of rope—some 1,700 miles of it—in one year. Most of the packaging was done by Japanese, and they were good at it. Without their help we could have never packaged the loads we did.

Parachutes are expensive, the large G-11 costing $1,300. Some idea of the cost of our operation can be obtained from these figures: we dropped 73,000 G-1 chutes (24 feet) which cost $43 each, and 70,000 G-9 chutes (18 feet), each costing $25. Dealing in those numbers and costs, it was essential to get the chutes returned from the drop zone whenever possible. Each division receiving a drop was supposed to get the parachutes to the nearest air base, and from there it was up to the Air Force to return them to Ashiya. No one really knows how good our recovery rate was, but I'd guess perhaps 40 per cent.

Although the Air Force was given the drop-zone location, the exact spot was marked on the ground with a T panel. Soon the Chinese got wise to this system, and they placed panels and received several of our drops. Then it became customary to have an Air Force Mosquito plane meet the C-119s ten minutes away from the drop zone and escort them in. On rear-area flights we sometimes dropped cargo along the sides of airfields.

Our men tried to see how close the drop came to the T and sometimes they could see that it went wide. When the unit being supplied was on the line this sometimes meant they could not gather the supplies. They immediately notified army G4, who passed the message to the 8247th, and then we got it. The notification of a bad drop normally reached the company before the planes returned. If it appeared to have resulted from a pilot failure, the Air Force usually made the same crew fly the second mission and hit the drop zone. Usually we sent our same men along. But when a plane developed engine trouble and had to jettison its cargo and limp home, we had someone else go on the replacement flight.

Sometimes the first effort to drop the cargo would be ineffective and the plane would have to make several passes over the DZ. One officer normally flew each day for morale purposes, and when an officer flew he took the place of an enlisted man and carried out the same duties. In November 1951, CWO Byron Kirkman and I were flying a mission together. We carried concertina wire for use along the Imjin River. The coils were wide and the bundles overlapped in the center of the plane. Just as the plane started to dump its load we hit an air pocket and the wire jammed. Nothing went out on that pass, so we notified the crew chief, then went to the rear to loosen the wire. The best we could do was to drop one bundle from each side of the plane on each pass. It took five more passes to complete the job.

On my last flight there were six planes in the flight and the drop was on the front line. To hit the DZ we had to cross into enemy territory after the drop. The lead pilot did not give the signal to drop. Maybe the DZ wasn't marked, because the other pilots followed his lead. We moved over enemy territory going 110 miles per hour at 800 feet. Enemy small arms cut up to thirty holes in each plane. In my plane, the Plexiglas windshield was shattered and both pilots were seriously cut in the face. The sergeant with me was wounded, and only the chute he wore saved his life. One other dropmaster was injured. In spite of the fire and their wounds, the pilots turned, made another sweep over the DZ, dropped their cargos, went again over the enemy, and flew back to Japan. When we reached Ashiya Air Base all the emergency crews and ambulances were waiting and I felt as though we had returned from a bombing mission.

While no one was killed on this flight, we did have two dropmasters killed in May 1951, when a failure to stop our artillery fire allowed one C-119 to be hit. A second plane crashed right behind the first. On this day, fortunately, we had only one soldier in each plane. We had five other emergency free-fall drops when our men bailed out of falling planes. We had three or four more men wounded on flights, and of course we had the famous case of Sgt. Robert Hale and Corporal Page who "just happened" to fall out of their plane right after they had dropped a cargo to the 187th Airborne RCT. Page was back in two days, but Hale was wounded by a sniper and did not return to duty for weeks. We took no disciplinary action, but we never believed their story of their "fall."

Jumping wasn't much to these men, for all were rated. We did a lot of jumping—even on Saturdays and Sundays if business wasn't too heavy. We landed on the beach along the ocean, and sometimes we alerted the air-sea rescue people and jumped into the ocean for practice. We never had any casualties in our unit, but one lieutenant colonel who got permission to jump with us was killed on a water jump when he became confused and inflated his Mae West before he got out of his harness.

We tested a lot of Japanese parachutes for G4, and some of them were pretty good. We also ran a lot of tests to determine what items could be given a free drop. Concertina wire was dropped free but broke its securing wires and unraveled. What a mess! To counteract this we placed small chutes on the wire—just enough to slow it down. Canned rations smashed badly when dropped free. The new rubber containers for water landed in good shape, but they were small and frequently were lost. Blankets and all types of clothing came through the free-drop process very well.

One of our men (Sergeant Gordon) devised a bomb-shackle release that worked well in loosening cargo. The load was emptied by nosing the plane up. This was simpler than the standard practice of having the pilot operate the glider-tow device and sending out a pilot chute to pull out the cargo. We showed the Gordon device to one observer who came over from The Quartermaster School, and we even gave him one, but it hasn't been adopted.

One thing our men were proud of was the magazine drops. Knowing that men on the front appreciate any kind of reading, we used to tie bundles of magazines into the cargoes we dropped. We heard from those men at times, and their appreciation made us feel good. In spite of continuous hazards and combat rating, we lived the Air Force life and came home to clean sheets, hot meals, and movies. Helping the infantry out there made us feel more a part of it.

4. Service Company Runs Depot

Lt. John Douthitt, 545th Quartermaster Service Company

The 545th Quartermaster Service Company was an integrated unit with Negro and white officers and enlisted men. At various times men of both races held the positions of company commander and first sergeant, but the whites held a greater relative proportion of the non-commissioned ratings. There was no problem of the men getting along, although some dissatisfaction existed among a small minority of whites because they were serving in an integrated unit. We had only one period of tension—after a fight—but it did not last long. At no time did race antagonism impede our work.

The mission of a quartermaster service company is to provide a labor force for attachment to depots and other installations. But from the time the 545th withdrew from Pyongyang, it was assigned missions very different from its intended one. For a year we operated major supply depots ourselves. This difference was especially evident at Chunchon.

The company reached Chunchon on 23 July 1951, with instructions to open a class I and class III supply point. When we arrived we found only a rice paddy. We had just three days in which to receive our supplies, organize our depot, and begin to issue rations. On the 26th we issued rations to 26,000 troops, and on the next day to 50,000. During the fall of 1951 we were supplying 90,000 troops, including three divisions and adjacent units.

As soon as we arrived at Chunchon, we received ninety rail cars of supplies, and our battalion commander was yelling for the return of the empties. Little local labor was available, so we put every man on the job, including the first sergeant and the cooks. We cleared our siding in forty-eight hours!

On the 25th we received our first refrigerated supplies, and by the 26th we had ten to twelve carloads of perishables. We had no refrigeration facilities or additional ice, and this was the hottest part of the summer. We issued perishables as fast as we could, and salvaged ice from every car unloaded. Eventually we received a half car of ice, and that was a help. It was a close race between issuance and spoilage, but we won. We kept a veterinarian busy inspecting the food before we released it. A month later we received a number of permanent refrigerators and an engineer to service the machinery.

We opened our Chunchon supply point with 3 officers and 165 men. In the next few months we received 3 additional officers while the enlisted strength varied between 170 and 190. This becomes significant if two facts are kept in mind. First, this company was doing a job not suited to its organization, training, or strength. Secondly, 90,000 troops were being supplied by one company. At Wonju, 8,000 to 10,000 troops were supplied by a service company minus one platoon, a subsistence company minus a platoon, a petroleum platoon, and a refrigeration platoon.

While we carried out our mission, our overload of work led to certain problems. Security was one. We were augmented by a few Korean National Police, but they controlled only Koreans and would not halt Americans who entered our area illegally.

Our men also suffered from a lack of time off. They worked seven days a week and had no other outlet for their energy. A leave in Japan every six months was not enough. Some visited that inevitable Korean shack which was set up in the neighborhood of our installations. There they found liquor and prostitutes. We had several men ill from bad liquor and several cases of venereal disease. We also had several cases of drug addiction.

A few men of the 545th were difficult to control. The working, living and recreational facilities could not be improved, and Eighth Army would not allow us to use confinement to enforce discipline. Company punishment meant nothing, yet confinement was not authorized unless a dishonorable discharge or a bad-conduct discharge followed. Our battalion tried to bring pressure on offenders by ordering a delay in rotation for a man who committed a court-martial offense. This was countermanded by Eighth Army, even though it brought results.

In Korea the 545th had no shortage of reports. The company commander, the first sergeant, and two clerks were kept busy with paper work, and later an administrative officer was assigned to us full-time. We had to prepare twenty-one different monthly reports, and many daily and weekly reports. Battalion finally had to send us a calendar each month showing the date on which each report was due.

5. Testing Equipment in Korea

Capt. Fred C. Jacoby, Observer for The Quartermaster Board

I was sent to Korea with a detachment of enlisted men in March 1951 to conduct a special series of on-the-spot tests of equipment for The Quartermaster General and The Quartermaster Board. After I received my instructions in Washington and Fort Lee, I entrained for Oakland, California.

At the Oakland Quartermaster Depot the equipment to be tested arrived direct from the manufacturers. I received the following untested items: 130 unit burners for field ranges, 5 cabinets for a new field range, 1,000 one-burner stoves for small detachments, 5 cleaners for 55-gallon drums, and 150 rain suits. All this material was loaded on board a cargo vessel.

My men accompanied the equipment but I flew to Japan to report to the quartermaster of General Headquarters, Far East Command. In Tokyo I was told to report to the quartermaster of Eighth Army and work out the details of the testing program direct. Eighth Army designated the 7th Infantry Division as the testing organization.

When the test equipment arrived at Yokohama it was transferred to a ship sailing to Korea. At Pusan all of my equipment, except the drum cleaners and field-range cabinets, was loaded on trucks and taken to the 7th Division.

The men of the 7th Division were pleased to have been selected to make the test. The division commander personally assisted in the selection of units to use the equipment. The burners for the field ranges (which were installed in the standard-type range) and the one-burner stoves went primarily to the infantry. The rain suits were issued to the engineers, military police, and the reconnaissance company. I stayed most of the time in the division's area, checking the users' opinions of the equipment and examining items for evidence of wear.

The one-burner stoves, the burners for field ranges, and the rain suits were well liked. I recommended one modification to the field-range burner as the result of a fire. I left all the test items with the 7th Division when I returned to the United States, except representative samples brought back for study.

The gasoline-drum cleaners had been distributed in Pusan and Osan and were well liked except that they would not work on nonstandard drums manufactured in Japan. I recommended a slight modification that would allow the cleaners to be used with any drum. The cabinets for the field ranges were recalled for modification before I finished my testing.

I feel that this testing program was quite successful. The realistic conditions were the key to this. The trip overseas, with its transshipments, demonstrated that the test items were capable of standing actual wear and tear. The men who made the tests lived or worked with each item all the time and not just during work hours. Troops in the field are always critical in their judgment of equipment and most outspoken in expressing their likes and dislikes. When they said they liked a fire-burner, I knew they weren't trying to spare my feelings or hold onto their jobs.

One element of the testing program deserves some consideration. The men who came into contact with the program felt that the United States Army was sincerely interested in their welfare. They felt they were being consulted by the high command about an item, and not being given something that looked good to a desk soldier being pressured by a manufacturer's agent. The final seal of approval of a product came when men from adjacent units asked me when each item would be available for issue. I could only give the stock answer: "Soon, I hope."

6. Rations in Korea

Major Lawrence Dobson, Observer for The Quartermaster General. (From an oral report, 25 April 1951.)

To accomplish my subsistence and packaging mission, I visited the three corps headquarters, all division headquarters, and units within the divisions. In addition, I visited all the army supply points and the mobile bakeries.

I would like to start with a discussion of the operational ration since I feel that was the major portion of my mission. As you have heard, the troops in Korea are fed two hot meals a day whenever it is tactically possible. It is desirable, of course, to have three hot meals, but we say a minimum of two: normally, breakfast and supper. Noon meals are an operational ration. Hot meals were started by necessity because of a shortage of operational rations. Today we have plenty of rations, but the troops and the leaders appreciate the benefit of kitchen-prepared meals. It is a terrific morale builder among the forward elements.

First, I would like to discuss the 5-in-1 ration. During the last part of February 1951, Eighth Army asked that no more 5-in-1 rations be sent to Korea. That was quite a shock because we in the States had always considered the 5-in-1 our most acceptable ration.

Its military description said it would be used to serve small detachments—tank crews, gun crews, isolated units. I found that Eighth Army did not want the 5-in-1 ration because it was not satisfactory for the forward units. The men of these units do not have their mess gear or heating equipment with them; they travel as light as possible. Therefore, the 5-in-1 was difficult to break down and eat. I found that the ration was unacceptable when consumed cold. Still, that was the way it had to be consumed when it was issued to forward units.

I found that the armored battalions followed the same system of two hot meals a day, so that a case of 5-in-1 rations would be the noon meal for three days for the five men of a tank crew. The first day they cooked a pretty good meal; on the second day it was fairly good; by the third day they had no food left. The tankers had to draw another ration, and there we have a terrific waste. Also, the men did not want to cook when they could take the C ration, open one can, and be done with it.

The 5-in-1 was used in several cases as an emergency B ration. For example, the 31st Infantry was well advanced when a thaw hit. Roads were impassable, the regiment's kitchens were forward, and the men had to be supplied by air. So the 5-in-1 ration was dropped and used as a B ration. It was quite successful, but the mess stewards complained that there were not enough vegetables.

Before its cancellation request, Eighth Army decided there was insufficient food in a case for five men, and changed the basis of issue from 5-in-1 to 4-in-1. That again caused waste, since the accessory items—candy, chewing gum, cigarettes, peanuts—were put into the ration on the basis of five men. Still, four men used it.

I said that the 5-in-1 was unacceptable cold. When heated, the men did not care for the beef and gravy or the pork and gravy. They complained that there was too much fat, too much gravy, and that the meat appeared over-processed—just a mess of shreds and nothing to chew on.

As for fruit and jam—well, the best-accepted item is canned fruit. You can't give the men too much of it and, if you ask which is the most acceptable, they will think a while and then they might say "peaches," or they might say any of the other fruits. Vegetables are the same as in the B ration, and are a matter of preference. Canned puddings and desserts were well received. The precooked cereal in the ration was rated very low to fair. If the men had to add hot water to it themselves, it had poor acceptance. If the mess sergeants added milk and heated the cereal, it had very high acceptance. If only cold milk was provided, it had fair acceptance.

In addition to the use of the 5-in-1 as a B ration, and because there was a surplus on hand, Eighth Army at present is making some forced issues of 5-in-1 to the troops, and is also utilizing it as the ration to feed troops on trains. For troop-train feeding it again had very poor acceptance because of absence of heating equipment and, in many cases, lack of mess kits.

I would therefore recommend that the 5-in-1 no longer be considered a combat ration, but rather a ration to be used by small detachments in a semipermanent location with ample cooking facilities available to them; and that the ration also be considered an emergency B ration— one that can be moved in as I have explained.

When we started, we had the C-4 ration. We procured the C-6 ration and, later, we had a C-7.

The C ration is the most acceptable ration we have in use in Korea. Everyone likes it. The relative acceptance ratings of the meat items are: (1) beans and frankfurters; (2) beans with pork; (3) meat and beans; (4) ham and lima beans; (5) spaghetti and meat; (6) hamburgers with gravy; (7) pork sausage patties with gravy; (8) meat and noodles; (9) chicken and vegetables; (10) beef stew; (11) corned-beef hash.

This ration is a combat ration, and one of its characteristics is its capability of being consumed hot or cold. The reaction of the men was that the only items acceptable cold were the three bean items. The principal complaints were against the meat-and-spaghetti and the meat-and-noodle combinations. Both items were too dry, and when heated they would burn. The hamburgers and the sausage patties had too much fat and too much gravy. It is difficult to determine the acceptance of the chicken and vegetables. In the C-4 and the C-6 we had a chicken-and-vegetables combination. The men disliked it. We had previously received reports on this, and in the C-7 we have a product of the same name but from a different formula. The men interviewed who have eaten the C-7 reported that the acceptance on the chicken-and-vegetables was very high. It is a very good product.

The corned-beef hash and the beef stew had very low acceptance ratings. Part of this can be attributed to the fact that, when operations started in Korea, we had a limited stock of meat items to be issued in the B ration. Supply Bulletin 10-495 has the menus we had planned to use, but we didn't have the items in stock. We had quantities of beef stew and corned-beef hash on hand, so they were shipped. The men had corned-beef hash and beef stew; beef stew and corned-beef hash. So the principal objection to the corned-beef hash in the C ration is that it has become the Spam of the Korean campaign. Beef stew—well, too much fat; very poor acceptance when cold.

It had been reported previously that there was too much meat in the C ration. I found that for those men in the rear areas—those who used the ration only when they were making a movement—there may be too much meat. But we must remember that this ration was designed for the fighting man. He is a young man—old men cannot climb hills. Fighters work hard. They will eat practically all you can carry up to them.

When talking to them, I asked, "Is there too much meat?"

"No."

"Is there too much in the ration?"

"No; we will eat it all."

Even to the cocoa disc and the coffee. If they cannot prepare them at the time they are eating the ration, they will save them for later. An interesting comment was that they liked the cocoa but sometimes do not have the fire to heat the water. So the cocoa is being eaten as a chocolate bar. They wondered if we could not improve the eating quality of the cocoa disc and still save its quality for reconstituting it into cocoa.

The B units—that is, bread-type units in the C-7—were slightly different from those in the C-4 and the C-6. In the C-7, we attempted to put in each can all the components that would be required for a meal, so that a man would not have to open a second can or open an accessory packet. As a result, the arrangement of components within the C-7 was very well received and liked better than our previous arrangement. Also, in the C-7 for the first time we had a soluble milk product for coffee and that had high acceptance.

The chocolate and the starch-jelly discs are liked. Complaints were made of the starch-jelly discs being too hard to eat during the cold months. Also, the men got a little tired of having the same thing repeatedly, and requested additional types of confection.

Before I went to Korea, complaints had been reported that there were not enough crackers. I could not substantiate this. Colonel Jackson, of the Quartermaster Section, Japan Logistical Command, stated that some of the men wanted more crackers with the hamburgers and sausage patties. I heard one medical officer say he wanted more crackers, and he didn't like the candy. He was the exception to the rule. I would say the quantity of crackers we have is just about right.

I would ask a soldier, "Do you want more crackers?"

"Well, maybe."

"What would you want us to take out of the B units so that we can put in crackers?"

"Don't take out a thing. Leave it all in and don't increase the weight."

The most acceptable item is fruit. In the C-4 and in the C-6 we had two 6-ounce cans of fruit. In the C-7 we had one 8-ounce can of fruit. The first reaction soldiers have to the C-7 is: "What? Only one can of fruit?" Mess sergeants, platoon leaders, and everyone else complained. It was too difficult to divide the ration. They tell of fights among the men over who is going to get the fruit. So I would recommend that in the future we change from the one 8-ounce can back to our two 6-ounce cans.

When I asked, "What do you think of the individual combat ration?" the first thing said was, "Where is the spoon in the C-6?" And the next thing: "The C-7 is a lot better ration; it has a spoon."

As I mentioned before, the men carry nothing. Mess kits are kept in kitchen trucks. Soldiers are stripped down—no packs—just the clothes they wear. We also used to think a man would never lose his eating utensils. That is not so. They lose them, and unit commanders cannot have them resupplied as fast as they are needed. In many cases knives, forks and spoons are kept in the kitchen. At first the C ration came without spoons, and we got reports of men eating beans with their fingers. One Marine colonel cut his finger in trying to make a spoon from the top of a can. I would say—and I am stating the opinion of everyone I interviewed—that plastic spoons are a *must* in the operational rations.

In the past we included a can opener in each accessory packet. Every soldier I saw had a can opener in his pocket or on his dogtag chain. He was afraid he would not have a can opener when he wanted to eat. If he had a can opener and got hold of another, he saved it. My prize example is a colonel who had one can opener on his dogtag chain and nine in his pack. So my recommendation is that the can openers be reduced to either two or three per case and that they no longer be packed in the accessory pack, but be placed on top.

The condiment issue in Korea has been very poor. The troops did not have enough spices, and those they did have arrived spasmodically. Condiments reached Pusan in bulk, but there wasn't time to break them down. In Japan a spice pack was made up—three thousand rations to a pack. I feel there is a definite need for a spice pack. If we ship loose condiments, they will get lost at a depot. They will not be broken down and sent forward. Supply points have difficulty in issuing them to small units.

The cooks were doing a great deal of extra baking, but they were not getting condiments. I found, in some companies, that when a soldier was going on rest and recreation in Japan, his company commander would have him report to the mess sergeant to determine what was needed. The company commander then gave him money from the company fund and the soldier bought condiments in Japan so the company's kitchen would have nutmeg, cinnamon, cloves, vanilla, maple, and the like. I think this shows a definite requirement for a spice pack.

The fire units actually are holding up well, but spare parts are a problem. For instance, the 3d Infantry Division followed the book and issued all the spare parts. As a result, spare parts were all over the division but not in the place where they were needed. In the 24th and 25th Infantry Divisions, the food-service supervisors set up equipment repair shops. Faulty field ranges, Coleman lanterns, and one-burner stoves were turned in to the regimental supply officer, taken to the quartermaster when the regiments drew their rations, and exchanged for serviceable units at once. It was surprising how few unserviceable units were in these divisions. The repair men are better mechanics and better at improvising than the average cook.

The cooks in the forward areas appreciate their position. Part of that might be attributed to the policy in some divisions that each cook must go forward once a week and spend twenty-four hours with the riflemen of his company.

I found that the cooks are really doing more than I thought they would. Our cooks are doing a marvelous job. They know how to prepare dehydrated eggs and milk, and have made granular potatoes more acceptable when mashed than fresh potatoes. I recommend we reduce the quantities of fresh potatoes and limit the use of fresh potatoes to French fries and an occasional boiled potato. Cooks are baking pastry and rolls far more often than the menu calls for. The men like the baked products.

I hope I have not left the impression that our cooks are perfect. Not all our replacement cooks are adequately trained. They can cook, but some do not know how to clean a field range. Others do not know how to light one. On care and maintenance of field equipment, not all have the knowledge and training. Some do not know how to put up a tent, and it is quite difficult for a person who has never erected one himself to direct a crew of Korean laborers who don't know either. Field sanitation is sometimes poor. The plea of the people in the field to the food-service school is, "Give more field training."

The farther forward you go in Korea, the better you eat. In Pusan menus are planned for three areas: Pusan, Taegu, and north of Taegu. In other words, north of Taegu is the fighting front; Taegu includes Eighth Army headquarters and its supporting units; and Pusan is the dock area. When any item is in short supply, it is distributed first north of Taegu, then to Taegu, and finally to Pusan. If the quartermaster had limited supplies of frankfurters and frozen turkey, the frozen turkey would go north of Taegu, the frankfurters to Taegu, and corned-beef hash to Pusan.

I am sure you have been told before of the method of feeding forward elements in Korea. The meals are cooked in the battalion areas, then carried forward in jeeps as far as possible, and finally packed by the Korean bearers using carrier straps or A-frames. Now, there are problems involved. Bearers cannot carry water up to the top of the hill except for drinking, and they cannot carry a stove to heat mess-kit water, so no one on the hill keeps his mess kit. The kits are all kept back in the kitchen and are carried forward with the food. This is a problem, since the meat cans do not nest very well. Fifty mess kits to take care of an average platoon will fill a foot locker, so the mess kits are carried forward in foot lockers, boxes, or duffel bags. They are washed first in the kitchen, but they become dusty on the trip forward.

Everyone asked: "What are we doing with the mess kit? It is no good. Throw it out. Give us a tray."

All except one cavalry colonel who asked: "What would the men do if they found some eggs? How would they cook them?"

When I inquired where his unit carried their meat cans, his reply was that they kept the mess kits in the kitchen. I asked how they would cook the eggs then, and he answered that they *might* have the meat can with them.

The bakeries are operating in the vicinity of the supply points. The bread is very good and the bakeries are doing a fine job. They are having terrific maintenance difficulties, but I found an additional problem. When I visited the 1st Cavalry Division, it was 93 miles from its supply point. Its infantry regiments were 40 miles from the rest of the division. That meant the bread was hauled about 130 miles over the dustiest roads I have ever seen. All the bakery had to pack the bread in was kraft-paper bags sealed with gummed tape. Well, I'll grant the bags could have been handled a little more delicately, but it was amazing to see the number of bags that became torn between the bakery and the units. Several times the surgeon came along and condemned some of the bread.

There were a few people in Eighth Army who felt that the bakeries were not far enough forward. In one sense I agree with them. The main problem was that the road nets are so terrible and the bakery had to supply so many units that it could not get close to one division, because the other divisions would have too far to go.

The average age of bread was five days when it was consumed by the men and, in some cases, it was running to seven days. Still, they liked it. To give you an example of how well it is liked, the French and Belgians, when they first came in, would not accept our bread, but would take bread ingredients and do their own baking. They are either getting accustomed to our bread or their cooks are getting lazy, because gradually they are reducing the quantity of bread ingredients they are drawing and increasing the quantity of bread baked by us.

7. UN Approval of U.S. Products

Capt. Richard A. Johnson, Observer for The Quartermaster General. (From an oral report, 22 August 1951.)

My primary mission was to determine the degree of acceptance of Quartermaster Corps clothing, equipment, and subsistence items by United Nations troops in the Far East Command other than those of the United States. I visited troops from Turkey, the Philippines, Thailand, the United Kingdom, Australia, New Zealand, Canada, India, Norway, Sweden, Belgium, and some forces of the Republic of Korea.

There is an expression in Korea that if anything is "tops"—if it is really good—it is called "Number One." When talking to UN soldiers, I asked how they felt about U.S. clothing, equipment, and subsistence. They answered, "It is Number One." But we know there is still room for improvement on everything we have.

First, I will talk about subsistence. The remark was made to me several times that no army has been as well fed as Eighth Army in Korea. I think the Quartermaster Corps deserves a hand for the amount of food being supplied and the way it is prepared.

In my opinion, the U.S. rations are suitable for all UN troops with minor changes, except for Oriental troops. The Turks will not eat pork, and the Greeks delete sweet potatoes, corn, peas, and other items. Most European soldiers draw additional bread, and those from Mediterranean areas draw vegetable oils and olives. Some of the extra issues are made from U.S. stocks, and others are shipped to them from their own countries. The Greek Government, for instance, ships olive oil to Pusan. It is then forwarded with the regular rations to the division supplying the Greeks. These supplementary foods are not a problem that need worry us in the United States unless we feed a much larger number of UN troops.

Our rations are not suitable for Oriental troops because their basic food is rice. If they get rice they are happy. Anything else they draw merely supplements the rice portion of the meal. If you give them a fine steak, they cut it up and boil it with rice, so I don't see the necessity of issuing them steak when they are going to cook it in that way. I feel some work should be done to develop a menu for Oriental troops if we are to continue to supply them. Start from scratch, find out what they like, and issue that instead of the U.S. menu plus rice. In our present system a lot of items are wasted.

A special operational ration has been developed for the South Koreans called the 12-in-1, or J, ration. It is made in Japan. The Korean soldiers like it; however, like all combat rations, it becomes tiresome when eaten over long periods.

No particular difficulty is found with the package marking. At first, when a Turkish soldier got a can of U.S. food, he wouldn't know what was in it. However, after using a particular item for a month or so he learned to associate the writing on the can with its contents. So, if the troops are going to use an item over an extended period, there will not be any particular difficulty with markings.

Next, I will discuss clothing and equipment. I am not blowing the Quartermaster Corps horn by saying everything the U.S. has is the best in the world. But the U.S. items are generally of better design and of better quality than those manufactured in other UN countries represented in Korea. For that reason, the UN troops prefer the American items. The Turks, in speaking of many items will say, "We like the U.S. item because it is more convenient to use." In other words, our design is better.

The main difficulty with U.S. clothing for UN troops is sizing. The Turks and Greeks are about the same size as American soldiers except that their feet are quite a bit wider. Oriental troops are smaller than the average American soldier and their feet are small but wide.

So far as equipment is concerned, many of the UN troops are not mechanically inclined or have not worked with mechanical equipment. For example, Thai officers say that many of their soldiers come from farms and have never used anything mechanical. They probably have been following a plow all their lives—and a wooden plow at that. So you will find they have difficulty with what we consider simple mechanical items such as the immersion heater, the Coleman lantern, and the fire unit. Rather than go through the ordeal of setting up the immersion heater, they go down to the nearest stream and wash their mess gear.

Many UN troops do not understand the layer principle as we apply it to our winter clothing or, if they do understand it, they don't agree with us. They told me they like American equipment because of its lightness, but they felt that for warmth they should have much heavier clothing—something that will keep out the cold. They don't believe that two layers of light clothing keeps out the cold much better than one heavy layer.

As much as the UN soldiers like to wear the U.S. uniform, when they go on leave to Japan they want to be known as Turks, or Greeks, and not as U.S. soldiers. They are, however, very proud of their association with a U.S. division, and will wear the shoulder insignia of their own country on one shoulder, and that of the U.S. division on the other.

I want to mention that I think the United States Army has forgotten that the American soldier is also proud of the fact that he is an

American soldier. Many American soldiers in Korea remarked, "Why doesn't the United States Army have a uniform of its own—a uniform that every Tom, Dick and Harry in the world isn't wearing?" So I believe some thought should be given to *esprit de corps* in the U.S. Army, to give the American soldier a uniform he can be proud of—and that *only he* will be wearing.

8.   Wet-Cold Clothing Indoctrination

William F. Pounder, Civilian Observer for The Quartermaster General. (From an oral report, 19 January 1951.)

The primary reason for my trip to the Far East was to establish and execute a broad training program for all troops in Korea in the proper issuing, fitting, use, and maintenance of the wet-cold and dry-cold climate clothing. I left the United States for this mission on 22 September 1950, with 6 officers and 3 enlisted men.

After arriving in Japan our party set about establishing a wet-cold training program. Since we sent troops to Korea through the replacement training center in Japan, we first had to set up a training program in Japan itself. At Camp Drake we had our most experienced officer (Capt. James D. Norman) establish a wet-cold training program. We worked in spurts—sometimes from 0600 until 2100 or 2200—then waited until new troops arrived. Sometimes we taught as many as three thousand during two-day periods.

During the slack periods we trained new instructors, for we realized that six teams would not be adequate in Korea. After the training team had its program well under way in Japan, the remaining teams left for Korea.

There we established a training program within Eighth Army, and within every corps, division and separate unit. We had training teams in the 1st Cavalry Division, in the 2d, 3d, 7th, 24th, and 25th Infantry Divisions, and in the 1st Marine Division. As we moved from division to division, the unit "next door" would hear that we had trained instructors, and would immediately request a team. We kept calling on the replacement training center for additional instructors and assigned them permanently to divisions.

We also worked with the logistical commands because personnel were being taken from rear-area units and sent into the combat zone. We didn't have enough instructors for every unit, so we used "indirect training." We did this in a large church in Pusan, where we spread the gospel of wet-cold and dry-cold training to the 2d Logistical Command. At least two persons came from each separate unit, and we trained 86 instructors. To help them conduct training in their own units, we equipped each with complete issues of clothing, an outline of his talk, and all his training aids.

As the training progressed we realized there would also be the problem of instructing the other United Nations troops, so we began to expand even further. The first UN troops we came in contact with were the South Koreans. To augment U.S. units, there were as many as eight thousand ROKs interspersed in each of our divisions. Only a few of these could speak English. We had to translate our talks and our outlines into the Korean language and have them published. We also had the talks distributed to the ROK divisions.

Later we got in touch with the British brigade, the Turkish brigade, the Thai regiment, the Filipino battalion, and the French battalion. I have just received a letter saying they are now working with the Canadians and New Zealanders. In all, the wet-cold and dry-cold gospel has been translated into Korean, Turkish, Spanish, and French.

I said that we had six teams. When I left Korea there were seventeen teams in operation. We are proud that when the Chinese Communists attacked, we had teams with the 7th Division at the Yalu River, with the 1st Marine Division in the Changjin Reservoir area, with the 1st Cavalry Division in the northwest, and at the front line with every one of our divisions.

It was difficult to operate a wet-cold indoctrination program in the field, especially near the front lines, where we had to instruct units as they came into reserve for an overnight rest. In Japan, where we could seat 700 or 800 men in a theater and show our movie, it was far more satisfactory.

Our teams did more than just instruct the troops. Sometimes they helped the quartermasters prepare requisitions. At other times they aided in locating and expediting shipments of winter clothing. It was a terrific problem to haul all this clothing long distances, over a disrupted transportation system, and a few shipments did get lost. Sometimes a unit had the clothing but could not move it forward because of the presence of guerrillas. Since the division quartermasters were short of personnel, they gave our teams transportation and sent them hundreds of miles to locate the shipments and bring the clothing forward.

We made physical inspections of clothing and equipment to separate superior items from old or inferior ones. This was extremely important, because we had several types of footwear and clothing. The old shoepac is not as good as the new type, and our men made sure the best were issued to combat troops.

The teams made certain that circulars about the prevention of cold injuries reached the company level. Then we made spot inspections, beginning with the front-line private, to check on understanding and compliance with the circular. When our teams found noncompliance, they reported it to Eighth Army. We also checked to see that each company had a cold-injury prevention team of its own.

Our teams checked the progress and adequacy of the sock-exchange system within the combat elements. Clean, dry socks are important in preventing cold-weather injury. It is not enough to put this in a circular. You must go forward and actually see that the units have set up a sock-exchange program. Our teams assumed almost complete responsibility for getting changes of dry socks up with the rations.

We worked hard to insure adequate numbers of warm-up and drying-out tents and rooms. Again, you must go up there and be sure there are tents or rooms, and that there are stoves. When a soldier feels or sees that he is getting a cold-weather injury, he needs a place to go where he can warm up and get a change of socks.

The last function of our team was to report the cold-weather injuries that occurred. The 24th Infantry (25th Infantry Division) in a two-week period had 169 cases of trench foot and frostbite, while a unit operating right next to it had only 20! These units were in reserve. When this report arrived, it was relayed to the surgeon of Eighth Army. A member of his office and one from the quartermaster's office visited the regimental commander.

Now let's look at the results of the cold-weather indoctrination. We have long been trying to get complete casualty reports from Korea, but it is difficult and we are getting them only periodically. While I was there I made a check into weather casualties and I found that from 28 November to 7 December 1950—the period of the Chinese Communist breakthrough—there were 1,500 such casualties. Of these casualties, 1,100 had to be evacuated to Osaka General Hospital in Japan. We have another report on weather casualties after things quieted down. For the week 22-29 December, we had 223 casualties, 184 of which were frostbite cases.

At the time I left Japan, we estimated that weather casualties during the worst of the fighting in Korea totaled about 4 per cent. In winter campaigns in Europe and Italy during World War II, under conditions not so severe, we found there had been an average of 8 per cent of such casualties. We like to think that part of this reduction was due to our wet-cold indoctrination; not only by team instruction, but by making sure that the sock-exchange system, the dry-out tent, and proper care were forced on the individual soldier.

Now let's look at some causes of cold-weather injuries in Korea. First, I feel that many staff officers are ignorant of proper clothing needs for cold-weather warfare. In October 1950, at the time of our northern push, the troops left Seoul, Taegu, and Pusan—areas where the weather is comparable to that of Washington or Baltimore—and moved 150 or 200 miles north into areas with the climate of Maine—with only one layer of wool clothing. We discussed this with the staff while I was there, and told them that cold weather was coming soon. We explained that the supply of cold-weather clothing was a complex affair. I was told that, at this time, ammunition, POL, and rations had No. 1 priority, and that when the cold weather came the supply of overcoats would be taken care of in due course. "The supply of overcoats"! The supply of overcoats is not all that is concerned in cold-weather clothing.

The second cause of cold-weather injuries was ignorance and lack of supervision by troop officers in the wearing of winter clothing. In some areas, where the temperature was zero, the officers told the troops to wear the combat boot in snow rather than the shoepac because it was lighter and would be better for marching. They did not know that a leather boot will get wet and soon freeze. No matter how many times you change your socks, you do not get a dry change of footgear.

The third reason for injuries was that the temperature was extremely low at a time when enemy pressure made it almost impossible for some men to take proper care. We made a survey at Osaka General Hospital to find out how the patients became casualties. We found three hundred of the weather casualties were men who had been wounded and, in some cases, had been lying on the snow, ice, and frozen ground for as long as two or three days. These men were in very serious condition and some needed amputations.

We talked to others who had been wounded, and asked if they had had the two-hour training. We found no one who had not been indoctrinated in proper clothing. We asked why they didn't carry out their training and they gave several reasons. First of all, they didn't know how close the enemy was to them and they didn't dare take off their shoepacs for fear they might get caught in their stocking feet and have to continue without footgear.

Others, in the Marine division, had to go through a river about sixty yards wide and partially frozen over. One ten-yard section forced men to wade through water almost up to their knees. Some of the men were fortunate enough to get on vehicles and get through. Those who were well trained knew enough to take off their footwear and walk barefoot through that water, dry their feet, and put on their footwear at the far side. Others, who were not so well trained, walked through the water with their footwear on. They might just as well have been hit by machine-gun fire. To make it worse, some of those who walked through the water got on vehicles and rode for several hours without giving their feet any exercise.

These were the main causes for the cold injuries, and it showed that we needed training. Before Korea, our troops did not receive wet-cold training.

Most of the troops we are sending into arctic and wet-cold areas have been trained in the South.

We visited the units that had trained in cold-climate areas. In the Marine units that had trained in Greenland, the 2d Infantry Division units that had trained in the mountains of northwestern United States, and the 7th Infantry Division units that had trained in northern Japan, not one man became a cold-weather casualty! Think that over.

You cannot make clothing and equipment foolproof under all conditions, so we must train our troops. That does not mean a two-hour instruction period. It means living under actual wet-cold conditions. And living under those conditions is an acquired skill you can get only through training.

9. Command Action in Korea

Prepared for the Army Field Forces Commanders Preventive Maintenance Course, Aberdeen Proving Ground, 1952

Soldiers of the United States Army are issued large quantities of clothing and equipment in accordance with existing tables of allowances. The soldier stores some of them in his duffel bag, some in his cargo pack, and some in his combat pack. When the time comes to shake down to minimum essential equipment for his first combat, the average soldier is reluctant to part with many of the articles he has been issued. As a result, he attempts to carry on his back everything which will contribute to his comfort in the field.

The soldiers of the 7th Infantry Division were no exception, and they were overburdened when they landed at Inchon in September 1950. The inevitable soon happened: equipment was abandoned. The commanding officer of the 32d Infantry (Col. Charles E. Beauchamp) determined to do something about it. During the planning phase of a later amphibious operation in which his unit was to land at Iwon, Colonel Beauchamp limited the items his men could wear and carry to: helmet, complete with liner; cotton field cap, with visor; wool muffler; two sets of winter underwear; high-neck sweater; pile field jacket; M43 field jacket, with hood; a pair of wool field trousers; a pair of cotton field trousers; four pairs of ski socks; a pair of combat boots, fitted over ski socks; a pair of shoepacs, with two pairs of flat insoles; poncho; mountain sleeping bag, with case; cargo and combat field pack; cartridge or pistol belt;

canteen, with cup and cover; first-aid packet, with pouch; toilet articles and insecticides; individual arms and ammunition; C ration (three meals maximum).

Colonel Beauchamp compiled his list after a consideration of what a soldier could carry and what was absolutely essential. Shelter halves, pins and poles, and intrenching tools were eliminated because the frozen ground would make them useless. Flannel shirts were omitted because of their binding qualities.

In a showdown inspection, Colonel Beauchamp collected all items in excess of his list and turned them over to his S4. With the concurrence of the division quartermaster, quantities of some items were retained. Among these were 2,000 suits of woolen underwear, 4,000 pairs of ski socks, and 2,000 pairs of woolen trousers.

A standing operating procedure was developed that established the various articles and combinations of articles to be worn. Experience had demonstrated that the combat boot was better than the shoepac for marching and climbing the rugged terrain; therefore, Colonel Beauchamp directed that combat boots be worn under these conditions. When the march ended, or a static situation developed, the shoepacs, with two pairs of ski socks and a pair of felt insoles, were substituted for combat boots.

The regiment initiated a training program to insure that all troops understood the layer principle of insulation. This was conducted by a wet-cold climate instruction team assigned to the 7th Infantry Division.

Finally, Colonel Beauchamp directed that officers and NCOs make frequent inspections of their men to make certain his instructions were strictly obeyed. He placed particular emphasis upon the importance of foot care, including changing of socks at the conclusion of each march, and massaging the feet to restore circulation. Troops were also required to change underwear after each period of exertion, when the situation permitted.

The results obtained in the 32d Infantry were noteworthy. Wanton abandonment of equipment was practically eliminated; care and maintenance of clothing and individual equipment improved. The incidence of frostbite, frozen feet, trench foot, and other cold injuries was extremely light. Through experience, the regimental S4 further reduced his clothing stocks. In time, other commanders in the division adopted Colonel Beauchamp's methods.

10. Clothing Exchange

Lt.Col. Kenneth O. Schellberg, Quartermaster, 7th Infantry Division

We learned that the quartermaster's shower and clothing exchange was a great economy in spite of the additional equipment necessary to allow the men to bathe and to launder their clothing.

The 7th Infantry Division began its clothing exchange in February 1951. Before that each man wore and carried two sets of clothing, and reserve supplies in the division held at least one other complete uniform per man. When the clothing exchange began, we collected all the duffel bags and limited each soldier to the clothing on his back plus a change of underclothing and socks. Clothing at the shower points and laundry equaled one half uniform per soldier. Thus the total number of uniforms per man dropped from three sets to one and a half.

Our quartermaster company drew its four shower units in Japan just before embarking for Korea, but we didn't establish a clothing exchange for six months. This delay was caused partly by inadequate laundry facilities. It was also a matter of selling the idea to regimental commanders.

There were many advantages to the clothing exchange system. It cut down the weight the soldier had to carry; it also eliminated duffel bags and the thirty-man detail in each regiment to guard and handle them. This increased our mobility. The cleaner clothing improved the hygiene of the troops, and the automatic exchange of clothing eliminated all requisitions below division. Exchange made possible early repair before shirts and trousers became unsalvageable, and it eliminated the old practice of mutilating Government property in order to get the supply sergeant to issue a new item. Reduced stocks also lessened the possibility of the enemy's capturing valuable supplies.

We learned that in combat there is no need to publish a shower schedule because company commanders preferred to send men to get showers whenever the tactical situation permitted. From experience we learned that the shower units should not be moved farther forward than regiment. Some regimental commanders tried parceling out the showers for several days at a time to each battalion. This made for time lost in moving, wear on equipment, and irregular treatment of the operators. Moving the shower into a battalion zone made it unavailable to most of the regiment; yet it was not always busy at battalion. It was easier to transport the men than to move the equipment.

The shower and clothing exchange was a great morale builder for the men. After an attack in which a regiment was unable to release men to get showers, we would augment its bathing facilities and see that every man could bathe and change within four days. Normally, however, the men had a shower once a week.

Company commanders watched their men for signs of excessive fatigue and sent them to the showers when a relief seemed necessary. Often a shower and a hot meal at regiment were enough to restore a soldier's efficiency. If the fatigue were dangerous, the soldier could be sent to the regimental rest camp for a day or two of sleep, hot meals, and regular baths. This was an excellent way to prevent combat fatigue.

11. QM Service Center No. 3

> Lt. Bevan R. Alexander, 5th Historical Detachment. (Narrative based on interviews of the following personnel of Service Center No. 3: Capt. Alfred G. Rollins, Capt. Henry L. Cody, Lt. Dewey Washington, Jr., and Sgt. Carrol L. Veach.)

During World War II, U.S. Fifth Army in Italy developed what became known as the quartermaster service center. The service center is a grouping, in one area, of separate quartermaster units that provide related services. After World War II, no service center was established until the spring of 1951, when Eighth Army activated one for each of its corps.

The first to begin operations was Quartermaster Service Center No. 3, serving X Corps. From Eighth Army were assembled two and one half platoons of the 549th Quartermaster Laundry Company; one platoon of the 505th Quartermaster Reclamation and Maintenance Company; one section of the 821st Quartermaster Bath Company; and the 580th Quartermaster Office Machine Repair Detachment. Officers of the several units took over duties in the service center, with the commander of the laundry company (Capt. Alfred G. Rollins) as officer in charge. The officers and men of each unit cooperated so successfully that, to all intents and purposes, the service center became a regularly constituted unit.

The service center was laid out in a compact area near a stream. The laundry was close to the repair and maintenance platoon. The clothing exchange of the bath company was near the laundry. Mess facilities were centralized but apart from the operations area.

The most important service of a center is laundering. During the first nineteen weeks of our operations (1 May to 8 September 1951), the laundry averaged 13,617 pounds of wash daily, for a total of 1,968,730 pounds. Thus, 1,462,890 individual items were cleaned.

The wash is normally received in bulk, laundered, put in stock, and reissued. When a unit or individual brings dirty clothing to the laundry, an exchange is made from the company's stocks.

Trucks bringing soiled clothing arrive at the laundry's check point. Here a checker counts the individual pieces. The agent receives a turn-in slip which he takes to the nearby stock tent and exchanges for an equal number of items of clean clothing.

The clothing is exchanged rather than returned because of the time lag and accounting. Since all clothing is of the same design and material, sizing is the only problem. In addition to the bulk laundry, a small amount of bundle work is provided for units or individuals near the service center.

At the laundry there are five separate washing machines. Each section contains a washing machine and a dryer, which are individually mounted on trailers. Dirty clothing is sorted and placed in front of each of the washers. After loading, it goes through a nineteen-minute cycle, during which it is completely washed and 75 per cent dried. Then the clothing is placed in a tumble dryer for eight to ten minutes. The entire laundering process lasts less than a half hour.

The dry clothing is next taken to a nearby inspection tent. Here each item is checked to determine whether it should be placed in stock, repaired, or discarded. If a piece of clothing needs repair, it is sent to the reclamation and maintenance platoon.

The reclamation and maintenance platoon repairs clothing, canvas and heavy textiles, and shoes. A secondary function of office-machine repair is handled in conjunction with the center's office-machine repair detachment.

The clothing section is equipped with fourteen standard textile-sewing machines for use in repairing uniforms. All clothing received is inspected to determine if it can be repaired. Most of the clothing received comes from the laundry, but some repair work is submitted directly by units.

The textile section is equipped to repair tentage and other heavy textiles. The section uses two heavy-duty textile-sewing machines and tent-repair kits, which contain rubber cement, glue, and patches.

The shoe-repair section is equipped to repair all types of service footwear. This section repaired 9,926 pairs of shoes and boots in nineteen weeks. Footwear is delivered to the section by the agents who bring laundry to the center. If the boots and shoes can be repaired, they are processed and returned. If they cannot be repaired, they are returned to the sender for salvage through the regular supply channels.

The office-machine repair detachment repairs all types of office machinery. The typewriter is the machine most frequently repaired because it is the most widely used. However, almost anything may come in for repair—adding machines, calculators, mimeograph machines—and the detachment has even repaired a time clock.

The greatest problem has been replacement of parts. Until the fall of 1951 the typewriter-repair kits received from the Zone of the Interior were not much use. Often only two or three parts of any of the kits were needed. For example, in one manufacturer's kit only the variable line-space clutch and the line-space-wheel assembly could be used, although the kit contained a hundred separate typewriter parts. This was more or less true of other kits. A change in the method of procuring replacement parts has been instituted, and all replacement parts are now requisitioned individually. Typewriter platens have never been available in Korea, however.

Expediency has proved the best way to obtain parts for office machines. Damaged machines have been cannibalized, and the machine shop of the reclamation and maintenance platoon has manufactured some unobtainable parts.

The heavy dust, the high humidity, and the extremes of temperature have reduced the effective operation of office machines, but the greatest unkeep problem has been neglect.

"People just don't take care of their machines," said Sgt. Carrol L. Veach. "Sometimes I'll clean up a machine and tell the person who comes for it to keep it covered. They often reply, 'Why should I worry about it? It's not mine.'"

Another problem for the repairmen has been the misguided effort of the novice repair mechanic. This character, when his machine begins to work improperly, takes it apart. He usually has it entirely disassembled before it dawns on him that he cannot fix it. Then, in its still disassembled condition, he brings it to the detachment, losing about half the parts along the way. Sometimes such a machine can be repaired, but often it can only be used as a source of parts.

Showers and clothing exchange are provided for troops near the service center. The single shower unit is capable of serving 4,400 men in a ten-hour day. A man who wants a bath need bring only himself. The exchange provides clean clothing, hot water, free towels, soap, and even shaving cream and razor blades.

12. Pukchon Cemetery

Major Jacob W. Kurtz, Graves Registration Officer, 7th Infantry Division

The 7th Infantry Division did not have a graves registration section in Japan, and one had to be created before we made our assault landing at Inchon. I received ten men from various sections of the quar-

termaster company—none of whom had had any burial experience. I
organized the section with a section chief, two clerks, four body proc-
essors, two supervisors of Korean labor, and a driver. Although these men
developed competence in their work, one sergeant was disinterested and
one other soldier was an Army misfit.

Before leaving Japan I assumed that casualties might be high and
that burial items might not be supplied for several months. I requisitioned
five thousand mattress covers and large quantities of identification tags,
burial forms, temporary grave markers, personal-effects bags, burial bottles, a fingerprint kit, and an addressing machine. The supplies were carried jointly by the infantry regiments (as evacuators of bodies) and the
quartermaster company.

At Inchon the graves registration section learned how to receive
and process bodies. No channel existed for evacuating bodies beyond division, so we shared a cemetery opened by the Marine Corps. Our large
stock of burial items came in handy here, for the marines exhausted their
supply and called on us for more.

At Inchon we learned not only from our own mistakes, but also from
those of the marines. The cemetery was located only 250 yards off the
main supply road and in view of all who passed. In the first days it was
not possible even to screen off the bodies awaiting burial. I believe this
affected many who passed.

In October 1950 the 7th Division made its landing at Iwon. Here the
division's casualties were evacuated directly to Navy craft and the
graves registration section did not operate until the division headquarters was established at Pukchon. Our section contained seven of the ten
men who had been at Inchon, and we were familiar with our duties. We
remained at Pukchon, even though division headquarters moved to
Pungsan, and the infantry regiments were scattered from the Yalu River
to Chosin Reservoir.

Whenever possible, a division evacuates its dead to an army graves
registration detachment. At Pukchon we did not have this army support. On approval of the division quartermaster (Lt.Col. Kenneth O.
Schellberg) we established a division cemetery. I reconnoitered the
Pukchon area and quickly found an adequate site, a half mile south of
town and a half mile from the MSR. The dry, rocky soil had good drainage, and the area was not under cultivation.

In Pukchon my section was quartered with the other quartermaster
troops. We had a clerical office with the quartermaster company and an
obscure building nearby for processing the bodies. Our operation was so
quiet that few people noticed it.

When a body arrived we encased it in a mattress cover, if this had
not already been done. We checked to see that each body had an emergency medical tag, and, if it did not, that the unit of the deceased sup-

plied one. Fortunately, every American body received at Pukchon was identified. We then checked the personal-effects inventory to see that everything listed was present, and made an additional search to be sure no effects had been overlooked.

We hired a dozen laborers to dig graves. While a ten-man section is adequate for operating a division graves registration point, it is inadequate for operating a cemetery. The Koreans were employed voluntarily and worked faithfully at a wage of two canteen cups of polished rice daily.

We opened our cemetery on 4 November 1950. Four or five open graves were maintained at all times, and no body was taken from the processing building to the cemetery until all preparations were complete. At the cemetery we maintained a pyramidal tent to protect the crews against the weather, and to screen the bodies during the brief period between their arrival and burial. No equipment was ever left in the tent and no guard was left in the area at night.

When a body arrived it was lowered into the open grave, face up. Then one of my men would reach into the mattress cover and place the burial bottle, containing a report of interment, under the left arm. The grave was closed and a temporary marker placed.

Unless a chaplain happened to be present when the body was interred, there was no ceremony at that time. Sometime during the day of interment, however, a chaplain of the soldier's faith came to the grave for a short service. If the soldier's faith was unknown, chaplains of all faiths visited the site. Several times we had a ceremony in honor of an individual, but in each case it was after the grave was closed. A memorial ceremony was held each Sunday.

As division cemeteries are temporary, regulations do not provide for any beautification. In digging graves our laborers turned up many stones. With these we built a cemetery wall. Three flags flew over the cemetery: the United Nations color at the front entrance, the United States color in the center of the cemetery, and the Republic of Korea color toward the rear.

We closed our cemetery about 1 December 1950, as the division began its march toward Hungnam. During November we had buried 50 Americans and 24 ROKs. Sketches of the location of the cemetery and a register of those interred were forwarded to the Eighth Army's graves registration section.

13. Repatriation of American Dead

Lt. Bevan R. Alexander, 5th Historical Detachment. (Condensed from an article based on information supplied by Lt. William F. Wurz, Sgt. James H. Deisenroth, and Cpl. Paul R. Imwalle, 2d Quartermaster Company.)

The evacuation of the dead resembles other quartermaster operations—in reverse. Bodies of the dead are brought from their units to a division graves registration point, then evacuated through corps, army, and theater installations to the United States.

The remains are processed at a division collecting point and forwarded within twenty-four hours to a corps collecting point. Accompanying each body is an emergency medical tag, and with each shipment is an evacuation list. The list serves as a letter of transmittal.

At corps the remains are forwarded to the army's collecting point. Here the fingertips of the dead are embalmed and fingerprints are taken. The bodies are then packed in ice and shipped to Pusan, then to Japan.

In Japan, unidentified bodies are examined by experts in anthropology, chemistry, and dentistry. Careful records are kept in hope that identification can be made. The bodies are totally embalmed, placed in military caskets, and shipped to the United States for burial either in a U.S. military cemetery or near the soldier's home. Under present policy, no bodies are being permanently interred either in Korea or in Japan.

Personal effects follow a similar path. The property of persons killed, wounded, or missing in action, those who die of natural causes, and those who are evacuated through medical channels, is divided into two classes. Class I includes trophies, keepsakes, and items of sentimental value. Class II items are those of specific value.

An inventory of the property of each casualty is made by his commanding officer or some other officer. Every item is listed—even if it consists of only two pennies or fifteen pictures. If the money belonging to the individual is worth $4.99 or less, it is sent with his effects, regardless of whether it is in dollars, scrip, *won*, or *yen*. If the money is worth $5.00 or more, it is converted into a U.S. Government check.

The effects of a person killed in action must be forwarded to his division's personal effects section, usually within eight days. For a person missing in action, the time is twenty to thirty days. From the division's personal effects section the articles follow channels to the rear until they reach the Effects Center at Kansas City, Missouri. Here they are checked again and arrangements are made for transmission to the next of kin.

14. Supply Lessons

Lt.Col. Charles R. Scherer, Assistant G4, 7th Infantry Division

Korea made several things very obvious. We had forgotten many of the lessons of mobility and small detachment operations learned in World War II, and we had to relearn them. We found that units must expect to serve more troops and work with less corps and army support than Quartermaster Corps doctrine prescribes. Above all, we learned about distance.

The occupation of Japan prevented normal training. Understrength battalions and regiments were scattered in small garrisons around the islands. Regiments maintained separate posts and S4s operated the combined technical services. Commanders forgot that division would normally provide most of their supplies and services. Once the dependence on S4s was formed, it was hard to break.

In Japan some of our technical services were performed by Japanese civilians. This was necessary because of troop shortages and the lack of qualified Army technicians. Our own men were thus prevented from getting the necessary training and experience. This, coupled with inadequate SOPs and field training, prevented the technical service troops on occupation duty from being ready for combat.

The 7th Infantry Division was the last of the occupation divisions to leave for Korea. As the other divisions left, we were levied for personnel and lost many of our key officers and NCOs. This didn't hurt the service troops as much as it hurt the infantry and artillery, but it did lower the efficiency of our division. We were preparing to go to Korea with a strength of about 9,000 when, about three weeks before our departure, we received 10,000 American and 8,000 Korean replacements to integrate into our division.

The Koreans we received looked as though they had been herded together to get them off the streets of Pusan. They spent their first week in Japan in quarantine, since they had to be deloused and cleaned. Then we had to equip them completely. Japan Logistical Command did a wonderful job of getting the articles of clothing and equipment to us, but it was a real problem to teach the Koreans how to live in a camp.

They could not speak English and we had few interpreters. Our instruction was given primarily by sign language and making simple motions for them to watch and imitate. We had a long way to go in two weeks. These men had no idea of sanitation, let alone the more complicated activities of military life. Yet high-level policy dictated that we treat them as our equals in every respect. They were to receive the same clothing and equipment, the same treatment, the same rations. Later, they even had to have chocolate bars and "comic" books!

We Americans have much to learn about handling troops of the so-called backward nations who may come under our control. They do not understand democracy, our ideals, our methods of discipline, and the forces that motivate our actions. The Koreans have not lived as we have, and our easy-going discipline did not work with them. In their own army discipline was strict, arbitrary, and often brutal. They had been reared under such discipline and seemed to understand no other kind.

The integration of Koreans was unsatisfactory. They ate our rations, rode our trucks, used our supplies. But except for menial tasks, they were a performance cipher.

We lost a great deal of mobility because of our overload of supplies. Our men had too much equipment in Japan and they did not strip down to prepare for combat. Regiments committed the same error. Used to depending on their own S4 sections for garrison supplies, they continued to carry large stocks of clothing and equipment in their own trains. S4s made "deals" in Pusan and carried their acquisitions around in their trucks. At Pukchon we found one regiment hiding three hundred cases of C rations among the men's duffel bags, while the division quartermaster was trying unsuccessfully to obtain operational rations! When the 31st Infantry was overrun near Chosin Reservoir, it lost ten to twenty truckloads of clothing. Critical types of ammunition would be concealed by one unit while greatly needed by another.

During our first six months in Korea, the infantry regiments did not trust the ability of their divisional service units to keep them adequately supplied. Occasionally a regimental commander would test our ability to produce. One regimental commander, while advancing to the Yalu River against moderate resistance, insisted on 50 tons of 4.2-inch mortar ammunition. We figured he didn't need that much, but we piled it right in his front yard so he could see we could deliver it. Unfortunately, we could not evacuate it when we withdrew, and it had to be destroyed. The artillery battalions near the Yalu River requested two extra basic loads of fire to be stored in a division ammunition supply point, and they gave strong arguments for it. I had mental reservations about getting so much heavy ammunition so far forward when resistance was light. When the fighting around Chosin Reservoir forced us to leave our exposed position on the Yalu River, this ammunition too had to be destroyed.

All the hoarding and all the demands for extra supplies took extra transportation at the very time such great operating distances put vehicles in shorter supply. When we first came to Korea, division headquarters could move in 25 trucks, but soon it took 50. Everyone had acquired a

Korean desk and chair. Regiments called for 200 additional trucks when they made a move, although movement tables show they should have been able to motorize themselves with a 90-truck augmentation.

Lest it seem our regiments alone were guilty of poor supply discipline, I will point out that some of the patterns of waste were established at the top. Higher headquarters sometimes caused us to overload our units. Once, while inspecting a unit, a general officer found a man who had only two pairs of socks. He ordered that every man in the division carry six pairs! We had to issue these over the protest of commanders who knew that their men would soon throw away the extra pairs. Colonel S. L. A. Marshall (in *The Soldier's Load and the Mobility of a Nation*) is right in his statement that when you overload a soldier you decrease his efficiency. Yet we had pressure in 1950 to draw every piece of impedimenta that the Army designed.

In Korea there were some increases in our loads that were very necessary and justifiable, such as tents and stoves. The extreme cold of northern Korea made it absolutely essential to have shelter throughout the division. It was necessary that each infantry platoon have a squad tent and stove so it could rotate its men and allow them to get warm. But enough tents for a division certainly complicated our transportation situation.

The distance from army supply dumps to us made it necessary for quartermasters to carry more clothing, shoes, mess gear, stove parts, and other supplies than normal. We tried to get permission to store these stocks in boxcars on sidings, but this was refused.

We usually think of the company or platoon as being the smallest work unit among service troops. In Korea we learned the need to operate in smaller detachments. The quartermasters often had to maintain four or five class I and class III supply points, and maybe two II and IV points. It took a lot of detachments to accomplish this. Typically, one officer and a composite squad would run a small distributing point. The ordnance company sent semipermanent detachments to the regiments because of the distances separating them. Here was a place where leadership was necessary on the part of junior officers and NCOs. We often hear of the need for leadership among combat troops. It is no less necessary among service troops.

The rations in Korea were out of this world. I had more fresh meat in Korea in a month's time than I received in three and a half years of Pacific service in World War II. We also had fresh vegetables in limited quantities. The food was so good that we got few complaints from commanders except about an occasional shortage in Worcestershire sauce, catsup, or black pepper! I doubt if we could have maintained this quality of food were we operating on the scale of World War II.

15. The Failure of Support

Major James W. Spellman, Executive Officer to the Quartermaster, 24th Infantry Division. (Condensed from a statement written on 15 November 1950.)

From the first day they spent in Korea, members of the 24th Division's quartermaster section have had mixed feelings about quartermaster support. We remember with pride the difficult being done immediately, and the impossible taking a little longer. Then we shudder as we recall how often we failed in those hectic days of defeat, victory, and stalemate. We don't like to remember how many times we have had to turn down requests. "How about the mantle for my Coleman lantern?" "How about a generator for my field range?" "How about . . ." stencil paper, GI soap, trousers, tent poles, paper clips, underwear, cigarettes?

We seldom had to make excuses for lack of rations or gasoline. But yeast, baking powder, shoestrings, toilet paper, and forks were not available. It has been weeks since many of the small but very important items have been received. Shoes are tied with scraps of cord and kitchens are using toilet soap received from home by mail. I do not doubt that hundreds of soldiers are writing home for items of quartermaster issue because they are not available, or because they come more quickly by mail. After all, our requisitions are often still unfilled after a month of waiting.

From the tragic days in Taejon we have sensed a passive indifference to our requirements for individual and unit equipment. In the heat of summer we begged for even salvaged fatigue jackets and trousers to be shipped from Japan to cover our semi-naked soldiers, for salt tablets, and for mess kits to replace those lost by our troops as they withdrew over the mountains, carrying only their rifles.

It was understandable that supply confusion should exist at first. But I do not understand why the supply authorities should resist our legitimate requests with criticisms that we were using too much. How *were* we using too much? What known yardstick of modern U.S. logistics could be applied to this long series of defeats and withdrawals?

From the first telephone request—ignored—for minimum clothing and equipment, through the present requirement of six copies of every requisition, we have felt the antagonistic, unsympathetic reaction on the part of Eighth Army's minor quartermaster personnel. They have minutely questioned every item of even emergency requirements, and deliberately delayed supplies while they checked and rechecked requests against noncombat-type statistical status reports. There has been an almost comical questioning of requirements, delving into the microscopic details of why a company, outnumbered 30 to 1, did not evacuate kitchen equipment under small-arms fire. A directive stated that when damaged equipment was not submitted for exchange, a formal certificate must be submitted giving all details of loss.

So long as Pusan remained within truck distance, it was possible to bypass approving authorities and go directly to the mountains of supplies in the port. Often we obtained supplies in Pusan that were impossible to get through the red-tape maze of proper channels. Personnel in charge of warehouse operations frequently begged us to take supplies so they could make room for those being unloaded from ships.

After we crossed the Naktong River, efforts of the army quartermaster to supply class II and class IV items to the 24th Division were conspicuous by their absence. It is true that great efforts were made to supply class I and class III items, but it only made the indifference to II and IV more apparent. Even now, if a unit is willing to send its trucks 230 miles to Ascom City, or 400 miles to Pusan, supplies can be obtained. But the price in broken springs and deadlined trucks is prohibitive.

As the drive passed Kaesong, Pyongyang, and points north, frantically worded requests to Pusan awaited the opening of a shaky rail system for delivery. On 10 November, the 24th Division had just completed a forty-mile withdrawal of its forward elements. The quartermaster section, then at Sukchon, received a placid notification of a boxcar of class II and class IV supplies—complete with car, engine and train numbers, and hour of departure from Pusan on 9 November—destined for "24th Division, Waegwan." Our rear echelons had cleared Waegwan nearly two months earlier.

A long time would be required to list the major deficiencies in our supply line. In the prosecution of a war the lack of a generator for a field range is not vital. But the result of poor meals is lowered morale—which *is* vital. When repeated supply failures occur, when indifference is shown, troops often become discouraged and indifferent. Supply failures at this level cost men their lives.

PART VIII

Security, Combat, Morale

1. Refugee Removal

Lt.Col. William Luk, Provost Marshal, 24th Infantry Division.
(Interview by Major Robert H. Fisher.)

In the late spring of 1951 the 24th Infantry Division had joined the 7th Infantry Division at Chunchon after a twenty-mile plunge into enemy territory in a double envelopment. Thousands of Chinese Communist troops and Korean noncombatants were trapped!

The day had been heavy with rain and I was wrestling my quarter-ton through the gumbo when the commander of the 24th Division (Maj.Gen. Blackshear M. Bryan) flagged me down. I was wet and tired as I sloshed through the mud to the general's jeep. The Old Man was serious.

"I want these people cleared from the division area," he said, pointing to the struggling humanity moving by, "and I believe your military police can spark the effort."

The refugees were not as numerous as they had been during the big bugout of December 1950; nevertheless, their presence created serious problems. The retreating enemy invariably left line-crossers to foment unrest among Korean noncombatants and to gain information. It was next to impossible to tell the difference between line-crossers and friendly noncombatants. The only answer was to round them all up and remove the whole mass from the battle area. The refugees were also a serious traffic obstacle on our newly won but inadequate road net. I knew from previous experience that the presence of noncombatants in a division's area caused a sharp increase in pilferage, assaults, and other crimes. As General Bryan's provost marshal I shared his concern.

The order "Clear them out!" was flashed to the CP of the 24th Division's military police company, and the roundup began. As I drove along the overtaxed main supply road I saw military policemen accumulating groups of white-garbed Koreans at check points, traffic-control posts, and defiles. Once their motion was halted, these Orientals assumed their normal resting position—a docile squat. They stayed at the temporary collecting points until empty supply trucks could be halted and used for rapid evacuation. As the day wore on, motorized military police patrols directed an increasing number of persons into the temporary collecting points, and the road leading to the division's refugee collecting point, twenty miles to the rear, filled with trucks.

At the division's refugee collecting point I saw our civil assistance officer (Colonel Hanson) busily supervising the screening of the refugees. Those who were in obvious need were given treatment by Korean medical personnel. The Korean National Police maintained order and Korean laborers were preparing steaming kettles of rice so that refugees could be fed before further evacuation.

As I retraced my route toward the main line of resistance, I saw all the military policemen who could be spared from other duties fanning out into villages along the road to evacuate those Koreans who were not on the move but whose presence in a house made it a likely refuge for the line-crosser. It was during this phase that the big roundup slowed its pace.

The removal of thousands of reluctant refugees and noncombatants from their villages and farms in the division's two hundred square miles of mountainous terrain was a task that could not be performed overnight, nor was it a job that could be done by the military police alone. The commander of the 24th MP Company (Major Carl Clark) reported that his men had just scratched the surface, and he estimated that even an around-the-clock operation would keep his company busy for weeks. As I looked over Clark's shoulder at the two gaunt refugees in the back seat of his jeep, I knew that everyone was in on the act, although this operation was just one of our many jobs. We needed help.

In my report at the briefing next morning, I told of our progress and asked for additional help. Our G2 (Colonel Cates) and Colonel Hanson, who had come up from his collecting point, volunteered their support. Messages were relayed to all division units, and the big roundup moved into high gear.

Infantry units on the MLR took into custody all refugees in their area and notified the military police. Artillerymen engaged in surveying gun positions sighted refugees in their transits and sent parties to round them up. Trucks from the MP company, augmented by empty supply trucks from units of the division, moved rapidly to evacuate the refugees from combat units to collecting points. Men of the 24th Reconnaissance Company, although tired from their recent combat mission, screened remote mountain villages and valleys, adding their take to the steadily mounting stream.

As the days passed, the combined efforts of all units of the division turned the tide, and the flow of refugees was reduced to a trickle. Finally, the number of refugees sighted and taken into custody became so small that military police handled the chore. However, it was a constant duty. Military police motor patrols and MP officers inspecting traffic posts were often seen to dismount to investigate signs of life observed near the MSR. Usually a refugee or a Chinese soldier who had been hiding since our junction with the 7th Division was flushed out.

More than a month elapsed from the time General Bryan gave his clear-them-out order until we were able to claim an almost complete vacuum between the front line and division rear. Any line-crosser would now have to run a 37-mile gantlet.

To insure that control of refugees was maintained, military policemen took frequent observation flights in helicopters and other light aircraft. When smoke was seen rising from a chimney or clothing observed hanging on a line, MP ground patrols were dispatched to investigate. The investigations would frequently turn up some strange doings. One liquor salesman's thriving business in native spirits, two miles behind the MLR, was brought to a halt. And in another raid a busy Korean *bordello* within walking distance of the front line was put out of business.

By such vigilance the noncombatant vacuum was maintained. The control guaranteed real security to the division from line-crossers, crime, and impeding traffic. Even in this seemingly simple task, teamwork helped to spell success in combat.

2.   Ordnance Company Under Attack

> Lt. Edgar E. Dunlap, Lt. William E. Peter, Sgt. Claude H. Lusk, Sgt. M. J. Thomasson, Sgt. Thomas E. Griffin, Sgt. George A Batson, Sgt. Eugene F. McCracken, Cpl. Elio Battaglia. (Interviews by Capt. Edward C. Williamson, 4th Historical Detachment.)

The 38th Ordnance Medium Maintenance Company came to Korea in July 1950. Its mission was to take the ordnance overflow from the 2d Infantry Division.

On 19 September 1950 the company was in the rice paddies alongside the Chongdo River, a half mile south of the small, mud-hut village of Songso-dong. The main supply road from Chongdo to Changnyong ran by the company's position.

Earlier in the summer there had been some fighting in this area. However, the village was still in good condition. The war was at a standstill on 19 September. As a result of recent rain, the Chongdo River now contained some water, and the men of the company built a dam on the stream so they could bathe.

An experienced company commander (Capt. Francis P. Smith) had been replaced a week before by Lt. Chris Beaber. Smith had spent nineteen months in Korea before it was overrun by the Communists. He had not allowed Korean civilians into his company area because he thought most Koreans would steal and because he was fearful of guerrilla attacks. However, the attitude of the villagers of Songso-dong was friendly, and they sold the soldiers pigs and chickens.

On the afternoon of the 19th it was planned to move the company to a new location. The men loaded their trucks, policed the area, and threw all their trash into the foxholes. At the last minute the move was postponed, however, since an artillery battalion and a tank battalion had beaten the ordnance company to its new location.

While camp was being broken some 30 adult Koreans and 60 to 70 children gathered on the rice-paddy dikes near the river. Normally the guards would have ordered the civilians away, but in the company's preoccupation with its move, the Koreans were not disturbed.

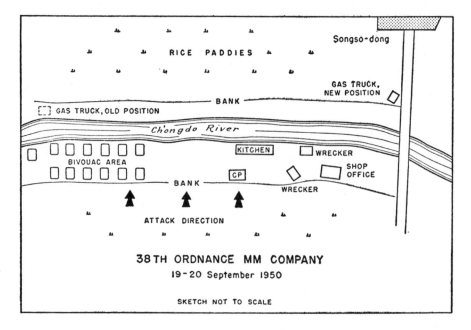

When it became apparent that the company would not move that day, preparations were made to settle down until a new reconnaissance could be made. The trucks were partially unloaded and the camp routine reestablished. No one took the precaution of cleaning out the foxholes or remounting the caliber .30 machine guns.

After unloading, three sergeants went down to the company pool to bathe. They noticed a Korean civilian who just sat on the bank and scowled at them.

Sgt. Burt Davis told the others: "I had a run-in with two Koreans on the dike an hour ago. I told them to shove off and they talked back. This made me mad, but I thought that if I harmed them I'd get into trouble."

All the men agreed that these actions by the Koreans were unusual.

The 135 officers and men of the 38th were armed with 7 truck-mounted, caliber .50 machine guns, 3 caliber .30 machine guns, 3 submachine guns, 3 bazookas, 45 carbines, and 76 pistols. The company's alert plan called for sounding the truck sirens in case of emergency. The men were to take their posts by sections. On the south and east sides would be headquarters, supply, service, and recovery sections. These 53 men were armed mostly with pistols. The carbines were primarily in the automotive section (48 men), and this section was responsible for the north and west sides of camp.

That evening a camp guard, consisting of 4 stationary and 2 roving sentries, was formed. The 800-yard rectangular company perimeter had a guard at each corner. Darkness fell at 2000 and it looked like rain. The company did not have electric lights, and the men customarily turned in early. About two thirds of the company slept in lean-tos, the remainder in the trucks.

A sergeant returned from a routine trip at 0030, drove into the bivouac area, and halted briefly with his jeep lights on. At 0100 the guard was changed. Along the main supply road there was an unusual quiet, as the South Korean National Police did not relay their usual messages along their chain of grass-hut posts. Only the sound of a howling dog disturbed the quiet of the night.

Shortly before 0200, a party of 35 or 40 guerrillas reached the rice paddies and began crawling toward the ordnance company. Unnoticed by the two guards stationed to the south of the company, they quietly reached the four-foot bank which bounded the company area. First realization of the attack came with the thud of grenades falling in the company area.

It seemed to the company's men that guns were firing all over the place. Bullets hit the trucks and rocks and ricocheted throughout the area. Men tumbled out of their trucks and lean-tos to find the guerrillas already on top of the south bank and some moving into the company position. The two guards were forced from their positions along the south bank, but fortunately were able to withdraw without being hit.

The enemy action was planned in detail and skillfully executed. The guerrillas centered their attack on the company's command post and the previous location of the gasoline truck. Because of the expected move, the 750-gallon gasoline truck and other POL supplies had been shifted closer to the MSR. A thermite grenade thrown into the old POL area thus did no damage.

A grenade or a tracer hit one truck and set it afire. This brightly illuminated the company area, and the men had neither cover nor holes in which to hide. The two trucks nearest the blaze caught fire, but were driven away while the fires were extinguished by Sergeant Ellis and Sgt. Paul Easlom. A machine-shop truck burned fiercely after a grenade was dropped into its gas tank. Making the best of an extremely bad situation, many of the men crawled under their trucks while others dispersed themselves behind the river dike to the north of the company position.

A light tank (M24) was inside the company perimeter for repairs, and was combat-loaded when the attack occurred. It could fire from its fixed position. The crew crawled into the tank and remained buttoned up without taking any part in the engagement.

Few of the ordnance company's men fired back at the enemy. Some were so poorly situated they could not fire without endangering their comrades. Some were scared. Others just didn't think of the importance of defending themselves. The entire company might have been overrun had not Sgt. Eugene McCracken taken a hand.

McCracken, dressed only in underwear, was under his wrecker. He helped Lt. Henry J. Moore, who was wounded, and then began to look around. The attack had now been under way for about five minutes, and McCracken suddenly realized that all the fire was incoming. He jumped on his wrecker and attempted to fire the caliber .50 machine gun mounted on it. The gun wouldn't fire.

McCracken could see ten or twelve guerrillas running up and down the bank throwing grenades while three others sat on the bank behind his wrecker and fired small arms. Finally he discovered that the headspace of the machine-gun barrel had not been correctly adjusted, and he re-adjusted it. The gun worked perfectly and he fired a burst at the three enemy on the bank. These three disappeared and McCracken continued to search the area with fire. Lieutenant Beaber came to the wrecker and shouted, "Can you see any more?" Just then the guerrillas cut loose with another burst of small-arms fire. It missed McCracken but damaged his wrecker. One bullet hit just in front of him, and he let loose some choice profanity. Several men under the wrecker thought he had been wounded, and one shouted, "Mac, are you hit?"

"No," he replied, "but they're sure trying!"

Another man who fired at the enemy was PFC Daniel LeGaspi, who used his caliber .25 pistol. LeGaspi was wounded during the action by an enemy grenade. Sgt. Guy W. Miller managed to set a second caliber .50 machine gun into action, but it jammed after only a few rounds.

The attack subsided after fifteen minutes. A lull followed during which the company moved into a close perimeter defense and section leaders organized their areas. But no more automatic weapons were put in order. McCracken put another box of ammunition (250 rounds) on his gun and then climbed down to wrap up in a blanket for a few minutes.

After five minutes the men of the company heard a whistle blow. Everyone hoped this was a signal to withdraw, but instead it proved to be the beginning of a second assault. Twelve to fifteen guerrillas charged down the bank firing small arms and throwing grenades. Eight to ten grenades exploded in the company area, one six feet from McCracken's wrecker. He again opened with his machine gun and fired a second box of ammunition. His gun suddenly stopped firing and he thought it had jammed. Checking it, he looked in the ammunition box to find it was empty. He put a fresh box on the gun, reloaded, and continued firing, spraying up and down the area.

About ten minutes after the second assault started, the enemy firing suddenly ceased. It was now close to 0230. The second assault had less intensity than the first. Damage was confined mostly to the vehicles. The guerrillas now began to withdraw, setting up a machine gun to cover their movement. Fire from this machine gun came high into the ordnance company area, and McCracken spotted the gun's muzzle blast. Turning his weapon on the flash, he silenced the enemy gun.

Near the end of the second assault a messenger left the company area to get help. Within a few minutes he returned with a patrol from the 622d Military Police Company, stationed in Chongdo. At about 0300 another squad of MPs also arrived, but did not immediately pursue the enemy since it was still dark and their route of withdrawal was not well defined.

In the meantime, the commanding officer of the 622d MP Company made contact with the local police. He learned that the police had been attacked before the assault on the ordnance company. A platoon of 25 to 30 policemen arrived shortly before dawn, went into diamond formation, and headed for an apple orchard where the guerrillas were last seen. Later they sent back for a caliber .50 machine gun, but the guerrillas managed to escape. After dawn the body of a North Korean officer was found, and his papers indicated he was the leader of the guerrilla force. No other dead were found. Seven guerrillas were believed to have been wounded but evacuated.

In the ordnance company, 1 man was killed and 5 wounded. In addition the company lost 3 2-½-ton trucks (one a machine-shop truck and another containing an L maintenance set), 1 quarter-ton truck, 3 trailers, and 26 cylinders of oxygen and acetylene. Several vehicles were partially burned or otherwise damaged.

The company made its move to another area at 1100 on 20 September. The men agreed that in the future no one would sleep in a truck and no one would undress on going to sleep.

3. Attacks Unwelcome

Capt. Frank D. Secan, 304th Signal Operation Battalion

One would expect that duty with an isolated radio-relay team would be extremely unpopular. I hear many persons express that idea. I also hear that relay men become careless soldiers and signal operators, that they have little discipline, and that they allow themselves to go unshaven and dirty.

There is no question about isolation, or rude living conditions. Yet the men of my relay platoon volunteered for such duty. I believe the disadvantages of this type of service can be largely overcome, and men kept clean, disciplined, and happy, if the right type of NCO is placed in charge of each team.

Isolation is a matter of degree. Relay teams are not completely cut off from the world; they have the monitor channel with which they can keep abreast of things. By this channel they can request supplies and call for help in emergency. Still, the isolation calls for much resourcefulness and men have to take care of themselves. This was especially true when we were in northern Korea.

In November 1950 I sent a team to establish a relay some twenty-five miles from the nearest military unit. The team was commanded by Sergeant First Class Rhodemeyer, an especially self-reliant soldier. Rhodemeyer's team consisted of 12 to 15 signal men, 10 ROK soldiers, and a Japanese interpreter. In addition to their individual weapons the team had two caliber .30 machine guns and a few grenades. They carefully established a perimeter defense with four or five guard posts, and set trip flares in all paths leading to the position.

One night a trip flare went off, and the men knew they were about to be attacked. The raiding party consisted of about fifty enemy with small arms. The attack was repulsed without casualties or damage to equipment. The next night a second attack was made. Again Rhodemeyer and his men were ready, and repelled the guerrillas without difficulty.

Following the second attack, Sergeant Rhodemeyer left a minimum operating and guard force at the radio site, took 5 signal men, 10 ROKs, and the Japanese interpreter and led his party to a nearby village. The men entered the settlement at gun point, but no resistance was offered. They carefully searched each building and found some sixty weapons and a good deal of ammunition. All this matériel was confiscated and destroyed. No prisoners or hostages were taken, but Rhodemeyer let it be well understood that there had better be no more attacks on the relay position.

The relay station stayed at the same position for ten days after this incident. The entire area remained quiet.

4. Fighting Medics

Lt. John Atkins, Lt. Fred O. Blair, Lt. David C. Copell, and Sgt. Vincenzo DiSanto, Medical Company, 21st Infantry. (Interviews by Lt. Martin Blumenson, 3d Historical Detachment.)

The juncture at Sinpori in May 1951, of the 24th Infantry Division, attacking north from Kapyong, and the 7th Infantry Division, attacking north from Chunchon, bypassed a good many enemy groups. On the 26th of that month the Medical Company, 21st Infantry (24th Infantry Division), set up its tents for the night about three hundred yards from the regimental command post and about the same distance from the position of Battery A, 213th Armored Field Artillery Battalion. The camp site was on the side of a hill in a narrow strip between the place where the steep slope ended and, continuing below it, the terraced rice paddies began. A little southeast of the company position a small stream came down through a defile in the hill mass.

The company had a permanent guard force of twenty men and, according to its SOP, set up four guard posts. Enemy troops were known to be somewhere close by, so two men were placed on each post.

In the early hours of the 27th, some remnants of the enemy moved down along the small stream and through the defile, obviously trying to find their way back to their own lines.

At about 0200, the foremost of the enemy soldiers ran into the medical company's guards along the stream bank. One guard challenged the first Chinese soldier he heard or saw, and got a volley of concussion grenades for his trouble. These explosions awakened the rest of the company. Some were sleeping in tents, some on cots or stretchers, and some in trucks. The first reaction of everyone aboveground was to get down. The second was to get dressed before going out in the mud and rain to meet the enemy.

The 5 officers and 63 medics were inadequately armed for combat. In fact, only a few had ammunition. Sgt. Vincenzo DiSanto had a little in the supply truck and put out the first 150 rounds to three guards who came asking for some. This left him with 250 rounds of carbine ammunition and 8 grenades. DiSanto decided to leave his truck and pass out the ammunition to those who needed it. He found that a firing line had already been built up.

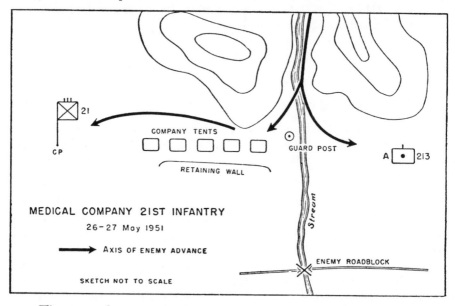

The ground was such that the only cover was behind a retaining wall a few yards west of the company. This put the company's tents and vehicles right between the firing line and the enemy. In a few minutes DiSanto distributed his small supply of ammunition. He kept one grenade for himself to supplement his pistol.

The enemy was not organized. One group moved down the stream bed to the road and set up a roadblock. Others fanned out and ran into Battery A and the medical company. In the confusion, our troops were fearful of hitting one another.

As Lt. John Atkins visited a post near the stream he heard the guard challenge, yelling, "Who are you?"

"ROK soldiers," the reply came, so Atkins shouted to the guard, "Hold your fire!" He quickly changed his mind when the "ROK soldiers" opened with burp guns.

Several enemy soldiers got into the company area and threw grenades. The grenades were ineffective and led only to the throwers' being killed. The cooks in their white clothing seemed to attract the attention of the enemy more than anyone else. In the shooting, enough rounds were fired by both sides to riddle all the company tents.

The firing line of the medical company was never seriously threatened. The chief effect of its fire seems to have been to deflect the enemy on the medical company's side of the stream into the line of the regimental command post on the left of the company area. A runner sent over to regiment to report the fight found that the command post was fighting too.

Sporadic fire continued until daylight. The company reorganized at dawn. A nose count showed 58 Chinese prisoners, and 23 enemy dead in and around the company position. Casualties for the company were 1 killed and 10 wounded, and the regimental chaplain (Father Francis X. Coppens) was killed in the company area.

Company F and G, 5th Infantry, came on the scene shortly after daybreak and, accompanied by two self-propelled guns, counterattacked. Several men of the medical company joined this force. A hundred prisoners were soon taken, and the prisoner bag for the 5th Infantry and the 21st Infantry during that day was 2,900.

The medical company continued to work as such during the fire fight. Lt. (j.g.) Edward Green, USNR (the acting regimental surgeon[1]) was wounded on the firing line. He went to the first-aid tent with two other wounded. There he treated these men and remained to treat others as they were brought in. An officer-patient, awaiting evacuation, was wounded as he lay on a stretcher.

The Chinese were more surprised than the men of the medical company. Intent on escaping encirclement, they were unable to launch an organized assault. Had they been able to do so, they would certainly have overrun the lightly armed troops. Nevertheless, the determination of the medical company to resist the assault helped prevent the enemy's escape.

By 0830 the company was extremely cocky. They were "fighting medics," and wanted to know "Who in hell says the medics can't fight?"

5. Task Force Baker

Lt.Col. Barton O. Baker, Ordnance Officer, 25th Infantry Division

Every service unit needs to be organized so that it can shift rapidly from its service mission to a security mission and, if necessary, to

---

[1] During this period the Army borrowed five hundred Naval Reserve physicians, some of whom saw active service in Korea. Whenever the Navy officer was the senior officer in a unit, he commanded it.

a combat mission. To reach this standard, training, discipline, and a good SOP are necessary. To show how effective a service unit can be in a security role, let me tell you about Task Force Baker.

In early September 1950, a small Signal Corps VHF detachment was stationed on a hilltop about five miles from the CP of the 25th Infantry Division and about twelve miles behind the infantry line. This party consisted of 5 U.S. soldiers and 3 or 4 South Koreans attached for labor and security. The night of 3 September was rainy and miserable, and all the men in the detachment crawled into their squad tent. No guard was posted.

At 2200 a party of guerrillas or infiltrators—it was not established which—from the North Korean Army stealthily approached the detachment and killed them all with small arms and grenades. The newspapers condemned this action as an inhumane massacre, but from a professional standpoint it could be called negligence—or even suicide!

The next morning (4 September) a CID agent and a reporter started toward the VHF site. Part way up the hill they were wounded by grenades. Though injured, these men returned and their wounds were treated at the nearby 8063d MASH in Changwon, at the base of the hill where the action had taken place. It was obvious the enemy had not withdrawn from the vicinity of the VHF station.

Later that day, I was driving through Changwon and stopped briefly at the MASH. Considerable excitement existed as the result of the two incidents nearby, and the hospital officers pointed out to me that mortar fire was falling on the hillside near the hospital. The enemy obviously was well armed, but what he was firing at I don't know. While I was talking, one of the hospital orderlies came in carrying a spent bullet that had just pierced his tent.

The location of a hospital, ammunition dump, railroad, and division main supply road made it vital that this area be protected. I phoned the division CP and reported the situation to the commanding general (Maj. Gen. William B. Kean). When General Kean asked for my recommendation, I suggested that since it was already 1700, we could do little now except post security. I told him 150 men should be adequate. The general asked where I proposed to get the men. I replied that I could use the men from my 725th Ordnance Company. He agreed, and said the division reconnaissance company would come as soon as it was available, and other units also would be dispatched. The force was designated Task Force Baker, and I was to command until the recon company jumped off against the enemy, at which time its commander (Capt. Charles Torman) would take over.

Immediately after talking to General Kean, I called the ordnance company and told the commander (Capt. Ira Snyder) to bring 3 officers and 150 men to my CP location in Changwon. These men arrived in sixty minutes, with their individual weapons, three light machine guns, a rocket launcher, and four radios. The group was already divided into three platoons, each with an officer.

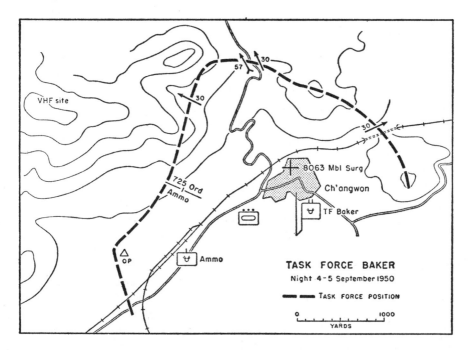

I had already planned my dispositions, and in the next forty-five minutes the platoons were spread in a semicircular perimeter extending from the ammunition dump on the west to a hill east of the hospital. The two most critical points in the area were given particular attention. I ordered a machine gun placed to fire northwest in a draw that was the easiest and most likely approach. At the point where our perimeter crossed an important north-south road I directed that another machine gun be posted, reinforced by the rocket launcher, and that an officer be there at all times. Radio communication from my CP to each of these platoons was established.

As these dispositions were being made, I went to the hospital and took charge of an engineer platoon that was indifferently providing the close-in security. I informed the engineer lieutenant of the formation of the task force, and directed him to tighten up his defense of the hospital.

Next, I visited the ammunition supply point and told the commander of the ammunition company of the situation. I directed him to form a security screen extending from the left flank of the ordnance position to well beyond his own installation. I also ordered him to place an observation post in a draw on his left flank. After this, I tested communications.

During the night an artillery officer called me and said he couldn't get any ammunition. I asked why. He replied, "They just won't issue it." I went to the ASP.

As I approached the railroad station that served as a CP, I met no guards but found waiting ammunition trucks lined up bumper to bumper. In the CP building I found the commander and all his men. This officer was scared, and his attitude had infected his troops. Although fifty carloads of ammunition sat in the marshaling yards, the commander would not allow any lights in the area and no identification or loading could take place. Under my direction the captain sent out the security force I had ordered earlier, and then I started him issuing ammunition. We had to take some risks, since we needed the ammunition.

During the night a tank platoon joined our task force. I split this and put half of the tanks in bivouac near the hospital and the others near the ammunition company. Toward morning we were further reinforced by a battalion of ROK marines who arrived from the Chinhae area.

We had one incident during the night. I had been informed that a civil-affairs detachment and some engineers were working north of us, and that they had not returned to the division area. Early in the evening a number of these people were challenged, and then came through our roadblock. We assumed all had returned. Later in the night a jeep came along the road but did not halt when challenged. The roadblock officer was a former infantryman, and he fired toward the jeep with his M1 as it came on. As the jeep sped by he grabbed two of the passengers and hauled them out. The jeep soon halted, and we learned he had wounded the local chief of police. I ordered him taken to the hospital, but he died from loss of blood on the way.

The following morning the division's reconnaissance company arrived and, as agreed, Captain Torman took charge. The division's ordnance company, the ammunition company, and the engineer detachment held fast while the tanks encircled the enemy and the recon company and the ROK marines moved into the area on foot. At the location of the VHF station the enemy put up strong resistance, using machine guns and mortars. Two American soldiers were killed, but I don't know the casualties among the ROKs. Seventeen guerrillas were captured or killed, including three women. The rest just melted away.

Had the reconnaissance company not arrived when it did, the 725th Ordnance Company would have swept the area. Still, the ordnance company's importance in providing security for the hospital, the ASP, and the MSR should not be underestimated. It maintained the security until an adequate offensive force arrived. In so doing, the company showed that well-trained technical troops can be of decisive importance during critical periods.

6. Secondary Mission

Capt. Robert L. Strouse, 65th Engineer Combat Battalion

During the Naktong perimeter days, the 65th Engineer Combat Battalion (25th Infantry Division) was split among three infantry regiments. Each regiment operated as a separate combat team. Occasionally they used the engineers as infantry—not only in defensive operations, but also in limited objective attacks undertaken as part of the general defense.

Near Chungam-ni, Company E, 35th Infantry, failed to take a hilltop after three successive attacks. The crest was an isolated strongpoint in the enemy line, and was strongly defended. On 14 September 1950, the regimental commander ordered Company B, 65th Engineer Battalion, to make a supported attack and capture the objective. Only two hours were given the company to prepare for this operation.

In addition to weapons organic to a combat engineer company, Company B's personnel had 2 caliber .30 heavy machine guns and 3 60-mm mortars. These were a special issue to the engineers in view of their frequent commitment as infantry. Company B did not use its mortars but relied on the infantry for this supporting fire.

The attack lasted only thirty minutes, and the objective was taken. The value of the men can be seen in 2 awards of the Distinguished Service Cross (one posthumous), 3 of the Silver Star, and 10 of the Bronze Star. Casualties were heavy, the company suffering 14 killed and 21 wounded, including an officer killed and another wounded. The 3d Platoon suffered particularly, having its platoon sergeant wounded, 2 squad leaders killed and another wounded, and 3 assistant squad leaders wounded.

The loss of leaders was particularly felt when the company returned to its primary engineer role. It meant a complete reorganization and training of NCO specialists. The 3d Platoon had only 13 men left after the attack, and could not carry out a platoon task until it received replacements five or six weeks later.

7. Combat Comes Suddenly

Lt. Norman R. Rosen, 10th Engineer Combat Battalion

Company D, 10th Engineer Combat Battalion (3d Infantry Division), landed at Wonsan on 20 November 1950—one of the last units of the division to arrive. It spent its first week ashore doing road maintenance work near the port, and was then detached from the 3d Division and ordered to report to X Corps headquarters, at Hamhung. I was in charge of the advance party.

On arrival at X Corps headquarters on the afternoon of the 27th, I was briefed on our future operation by the executive officer of the 8224th Engineer Construction Group and the S3 of the 185th Engineer Combat Battalion. Company D was attached to the 185th and ordered to proceed immediately to Hagaru-ri at the base of Changjin Reservoir. There our mission was to build a forward command post for X Corps. I was given the location of the proposed CP and told that a platoon of the 4th Signal Battalion was already on the ground to install communications. Nothing was mentioned in the briefing about the tactical situation, so I raised the question.

"Everything is perfectly secure," the executive officer replied. "I was up there yesterday in my jeep. The marines drive up and down the roads with their headlights on."

The company arrived at Hamhung by motor convoy at 1500. The men had all their equipment except the bulldozer. I passed on the information I had received to the company commander (Capt. Philip A. Kulbes), we refueled our vehicles, and started off on the last fifty miles of our trip.

At Sangtong-ni the convoy was delayed six hours by traffic control on a one-way mountain pass. While we sat along the road we listened to a battery of Marine artillery firing at a target over the first mountain. At that point I began to wonder how secure things really were.

At 0200 we arrived at our bivouac location south of Hagaru-ri. We knew no more of our situation than we had gotten in Hamhung, so we posted security and bedded down.

To us the most pressing problem was the weather. Company D had been in Korea only a week and was not acclimated. In one day's drive of 150 miles we had experienced a temperature drop of from 20 degrees above zero to 15 below zero. In spite of our heavy winter clothing we were miserably cold. We'd have been concerned with more than the cold had we known the tactical situation. Five of our trucks with 1 officer and 20 men did not arrive. These vehicles had engine trouble, and before they could catch up, the road from Hamhung was closed by the enemy.

At 0900 we roused the company. It was a slow start and the cooks rolled out with the rest. While we were waiting for breakfast a Korean civilian came into our area and told us the enemy was on the road behind us. We were impressed by this civilian's persistence, so we sent a patrol to investigate.

At this time a Marine Corps officer and his driver walked into our bivouac and informed us they had driven into an enemy roadblock in a defile only a mile south of our bivouac. They had to abandon their vehicle to escape. The driver was slightly wounded and both were wet and cold.

Captain Kulbes and I quickly organized a platoon-sized patrol and moved down the road. We met heavy fire from dug-in enemy. Soon we received word that the marines were sending a force to deal with the enemy, so we returned to our company position. Security was maintained and the men began to dig foxholes. Breakfast was served to small groups.

At 1400 the G2 of the 1st Marine Division arrived at our CP. By this time we had finished our holes and were hauling materials for the construction for the corps forward CP. This may have seemed a little amusing to the Marine major, as the tactical situation was not what we believed it to be. He told us Hagaru-ri was surrounded; that enemy heavy attacks were expected that night; that the Marine lines were thin; and that we should occupy a portion of their perimeter. The position he pointed out on the map was only three hundred yards from where we were, but it was a ridge and almost three hundred feet straight up. We were told there were prepared positions to occupy and that we would tie in on our left with a platoon of the 4th Signal Battalion and would anchor our right on the steep slope which overlooked a Marine Corps roadblock.

There was never a question raised about postponing our mission, or of coming under Marine control. Still, we didn't realize the gravity of our situation and did not move immediately to our new position. Instead, we moved all our vehicles and equipment to a Marine equipment park in their perimeter. We left our tents and stoves in position at the bivouac for future use.

Company D at this time had 3 officers, 1 warrant officer, and 77 enlisted men. In addition, we had 90 men from KATUSA integrated into the squads. Actually we had more acquaintance with Koreans than most American soldiers had. Before going to Korea our division had been levied several times for replacements. The Koreans had joined us in Japan two months before we embarked. Many of the Americans had arrived only days before we sailed.

In addition to individual weapons, our unit had as combat equipment 4 caliber .50 machine guns, 5 caliber .30 machine guns, and 6 3.5-inch rocket launchers. We had no mortars or recoilless weapons. We issued every man three units of fire (288 rounds per M1 rifle), two grenades, and all the machine-gun and rocket ammunition we could load on him.

The weight of the ammunition and weapons made our march up the steep slope very slow. It was late when we started, and it was dark when we arrived.

The ridge on which we organized fell off sharply on all sides except our left. There were lots of holes in the ground, but we found nothing that could be called an organized position. In the dark we could not organize a final protective line, so we did the best we could. The 1st Platoon (SFC Leonard J. Best) was on the right and some fifty feet below the crest. The 2d Platoon (Lt. George E. Smith) was in the center. I had the 3d Platoon on the left. Headquarters Platoon (WO Richard J. Dalke) faced to the rear. Thus our company formed a small perimeter. The company commander (Captain Kulbes) and a Marine Corps liaison officer were in the center of it.

Communications were poor. We had our full allowance of radios, but the SCR-536 sets did not work in this country. Each platoon had its SCR-300, and these happened to be on the same channel as those of the Marine Corps. My own set would not make contact with the company commander, but I did have good contact with a Marine officer who seemed to know the score. It wasn't until later that I learned the marine was our own liaison officer, and that he occupied the hole next to Captain Kulbes.

After I got my squads assigned to their positions I went out on our left flank to tie in with the Signal Corps platoon. Instead of finding Americans, I located a KATUSA labor platoon commanded by an American captain and three or four U.S. soldiers. I made arrangements to coordinate our fire with theirs, and returned.

Our company was in position by 2030. At about 2200 we began to hear firing near our position. Thirty minutes later it was evident that the enemy had cut through the KATUSA platoon on our left and was coming at us from both the left and rear (east and north). My platoon was the first in our company to become closely engaged, and with our flank in the air it was necessary for us to reface the squads, under fire, some ninety degrees. My men were not trained for this type of maneuver. In this change of front I lost most of my left squad.

We held fast during the night, although the 3d Platoon, and the 2d Platoon behind it, had to withdraw 250 yards. The company ended up with all four platoons in a tight knot on the crest of the hill by 0300. The closeness of this position was bad for us when we began to receive heavy concentrations of white phosphorus shells.

The enemy executed a great number of banzai-type attacks on our positions. The American engineers countered this with everything they had. They fired most of their 288 rounds of M1 ammunition, most of the machine-gun ammunition, and at times even fired the 3.5-inch rockets point-blank at human targets. We would stop an attack, things would slow down for a short time, then the enemy leader would blow a whistle and another twenty-five or thirty would rush us. In the morning we learned these were Chinese Communists—our first information that another nation had entered the conflict.

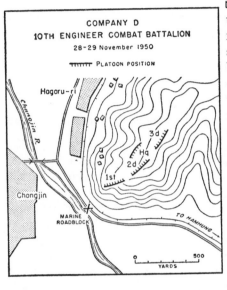

COMPANY D
10TH ENGINEER COMBAT BATTALION
28-29 November 1950

ттттт PLATOON POSITION

Hagaru-ri

Changjin R.

3d

Hq

2d

1st

Chongjin

MARINE ROADBLOCK

TO HAMHUNG

0   500
YARDS

While our Americans did well, the KATUSA soldiers did not measure up to the situation. We had difficulty communicating with them, and under the stress of battle they became demoralized. The most incomprehensible thing about them was that when we ran low on ammunition we asked the KATUSA soldiers if they had any, and they replied negatively. Weeks later we discovered that most of them had not fired their ammunition this night, but continued to carry it.

At the beginning of our fight we had a great deal of difficulty with our weapons because they were cold and fired sluggishly. We had gone into action so unexpectedly it had not occurred to us to clean the oil off our weapons. Several of our men abandoned their own weapons and took those of the enemy dead who littered the ground around their foxholes. The enemy, too, had U.S. weapons—mostly Thompson submachine guns and carbines.

During the night our Marine Corps liaison officer was killed, but not before he radioed division headquarters of the seriousness of our situation. We were ordered to hold the position at all costs. No help was at hand and it was almost dawn before a composite force of a hundred Marine Corps rear-echelon personnel reached our position. At 0900 we received an air strike to our immediate front, and it gave us a great deal of help. At about noon of the 29th we were relieved from our position on the ridge and moved to another sector of the perimeter.

Our losses for the night were almost 50 per cent of our total force. Casualties among Americans were 2 officers slightly wounded, 23 men wounded, 10 men killed, 9 missing. Among the KATUSA personnel, 50 were killed, wounded, or missing. Our losses were more serious, considering the key personnel lost to the company. The killed included the supply sergeant, two cooks, and two radio men. The wounded included the first sergeant, a platoon sergeant, an assistant platoon sergeant, a radio operator, and two cooks. The missing included a platoon sergeant and two squad leaders.

The marines tended to be critical of our company for its operations of the night—in spite of our holding the position. They estimated that we had been hit by an enemy battalion of 1,000, and we counted more than 400 bodies in front of our positions when daylight came. No account was taken of our inexperience, or that we were thrust into a combat role suddenly—without orientation or support. Months passed before the marines gave us recognition for even having been in their perimeter.

8. Efficiency Through Morale

Lt.Col. John E. Harbert, 314th Ordnance Ammunition Group

All battalion and company commanders of the 314th Ordnance Ammunition Group had a great problem of morale. A majority of the ammunition supply points were located within the division zones, manned primarily by troops who arrived in Korea poorly trained and jittery. Most of the ammunition personnel were selected from castoffs of units in Japan. The courts-martial and disciplinary rates were high.

The morale situation was further complicated by the rotation and recognition systems, which placed emphasis on unit assignment and not on geographic location, service, or hazard. Thus, service and supply personnel in a combat division were often located a hundred miles behind our ASPs; yet they received twice as many rotation points. Division service troops usually got more rest and had other advantages.

I felt that morale was the key to getting ammunition forward. I believed and proved that men who feel their work is important will produce under any conditions.

When I took command in mid-1951, I began working on morale from three directions. First, I demanded the highest standards of soldiering. Colors were brought into the field. Retreat formations were held weekly, formal security guard mounts practiced, cleanliness and neatness maintained at garrison level, and military courtesy required. I was nicknamed "Hard John" for my policies and, in fact, I encouraged the nickname. However, the men loved the soldiering and responded favorably. The neat clothing, proper uniform, and ceremonies gave the men a pride in themselves and in their units. The proof is in the result: 158,000 tons of ammunition delivered to the front in 60 days. This is a peak never before reached by any like group.

My second principle was to keep the men informed. The 314th Group developed a daily bulletin which was designed to appeal to the men. It told the history, tradition, and accomplishments of the Ordnance Corps. It also told in personal terms what their work was accomplishing in Eighth Army, and it stressed the slogan: "It is the piece of ordnance that kills the enemy." I had enlisted personnel from distant ASPs brought regularly to group headquarters for a three-day rest—plus a briefing on "the big picture" and the way their unit was helping.

The third approach was through recognition and reward. It is very well to recognize the combat soldier for his contribution, but this does not mean that recognition should be withheld from service troops. Divisional service troops share their division's accomplishments. Nondivisional service troops cannot wear the Indianhead, or say they belong to the Wolfhounds, or the Buffalos. Yet, for all of this, some of the ammunition service units have more dangerous jobs and even draw hazard pay. They disarm bombs and go into disputed territory on demolition work. On withdrawals from North Korea during the winter of 1950-51, the ammunition troops of the 314th Group shared the bitter rear-guard action. Often they escaped encirclement by walking over the Korean hills with infantry units. At other times they held positions in the line.

To overcome this lack of recognition, the 314th made "Andy Ammo" its official emblem. Andy Ammo is the man who doesn't question, but humps ammunition day and night. We plastered pictures of Andy Ammo at every ASP. We used his figure for a road marker, and many of our ASPs were called Andy Ammo by their "customers." A song was written about Andy, and our men sang it. Andy Ammo was a going tradition before I joined the 314th, but I encouraged his fame. He is now a legend and an inspiration to ammunition service troops who display the will to serve beyond the call of duty.

Recognition of our men on the rotation policy came partially as the result of a letter I wrote to the commanding general of Eighth Army. We finally received rotation points equal to those given divisional personnel when we operated in a division's zone. This made a favorable impression on the men. It was well deserved.

I gave recognition to individuals who worked hard, regardless of race. I recommended for promotion to lieutenant colonel a Negro officer who was one of my best field-grade officers. I brought Negro officers and men into the group headquarters on a merit basis. Each man was judged on his ability—an important consideration when more than 90 per cent of my troops were Negroes.

I remained with the 314th Ordnance Group only four months but I proved again that leadership is as important in ordnance units as it is in the infantry. The techniques are the same, yet they are often more difficult to apply when your men are spread over greater distances. Leadership and morale, efficiency and production, soldiering and recognition—all are tied together. They should never be overlooked in a service unit. These principles pay off in victory.

PART IX

Short Bits

1. Unification

Michael Slauta, Special Observer for The Quartermaster General. (From a speech, 16 November 1950.)

On the working level in the combat zone there are no unification problems. If two units from different services are together in an area for a time, you soon find they are wearing the same uniform—the uniform that was available in quantity sufficient to supply all. That goes for food and all other supplies. Eventually there will be standardization for all items and all forces in Korea, with perhaps the exception of the rum ration which the British demand.

2. How to Get Lit Up

Lt.Col. Olin T. Hinkey, Finance Officer, 3d Infantry Division

I consider that light and power were my major problem in Korea. It was solved by the Army custom of swapping some beer and whiskey to an engineer unit for a surplus generator. Repairs were made on the same basis. Without that generator normal operations could not have been maintained.

3. Speedy Refueling

Capt. Douglas O. Kennedy, 425th Traffic Regulating Group. (Interview by Capt. B. C. Mossman, 6th Historical Detachment.)

On 22 March 1951 the 425th Traffic Regulating Group was directed to handle a refueling and regulating point for elements of the

187th Airborne RCT moving north by land. To handle the refueling, we placed signs to indicate the interval between trucks when they halted. Five-gallon gas cans were stored at intervals alongside the road and an entire serial of fifteen trucks could be refueled at once. Each serial was under way within five minutes. In thirteen hours five hundred trucks were refueled.

4. What's the Score?

Capt. George R. Spreng, Korean Military Advisory Group

Korean engineers were the finest of the ROK troops. They had higher educational standards than the Army in general, and the selection was careful. Almost all of the enlisted and NCO personnel had some formal education. Like the American soldier, they asked many questions and worked best when they were told the exact situation. They needed a great deal of supervision, but they did well when given good leadership.

5. Loading in Flight

Capt. Homer W. Johnston, 8192d Helicopter Unit. (Interview by Lt. John Mewha, 8th Historical Detachment.)

On 14 August 1951 Capt. Homer W. Johnston, 8192d Helicopter Unit, received a message to evacuate two wounded men from the high ground east of the Punchbowl. It took him twenty minutes to fly from the 8224th Mobile Army Surgical Hospital to the French sector. As he circled the designated landing area, Captain Johnston noted that the area was small and slanted. He hovered down to test it.

The landing area was a pronounced slope that would cause the helicopter either to slip down the hill or topple over. To keep the copter upright, Captain Johnson kept the power on and tipped the craft slightly toward the crest. He was actually semi-flying while the patients were strapped on the carrying platforms.

As soon as the wounded men were ready, Johnston raised the helicopter vertically, scraping the right bunker as he did so. He dropped down the reverse slope until his craft reached the necessary climbing speed. Then he returned to the hospital.

6. VHF Ship to Shore

Lt. Robert T. O'Brien, 7th Signal Company

When the 7th Infantry Division's turn came to be evacuated from the Hungnam area, we began to set up special communications to expedite the movement. From others we learned that we could use AN/TRC-3 (very high frequency) radio sets for ship-to-shore communication. On the ship that was to carry the division's CP we set up an AN/TRC-3, but instead of using the directional antenna we substituted a whip antenna. This was necessary to keep our antennas aligned as the ship shifted with wind and tide. The expedient could only have worked over short distances, but it was satisfactory here.

7. Rescuing Wounded by Tank

Army Field Forces Training Bulletin No. 8, 16 November 1951

An instance has been reported of an infantryman being wounded and subsequently killed because he was unaware he could be pulled to safety through the escape hatch of a tank. He was lying wounded in the road, and efforts of the medics to get to him were ineffective. A tank commander moved his tank forward to straddle the man and get him into the tank. The wounded man misunderstood the intent of the commander, fearing he was to be run over, and kept crawling ahead of the tank. The enemy finally noticed the movement of the wounded man, and killed him. A set of signals or prearranged plans worked out between infantry and tank-platoon leaders and passed down to all troops may save lives in the future.

8. Time for Reflection

Lt.Col. John E. Harbert, 314th Ordnance Ammunition Group

The ordnance officer charged with getting ammunition forward has great problems of time, space, communication, and transportation. As commander of the 314th Ordnance Ammunition Group, I had over ten thousand square miles of Korea to cover in inspecting operations and troops. My units worked both laterally and vertically along the entire front of Eighth Army.

One must realize that army ammunition troops provide the only ammunition supply services to the combat trains of the using units. Unlike any other type of supply service, there is no counterpart organic to a corps or a division. This led to many problems involving command control and operational proficiency.

I tried many times to have a light plane assigned to me, but this was never allowed by higher headquarters. I spent well over half my time traveling from ammunition supply point to ammunition supply point over Korea's rough roads. Traveling like this had one value, however. I had plenty of time in which to contemplate my problems and to make decisions.

9. 5-in-1 Mule Ration

Sgt. David J. Fox, Radio and Message Center Company, 101st Signal Operation Battalion. (Interview by Capt. Pierce W. Briscoe, 2d Historical Detachment.)

The Chinese Communists used pack mules in their 1951 spring offensive. When the United Nations forces counterattacked, many of these mules were abandoned or escaped. Left to forage on the rice paddies and mountain slopes, they soon became thin and sickly.

The Radio Relay Platoon, 101st Signal Operation Battalion, gathered six of these mules for use in packing equipment up the mountains. The mules were fed candy, sugar, and cereal from 5-in-1 rations. After a short time the mules were fattened and resumed their burdensome life.

10. You've Got to Follow Through

Major Richard I. Crawford, Korean Military Advisory Group

The average ROK officer and soldier had received demolitions training—including how to calculate, prepare, and place charges. But they had had very little of the theory of defensive demolitions.

Before the Communist invasion, ROK engineers had packaged charges for the demolition of key bridges and roads in a zone forty miles south of the 38th parallel. We had held practice alerts, moved the demolitions to their sites, and prepared each site for demolition with gratifying success. However, we had not impressed the Koreans sufficiently with the importance of timely detonation and defense of their newly created obstacles. When combat came, trigger-happy individuals ordered key bridges blown before our vehicles had been cleared; on a few occasions the enemy made a flanking movement with small bands and killed the demolitions squad before the fuze was lighted. In at least six cases the tactical commander ordered that the bridge not be blown because he wanted to "counterattack over that route." In no case did such a counterattack ensue. Few, if any, of the obstacles created were defended. There was a great tendency for combat troops to fall well behind a blown but undefended obstacle to eat their rice, to sleep, or to regroup. That was fatal.

11. Recaptured American Wire

Capt. Rudolph A. Fallon, 5th Cavalry

In October 1950, the 1st Battalion, 5th Cavalry (for which I was communications officer), overran a North Korean signal dump. In it we found about thirty miles of single-conductor (strand) wire. We were particularly interested in this wire because obviously it was American-made W-110. We deduced this from the fact that it was the familiar four-copper, three-steel strands. Though the twisted pair had been separated and each strand individually rolled, the spiral marks where another strand had gone around and around were still plainly visible. Each roll of wire was wrapped in burlap and marked in what appeared to be Russian.

We were short of wire at this time, so we picked up the abandoned rolls on DR-4s and -5s. We often used the captured wire by rolling out two lines. However, ground return was used successfully by our artillery liaison officer. In one instance north of Kunu-ri, we laid about four hundred yards of single-strand wire along a railroad, using the rail for the return.

12. Intrenching Tools

Lt.Col. Arnold C. Gilliam, Quartermaster, 2d Infantry Division

During the winter of 1950-51, intrenching tools were discarded by combat units while they were actually engaged with the enemy. The reason was that the ground was frozen and the tools could not be used.

The quartermaster of the 2d Infantry Division did not become aware that these tools had been abandoned until the spring of 1951, when the ground began to thaw. Commanders then wanted replacement intrenching tools as rapidly as possible. But the number of replacement requests on this item was too great for the depot at Pusan to fill. It was necessary to airlift them from Japan. Unfortunately, this used air space vitally needed for gasoline and ammunition.

13. Bridge Assembly on Land

Major Carl A. Pollock, Liaison Officer to the Turkish Brigade

On the day before an assault crossing, we supplied the Turks with 340 feet of M38 infantry foot-bridging and instructions for its assembly. The crossing site was under heavy artillery and mortar fire. The Turkish engineer commander decided it would cost many lives to have his men work in the open, so he had the bridge assembled behind a small crest—150 yards from the river's edge. Once the bridge was assembled, several hundred troops picked it up and hand-carried it to the water's edge. During the carry, the bridge broke several times, whereupon everyone lowered it. When it was put back together, all lifted and moved on.

The bridge was put into the river at a 35- to 45-degree angle in the same direction as the current. At this angle it did not reach the opposite shore, but the men walked its length and jumped into the water to pull on ropes and bring the bridge astride the current. It was a smooth operation, quickly executed.

14. A Dilemma

Capt. George W. Spreng, Korean Military Advisory Group

During the offensive into North Korea the ROKs had few trucks with which to supply their divisions. To solve this problem my division commander ordered me to establish a railroad operating section in our engineer battalion. This put me in a command dilemma, for the U.S. authorities had ordered all locomotives and rolling stock returned to Hamhung. I was caught between the ROK decision to use the trains and the U.S. decision to move them back.

All KMAG advisers were hampered by the U.S. decision "to advise only" and stay away from command. This seemed impossible to me, and by agreement with the South Koreans I actually ordered people to carry out tasks.

But now I was faced with a direct order by the U.S. officials to countermand the order of an ROK division commander. I took refuge in my advisory capacity and suggested that these orders be sent through channels. I don't know that this was done. We did release a few trains for appearances' sake, but we kept eight complete trains for ourselves.

15. Integration

Lt.Col. Homer P. Harris, Quartermaster, 2d Infantry Division

I especially want to note that the 15th Quartermaster Company was integrated and that at least a third of my men were Negroes. I believe these were my best men. They held more than their share of the NCO ratings. They did skilled jobs. They knew they were getting a break on rotation points and were not being discriminated against in any way. They were good soldiers.

16. Broken Springs

Major John C. Bell, 13th Engineer Combat Battalion

There were times when we had as many as 15 of our 81 trucks deadlined—all for broken front springs. The breakage was so far from the normal expectancy that Ordnance was rarely able to supply these springs.

Most frequently the break occurred in one of the two bottom (long) leaves. The mechanics soon became adept at rebuilding front springs by throwing out a bad leaf and combining the rest of this spring with parts of another to make one good spring. If the breakage had been evenly distributed among the leaves, there would have been little trouble.

17. Language Problems

Capt. Robert F. Doolin, Korean Military Advisory Group

A frequent failing in ROK commanders was their refusal to use a common language. All Korean officers could speak both Korean and Japanese. But the use of Chinese was the sign of a good education. Consequently, an officer who understood Chinese would write his messages in that language and have them translated so they could be understood by the radio operators. At the other end the message was again rendered into Chinese before it was delivered.

18. Fire in the Hole!

Lt. William A. Champion, Lt. Charles H. Crossley, Lt. Weldon M. Gamel, and Lt. James E. Hunter, 2d Engineer Combat Battalion. (From interviews by Lt. John Mewha, 8th Historical Detachment.)

Company C, 2d Engineer Combat Battalion, sent the remainder of its demolition men to work on a pass in an access road. They progressed through the rocky sections at about a hundred feet a day, using a daily average of two thousand pounds of explosives. Every type of explosive charge available to the Corps of Engineers was used. Each time the demolition men finished blasting, from six to twenty rounds of enemy 82-mm mortar or 76-mm artillery fire hit the blasting site. For several days the men were able to blast only twice daily. The charges were placed in the morning with five- to ten-minute fuzes. As the men moved off the pass for lunch, they detonated the explosives. During the afternoon they cleared the debris and set more charges. As they withdrew for the night they blasted again. In this way they were able to avoid the enemy fire and proceed with their work.

19. Combat Boots

Lt.Col. Arnold C. Gilliam, Quartermaster, 2d Infantry Division

Some time before the Korean action, the new russet boot was adopted to replace the combat boot. As stocks of the combat boot in any size became exhausted, substitution of the new type boot was authorized.

News travels fast. Soon men requested sizes that did not fit so they would be equipped with the russet boot. The quartermaster of Eighth Army (Col. James M. Lamont) stated that, although he had exceeded the normal replacement factor by 269 per cent, the demand for boots continued high. It was apparent that many men had thrown away their combat boots in order to get the new type.

At an inspection of one regiment it was found that more than half the men equipped with the russet boot were wearing the wrong size. It was necessary to airlift foot-measuring devices so that commanders could be sure their men were wearing the proper footwear.

20. Need for Trained Personnel

Michael Slauta, Special Observer for The Quartermaster General. (From a speech, 16 November 1950.)

Handling supplies at the Pusan port was quite difficult at the start. It wasn't because we didn't know how to handle supplies; the personnel to handle them in quantity were not there.

The quartermaster section operated with a staff of six officers and a platoon of men. We had to depend on indigenous labor. The piers were soon piled high with unsegregated cargo. Loose cans filled a large warehouse. The problem did not diminish until service troops arrived.

21. Division Airdrop

Command Report, 23d Infantry, October 1951

Airdrops by liaison aircraft are successful only when the pilot knows where the target is located and dares to take his plane close enough and low enough to insure that most of the cargo will reach its destination. The airdrops in support of the 23d RCT consisted mainly of rations, water, fruit juices, and medical supplies (especially blood plasma). These drops were excellent, and there was at least 75 per cent recovery.

22. Who Wants to Serve in the Rear?

WO John Kinnaman, Jr., Finance Section, 1st Cavalry Division

A major problem in Korea was the lack of trained replacements. During the first six months we received only one trained finance man. Our main source of replacements were re-profiled front-line men, sole surviving sons, and men in similar categories. At the same time, a check

of the military pay records indicated that several finance school gradu-
ates were serving in front-line units as riflemen. After much discussion
with G1 and unit personnel officers, we finally managed to get some of
these men out of the front line and into our section.

We often operated by candle light in bombed-out buildings that
had little heat. Our workday started immediately after breakfast and
often extended to midnight. Because of the continuous moving of the
bulky equipment, our men had to assume the triple role of finance clerks,
stevedores, and guards. As a result of these working conditions, we received many requests for transfers to combat units. We had to deny
them for the good of the service.

23. The Sagging Bridge

Lt. William A. Champion, Lt. Charles H. Crossley, Lt. Weldon
M. Gamel, and Lt. James E. Hunter, 2d Engineer Combat Bat-
talion. (From interviews by Lt. John Mewha, 8th Historical
Detachment.)

About 12 August 1951, Company C, 2d Engineer Combat
Battalion, began constructing a Bailey bridge near the site of a washed-
out wooden bridge. The need for the bridge was so great that it was
begun before enough parts had been assembled for it. It was necessary to
launch the 80-foot span single-single (one panel wide and one panel high
on each side of the treadway) instead of a double-single. After the
single-single was across, the bridge sagged, and had to be made double-
single. To compensate for the sag in the alignment of the pins of the
outside panels, a D7 bulldozer was driven into the middle of the stream
and jacks were placed on its A-frame. By jacking one side at a time, the
bridge was brought into alignment. It took three days and two nights
to construct the bridge.

24. Carelessness is Expensive

Lt.Col. Clifford E. Roberts, Signal Officer, 7th Infantry Division

Service detachments of the 7th Infantry Division moved together from Seoul to Inchon in October 1950. A convoy moving along
the mountainous route in central South Korea was ambushed by the

enemy at 0200 one morning in a defile. The lead vehicle was hit and blocked the road.

The signal detachment had an SCR-193 radio, mounted in a jeep, which could be used to request assistance for the convoy. However, when an attempt was made to put the set on the air, the antenna would not load properly. For hours, the men made frantic attempts in the dark to get the transmitter into operation, but with no success.

When daylight came, it was found that the antenna terminal on the set was broken. Investigation revealed two important facts. First, the radio was a spare set and had not been operated recently. Second, the faulty antenna condition had existed before this operation.

Five hours and several lives were lost because of this carelessness.

25. Patrol Evacuation

Capt. Arne H. Eliasson, 8192d Helicopter Unit. (Interview by Lt. John Mewha, 8th Historical Detachment.)

On 18 August 1951 the 23d Infantry (2d Infantry Division) had a platoon-sized patrol in the Punchbowl area. Mortar fire struck the patrol and a number of men were killed and others wounded. The patrol immediately withdrew with its wounded and dead and notified the battalion surgeon. He called for two helicopters to aid in the evacuation.

The Punchbowl is a fairly level valley surrounded on all sides by mountains. Without helicopters it would be necessary to carry the casualties up the hills before they could be evacuated.

Twenty minutes after the call, Capt. Arne H. Eliasson was over the area. The patrol was withdrawing in single file. The men didn't have time to place the regular landing mark, but they had placed a panel in a nearby rice paddy.

Two wounded men had just been strapped to the stretcher platforms when several 60-mm mortar rounds landed fifty yards away. The infantry immediately scattered and Captain Eliasson flew the craft away. Later that day six calls came from the same area, and twelve men from the patrol were evacuated.

26. Problems of Sizing

Michael Slauta, Special Observer for The Quartermaster General. (From a speech, 16 November 1950.)

We had a considerable problem in issuing clothing and shoes to the South Koreans integrated into our ranks. They are very small people, standing only 64 or 65 inches, and are quite slender. Fortunately, they don't pay as much attention to size as we do. So long as an item was wearable, they would accept it and then trim it down.

Footwear, however, was another problem. During the summer and fall of 1950 we were issuing all our footwear smaller than 6-½ to ROK soldiers. There were some complaints on the fitting, so we ran a survey to see where we were going wrong. We found that 71 per cent of the ROKs have supplementary tariff size feet. The mean size was 6 EE; the smallest ran down to 3-½ EEEE; and the largest to 10-½ EEE.

27. Wire Recovery

Capt. Robert F. Doolin, Korean Military Advisory Group

The Koreans did not always understand our signal doctrine—or agree with it. Sometimes this made little difference. At other times the results were ludicrous. One ROK peculiarity was the refusal to use drums in the recovery of wire. Instead, a soldier would walk a wire accompanied by a cart. He would coil the wire around his bent arm as one does a rope. After he had as much as he could conveniently carry, he would cut the wire, carefully tie the coil, and place it in the cart. He would then repeat this operation until the entire length of wire was picked up. When he returned to his unit he would carefully splice the wire and rewind it on a reel. We just couldn't stop that practice.

28. Supply Guesstimates

Lt.Col. Kenneth O. Schellberg, Quartermaster, 7th Infantry Division

We didn't know what enemy resistance to expect at Inchon since this was to be the first offensive against the enemy. I had to reach into space for many of my estimates. I loaded rations enough for thirty days. Anticipating that water might be short until we captured Inchon, I included thirty gallons of water per man. On pure guess I included burial supplies for five thousand, and three loads of insecticides.

The quantity of supplies we carried may sound excessive in some cases. Actually, it wasn't. Although the division loaded them, the supplies were not to be unloaded while the battle was in balance. Initially we would have no supply base to turn to, but I anticipated that many nondivisional units would call on us for supplies. In this I was correct, for an ROK marine regiment was attached to us south of Seoul.

Our supplies, then, constituted the stock for the initial operation, and a beginning stock for 2d Logistical Command which was to come. Actually, the 7th Division did not meet an Eighth Army forward supply point until January 1951.

29. For Want of a Nail

Major Carl A. Pollock, Liaison Officer to the Turkish Brigade

The Turks are excellent in improvising when they lack a critical item. I recall one instance where they were building a bridge and did not have enough nails for the job. Their solution was to drill holes and insert wooden pegs. In the United States, hand doweling is used only in cabinet work.

30. Infantry Division Port

Lt.Col. Arnold C. Gilliam, Quartermaster, 2d Infantry Division

After the 2d Infantry Division crossed the 38th parallel we established a supply point at Sariwon. Trucks hauled supplies more than a hundred miles north of Ascom City. The main supply road was a second-rate road used by several other divisions. Because of the pressure, only class I and class III supplies could be moved.

At this time I learned that we could receive shipments directly from the sea if we could operate the port at Haeju. I moved to Haeju with Capt. Fred J. Tennant and a small detachment. Using prisoner-of-war labor, we unloaded one LST and several Japanese cargo vessels.

Supplies from Haeju were moved north to Sariwon over a narrow-gauge railroad. The smallness of the cars slowed the operation. We could load only 50 drums of gasoline in a car instead of the normal 150. As we were now in enemy territory, we placed two guards in the cab of each locomotive to be sure the Communist engineer moved his train to Sariwon. This operation relieved the pressure on the truck route.

31. Roadbound

Lt.Col. Ernest W. Chapman, Engineer Section, X Corps

I would say that our over-all concept of operations makes us roadbound to such an extent as to be dangerous. For example, we look at a road on a map and decide we cannot move a force over it. Yet in the next breath we concern ourselves with the possibility that the enemy will use the same road against us—which often happens.

32. Helmets for the 38th Infantry

Lt.Col. Arnold C. Gilliam, Quartermaster, 2d Infantry Division

In January 1951, I made a routine visit to the 38th Infantry (2d Infantry Division) near Andong. I asked the regimental commander (Col. George B. Peploe) if he had any quartermaster problem. He stated that there was one problem about which he was greatly concerned. Less than two weeks had passed since he had been assured that every man would be equipped with a steel helmet. Now his S4 advised him that the regiment needed 350 helmets. During this period the 38th had been engaged only in minor patrol actions.

I told Colonel Peploe I could take care of his requirements. He thanked me and said that stern disciplinary action would be taken against any man who, in the future, was caught without a helmet.

During the next month I again visited the 38th Infantry. The regiment had been engaged in heavy combat and there had been heavy losses of equipment in several companies. Nevertheless, the shortage of steel helmets was so small that only a few replacements were needed.

33.   Camera Patrol

Lt. Robert T. O'Brien, 7th Signal Company

The 7th Infantry Division was the only major unit to reach the Yalu River. We realized that we were very much exposed that far north, so we paid particular attention to combat intelligence. The civilians provided us with many rumors of enemy units between us and Hagaru-ri. To ignore any of these might have been dangerous, but to check them all by patrol would have been impossible.

Instead, the division G2 had our photo section make aerial photos of each suspected area and areas where enemy strongpoints might logically develop. These sorties were flown twice daily and the prints delivered to G2 within two hours. Comparisons gave the division a good indication of what was going on.

34.   Security Through a Swap

Capt. John M. McGuire, 1st Mobile Army Surgical Hospital

Although medical personnel had not been armed before our entry into Korea, by the time we left North Korea in late 1950 all our medics were armed with the carbine or the M1 rifle. Some of us thought this was a violation of the Geneva Convention, but we learned later that the Convention does not prohibit the arming of medical troops for the protection of their patients and themselves. Nurses were the only medical personnel who were not armed.

In February 1951, while four miles outside Andong, we felt that the possibility of an ambush was strong because enemy guerrillas were very active in the region. As our hospital was located within several hundred yards of two potential military targets—a main supply road and a railroad tunnel—we figured we were sitting ducks.

We felt that our individual weapons did not offer adequate fire power to protect us in an attack. Therefore, we exchanged some medicinal alcohol for ten automatic rifles from a division ordnance company. Needless to say, both units felt each had received the better bargain.

35. Flame-Thrower Tanks

Lt.Col. William C. Hammond, Jr., Chemical Officer, I Corps

It has been a hard job to sell the flame thrower to the armor people, but after they used it a while they became quite enthusiastic. The enemy fears fire. Recently, a tank went into a valley and fired one burst of flame. For a distance of a thousand yards all the enemy ducked down into their holes and stopped firing—including those way up on the sides of hills whom we could not possibly have reached. The psychological factor was tremendous.

36. Pick Your Method

Major Carl A. Pollock, Liaison Officer to the Turkish Brigade

The Turks did not always use methods that are part of our doctrine. They had with them American, German, and Soviet field and technical manuals in addition to their own. I gathered that their manuals were pretty much a synthesis of all of these. The Turks certainly were not doctrinaire in their methods.

37. Preparation for Action

Lt.Col. Kenneth O. Schellberg, Quartermaster, 7th Infantry Division

As soon as the 7th Infantry Division had closed in the Fuji area, the process of requisitioning equipment and bringing the division to wartime allowances was begun. Unfortunately, there just weren't enough supplies in Japan. The occupation divisions had been maintained at reduced strength and only a minimum of field training had been possible. Stock levels in the Far East Command had been related to both strength and losses, so there was little theater reserve of such items as mess kits, barber sets, and stove parts. The outfitting of the first three divisions for Korea had absorbed that reserve. The barrel was scraped clean before we got to Fuji. When we requisitioned carpenter sets, we first got the box the set comes in; then, from time to time, we received shipments of loose tools. Our requests for mess kits brought us a shipment of mess trays as substitutes.

38. Borrowing a Bridge

Lt.Col. James E. Linden, 14th Engineer Combat Battalion

The Kumho River appears as a small stream on a map, but it was wide and definitely unfordable in September 1950. As the attack progressed the 1st Cavalry Division built a 13-ton infantry support bridge across it. For the heavier traffic the division attempted a causeway of sandbags. This washed out as fast as the sandbags were placed.

The 24th Infantry Division faced a better prospect for its crossing of the Naktong River, as I Corps had attached to it a class 50 treadway bridge. A small margin of time existed before it was necessary to erect the class 50 bridge over the Naktong, and the 1st Cavalry Division borrowed the structure for its crossing of the Kumho.

The bridge over the Kumho River was 300 feet long and took four hours to erect. It carried critical supplies for twelve hours, then was dismantled and returned. So vital was the bridge in the plans of the 24th Division that the assistant division commander personally waited at the bridge to see that it was dismantled in time to be returned to the 24th Division. The treadway bridge was removed at 2300, and the next morning at 0600 the 14th Engineer Combat Battalion opened a fixed-span M2 treadway bridge across the Kumho.

39. Why Pay the Combat Soldier?

WO John Kinnaman, Jr., Finance Section, 1st Cavalry Division

It was intended that unit personnel officers screen their units to determine what portion of his pay each soldier desired. It soon became apparent that this was not being done, however, for turnbacks often totaled 75 per cent. Many men had no need or desire for their money.

I recommend that personnel in combat units not be paid until their departure from Korea. I suggest a gratuitous issue of ten dollars a month to cover cost of laundry and PX items. This program would cost about two million dollars a month. Since soldiers in the combat zone are given free cigarettes, beer, soft drinks, and candy, I feel that this expense is not out of line with Army policy. Furthermore, the cost will be more than compensated by the savings.

Savings and benefits will occur in many ways. Nonpayment would prevent military pay certificates from falling into enemy hands. The increased use of allotments would reduce the necessity for payment—and finance personnel. Limitation of money in the hands of troops would reduce the free spending that has been so damaging to the economy of the Republic of Korea. It is to be noted that the exchange rate on the ROK *won* rose from 1,800 to 6,000 to the U.S. dollar in the eleven months I was in Korea. To a large extent this was due to soldier spending.

40. Wire Cutters Caught

The Army Combat Forces Journal, February 1952

A wire "trouble" team usually fixes broken telephone wires. This crew also fixed some Communists.

When a recent trouble call was answered, wire men from the 25th Infantry Division in Korea found a break in the line and repaired it. Calling back to the switchboard was fine, but a call forward indicated another broken line.

As the men moved up the line and were about to advance over a ridge, they discovered the cause of their broken lines—eighteen Communists busily cutting the wire.

A quick call for reinforcements resulted in the capture of the wire spoilers and a return to trouble-free circuits.

41. What Do You Feed a Korean?

Lt.Col. Kenneth O. Schellberg, Quartermaster, 7th Infantry Division

Three weeks before the 7th Infantry Division shipped to Inchon, we received an augmentation of 8,600 Koreans. Before they arrived our division commander (Maj.Gen. David G. Barr) asked me, "What do you plan to feed these men?"

I countered, "How do you plan to use them?"

After some consideration he replied that the buddy system would probably work best. On that basis I recommended that we feed the Koreans regular U.S. rations, and make adjustments as we got complaints. I didn't believe it would be possible to set up a dual ration system within the units.

42.   Redesigning a Bridge

Capt. Francis S. Obradovich, 185th Engineer Combat Battalion, and Lt. George W. Brazier, Jr., 8224th Engineer Construction Group. (Condensed from interviews by Lt. Bevan R. Alexander, 5th Historical Detachment.)

The bridge over the Soyang River was well under way. The south abutment and the north approach road were complete and forty-one piles had been driven. On 24 April 1951, however, the engineers learned that the enemy offensive would bring a halt to their project. They began to evacuate the engineer equipment.

To hide as much of the progress on the bridge as possible, all the unused piling was buried. The south abutment was completely camouflaged to make it appear that the work on it had only just begun. The piling that had already been driven into the river bed was left in place because nothing could be done with it.

When the enemy offensive was halted, the UN forces counterattacked and reached the Soyang River approximately a month after the engineers had pulled out. The infantry reported that something had happened to the piles of the bridge. The message was vague. A construction officer flew to the bridge site and found that the Chinese had chopped the piles off at the water level.

The Chinese had used the chopped-off piles to build a low bridge about two hundred yards from our bridge site. The camouflaged abutment and the buried pile bents had escaped enemy observation, however, and had not been bothered. But the cut-off piles forced a redesign of our bridge.

43.   Infantry Replacements

Capt. Fred J. Tennant, 2d Quartermaster Company

The 2d Infantry Division entered Korea on 31 July 1950 and went into action immediately. The infantry regiments had high casualty rates in their fighting, and without replacements the infantry strength became dangerously low.

Here we learned that every man has to be a soldier. Division ordered all service units to transfer 10 per cent of their strength to the infantry. Some of our men had previous infantry experience, most had not. Often the men we transferred went into an attack two hours after joining the new unit. We gave the infantry good men—the enemy was too close to send out any 8-balls.

44. Eager Beaver

Col. Thomas A. Pitcher, Signal Officer, Eighth Army

One of the best cable splicers to work on the Mukden cable was Sergeant Van Atta of the 532d Signal Construction Company. Not only was he thoroughly proficient, but he was always anxious to get his job done. He carried his enthusiasm so far that, so long as the cable ran there, it seemed to make little difference to him whether or not we had captured an area.

Equal in zeal to Van Atta were the wire crews of the Republic of Korea's Ministry of Communications. They seemed to give allegiance to neither side in the struggle. Their interest and loyalty was to the cable. When it went bad they fixed it—regardless of whose territory it was in.

A strong bond developed between Van Atta and the Koreans. Once, north of Seoul, Van Atta went ahead of the infantry into enemy territory to get started on the cable. He was surrounded by Korean civilians and communications men. Suddenly several North Korean soldiers came on the scene and, seeing an American soldier, asked the civilians why an enemy soldier was here.

The communications men replied: "He's a prisoner. We're using him to repair the cable."

The enemy soldiers moved on.

45. Icebreaker, M1

Condensed from "Expedient River Ice Removal Practice," by Major Vernon L. Watkins and Lt. George W. Brazier, in *Engineer Lessons Learned in Korea*, June 1951.

Along with the rise in the Han River waters came floating ice. Combined, these forces of Nature destroyed all the bridges over the

Han in the X Corps zone except for a 300-foot timber structure near Chungju.

The floating ice varied from small bits to 40-foot sheets, and from 2 to 14 inches thick. It became apparent that the Chungju bridge would also fail if the ice could not pass. Already, clogging ice had raised the upstream water level 42 inches.

Demolition crews were unable to dislodge the mounting ice, and men with steel bars, tent poles, and native timbers were too slow. As the river continued to rise, the bridge began to fail. In desperation the engineers turned to any expedient, including one .that had been discussed earlier and passed over. Engineers fired M1 rifles directly at the jammed ice. Results were gratifying. A single fracture often broke the ice mass and allowed the fragments to flow under the bridge.

Throughout the night of 22 February 1951 and the next morning, squads of riflemen protected the structure, but subsequent rises in the river allowed water to flow over the treadway and forced the engineers from the bridge. Unattended, the ice clogged all openings and some of the larger sheets extended over the deck. The bridge failed.

Quick thinking and the use of an expedient had extended the life of the structure twenty-four hours. This was sufficient to permit the repair of alternate routes.

46. Curtailing the Money Black Market

Lt. Donald J. Horan, Finance Office, 2d Logistical Command

The main problem which arose in this rear area was the illegal trafficking in military payment certificates between members of the United Nations forces and Korean nationals. Within the means of the finance section we could practically wipe out this black market activity by making exchange readily available without any waiting.

We found that two cashiers could adequately handle the sale of *won*, which amounted to approximately thirty thousand dollars a day, provided they did not have to count the currency. Four Korean girls, money counters for the Bank of Korea, were used to count out the Korean currency in five- and ten-dollar stacks. Being more proficient than U.S. personnel at counting Korean money, their employment speeded up the counting and they proved far more accurate.

47. Temperature Adjustment

Michael Slauta, Special Observer for The Quartermaster General. (From a speech, 16 November 1950.)

The reaction of troops from tropical countries to wet-cold climate is unfavorable. When the Filipinos arrived in Korea on a September night, the temperature was a very comfortable 65 degrees. But the Filipinos felt cold. They were actually "freezing" and, before they moved away from the train, they had broken into their packs and had blankets draped over their shoulders. Before two days passed we had to issue them winter clothing.

48. Shortage of Spare Parts

Lt.Col. William C. Hammond, Jr., Chemical Officer, I Corps

We suffered all through the campaign from a lack of spare parts. I do not mean that the Chemical Corps is remiss; I mean that all spare parts are short. Korea is brutal on all types of mechanized equipment. It's because of rough roads and dust. The dust over here is terrific. It is highly abrasive—just like the dust we encountered at Salerno. The World War II replacement factor should be doubled, or even tripled.

49. Lead-in Wire

Sgt. Gene C. DeMont, 2d Medical Battalion

Around 15 September 1950 I was serving as advanced radio operator with the 2d Medical Battalion (2d Infantry Division) at Yongsan. The infantry was having a rough fight and we had a number of serious casualties in our clearing platoon in need of immediate evacuation. We were rapidly running out of medical supplies.

I was operating an old AN/GRC-9 radio with a whip antenna. I should have been able to get a range of forty-five miles, even in this rough country. The medical battalion was at Miryang—only thirteen miles away—and I could not reach them. I tried for an hour without success.

While I was trying to get the message through, a radio operator from the 2d Quartermaster Company came along. He looked at the lead-in wire between the radio and the antenna, and told me the wire was losing a great deal of power from radiation. He suggested I make a lead-in of coaxial cable—and even provided a short piece of it.

I made the lead-in and tried calling Miryang. I got them on the first call. Their signal was weak but readable. In turn, they read me strong.

I sent my message requesting supplies and asking for helicopter evacuation of the serious cases. Fortunately, the radio crew was located at a mobile army surgical hospital and a helicopter was available. The first flight reached us within twenty minutes of my message.

50. Feeding Koreans

Michael Slauta, Special Observer for The Quartermaster General. (From a speech, 16 November 1952.)

When Koreans first try the American diet they tend to overeat, and become ill. You could see the Koreans going through a mess line for a well-liked cup of coffee. They would fill the canteen cup quarter full of sugar and the remainder with coffee.

We began to control the amounts of food the Koreans could have. After they became accustomed to our rations they relished them.

51. Convoy Troubles

Lt.Col. Arnold C. Gilliam, Quartermaster, 2d Infantry Division

The haul from Masan to Chongju and back was 460 miles, and the turnaround took approximately 36 hours. Ten bridges were out and several rivers had to be forded. Guerrillas and bypassed enemy units attacked our convoys. One truck returned with nine bullet holes in its windshield and an unscathed driver.

We noticed that the guerrillas picked on the rear vehicle in each convoy, so we moved the convoy commander's jeep up from that position and placed a 2-½-ton truck in the rear. Then we rear-mounted a caliber .50 machine gun and stationed a gunner to return the fire. We had no more trouble with guerrillas.

52. Hot Food

Lt.Col. Kenneth O. Schellberg, Quartermaster, 7th Infantry Division

In the landings of the 7th Infantry Division at Inchon, I was particularly impressed by the speed with which food was brought forward. Each soldier carried a full C ration, but few used it. The kitchen trucks were among the first vehicles unloaded. Within hours of our landing most of the kitchens ashore were serving hot meals. Some of the messes even served hot rolls.

53. Never Put Off Till To-Morrow . . .

Major Edward Pooley, 25th Signal Company

The 24th Infantry (25th Infantry Division) was on field maneuvers in Japan in June 1950. During the last few days of the maneuver it rained constantly, and most of its signal equipment got thoroughly wet. At the close of the maneuver this equipment was loaded on vehicles and returned to the home station without being dried and cleaned. It was supposed this delay would not damage the equipment.

When the regiment arrived at its home station it was sent directly to Korea with no opportunity to service its equipment. Eight days later the regiment was in combat, and found its signal equipment operating at approximately 50 per cent efficiency, whereas during the maneuver it had been 95 per cent effective.

54. Supply by Cable

Lt. William A. Champion, Lt. Charles H. Crossley, Lt. Weldon M. Gamel, and Lt. James E. Hunter, 2d Engineer Combat Battalion. (From interviews by Lt. John Mewha, 8th Historical Detachment.)

The rains washed away a temporary bridge, isolating the front-line troops and our engineer company. Food and medical supplies were brought in for a 24-hour period by a cableway built by the 1st Platoon. Some men from the 3d Platoon, which had been left south of the stream, helped in the operation. A rock with telephone wire attached was thrown to the men, and to this a half-inch rope was attached. A three-quarter cable was attached to the rope. After the cable was pulled across, it was anchored on both sides of the stream. A snatch block, placed on the cable, ran back and forth, hauling supplies across the river.

55. Protecting Perishables

Lt.Col. Kenneth O. Schellberg, Quartermaster, 7th Infantry Division

We learned many tricks about shipping supplies while we were in Korea. One allowed us to protect perishables against heat and cold. When we needed—but didn't have—a refrigerated railroad car or truck, we used our standard vehicles and applied the layer principle. Frozen foods were maintained in standard trucks and boxcars for about three days during normal weather by placing cases of nonperishables on the bottom, sides, and top of the car, then placing the frozen product in the center. To insulate against cold we sandwiched loads of fresh vegetables between protective layers of products not likely to be damaged by the cold.

56. Finance on the Alert

Major Stanley H. Hendricks, 106th Finance Disbursing Section

While in Wonsan, we were required to remain on the alert twenty-four hours a day because of the limited number of troops available for perimeter defense. We were on the western edge of town and the enemy often infiltrated our positions. Several times I had to have my cash verified by two disinterested officers and necessary certificates prepared. Thermite grenades were attached to my field safes at all times so that the money, checks, and pay records could be quickly destroyed.

57. Napalm

Lt.Col. William C. Hammond, Jr., Chemical Officer, I Corps

Napalm mix has really come into its own over here. This is particularly true of its use in bombs. Last Christmas I was talking to the men of one unit who were mixing napalm at the Kimpo airfield, and they told me they had already mixed more than 375,000 gallons. The Air Force loves napalm, and for a while we had both smoke companies mixing it.

You very rarely see a flight of fighter-bombers take off in which at least one plane doesn't have two napalm tanks—and usually all have them. I believe more enemy tanks have been knocked out by napalm than by all other weapons combined.

58. A Real Convenience

Lt.Col. Arnold C. Gilliam, Quartermaster, 2d Infantry Division

During the time we were trucking supplies from Yongdungpo to Pyongyang, we found that the Air Force's C-119s were making a similar trip carrying drums of gasoline. But they could not return the empty drums because of the explosion hazard. One of my officers did some close liaison and worked out a deal whereby the south-bound planes would carry out 2-½-ton trucks. This saved a lot of time and effort during the week in which we were able to work this arrangement.

59. Radio Displacement

Capt. Richard M. Lyman, 8036th Signal Operation Company

In November 1950 we thought the fighting was about over, but soon we were ourselves displacing rearward. The radio personnel overheard enough messages to know immediately when things began to go bad. On the 29th, I was ordered to send a jump team back to Sunchon to establish a terminal.

I had been with the company only a few days, and had not moved the radios into this site, but I anticipated that moving four VHF stations with one truck would be difficult.

I was promised plenty of time to phase out my stations and pack the equipment, however. At 1300 on the 30th I got our march order from the corps signal officer. I was given lots of time—"Be in the column by 1500!"

Scouring the area, I found a North Korean fire engine and a 1-½-ton truck. Commandeering is the military term for what took place. I brought the vehicles up to our equipment and loaded. Everything got on board except an old Korean chair, but our appearance was none too military.

60. We Didn't Overlook Anything

Lt.Col. Kenneth O. Schellberg, Quartermaster, 7th Infantry Division

After the 7th Infantry Division landed at Iwon, its infantry regiments moved out very rapidly. The infantry was well on its way to Kapsan while the supply base was still being shifted from Iwon to Pukchong. We were able to supply the infantry only by the continuous use of our truck company, airlifts from Japan, use of the division's own light aircraft, and by operating a ten-mile mine-conveyor system we found. We used this to transport 55-gallon drums from the railhead at Honggun-ni over the very rough mountains to within twelve miles of Pungsan. We hauled gasoline all day and fought off guerrillas from our conveyor installations at night.

61. Seeing Is Believing

Lt.Col. Joseph Beaver, 2d Finance Disbursing Section

The sixty miles separating the finance section from the front-line troops brought no problem. A pay team took payrolls and cash forward to advance CPs on payday and remained until every service was completed. A battalion commander would advise our office when we could visit his units, and we would take the pay records for perusal or voicing of complaints by the men. Most complaints were without foundation; the men were just curious to see their pay records.

62. Who's Afraid of a Tank?

Capt. George R. Spreng, Korean Military Advisory Group

The South Koreans had an extreme fear of tanks. This was not without cause, considering how unprepared they were to cope with them. In time the ROKs came to realize how restricted the tankers were, and how frightened were the crewmen.

An incident occurred near Hamhung which pointed up the limitations of tanks. The Chinese Communists attached with four tanks out ahead of their infantry. Two of my ROK engineers each ran twice across the road dropping M6 mines in the path of the tanks. All four enemy tanks were knocked out, and the attack was stopped. The fear of tanks was much less thereafter.

63. Laying Telephone Wire by Air

Command Report, 23d Infantry (October 1951)

Liaison planes in three missions laid 11,000 yards of telephone wire. It was found that 2 miles of wire will cross 1.4 miles of ground distance. That is not excessive, for wire crews normally allow a 25 per cent slack.

Wire should be flown into position by 1530, as the wire crews must locate it and connect the wires before dark. To aid the wire men, a panel is tied to each end of the wire. It is suggested that smoke grenades be dropped from the plane at each end of a run.

We used the planes to lay wire only when the terrain was too rough for crews to do it on the ground. However, the wire crossed terrain where it could not be repaired. Alternate means of communication must therefore be established.

64. Payroll by Helicopter

Major Wilford E. Vidlock, Finance Officer, 24th Infantry Division

One morning I was due at the division's forward CP at 0900 to deliver the payroll to unit agents. I knew I could never make it by jeep, so I asked one of the pilots of a helicopter to fly me and my assistant forward. He very obligingly agreed. It took us an hour to make the trip that would have taken eight by jeep. So I claim for the finance section of the 24th Infantry Division the distinction of first having delivered a monthly payroll by helicopter.

We arrived on time, so everybody was happy. You should have seen the people at forward when I got out of the "eggbeater"! No joke. They were running every which way as we made our approach. When I stepped out it was really a picnic. They thought the helicopter was bringing General Ridgway!

Index

Index

☆ U.S. GOVERNMENT PRINTING OFFICE : 1986 O - 162-899